The State
They're In

Praise for *The State They're In*

'Matthew Lockwood's book is a real *tour de force*. It's a punchy and very intelligent read, covering everything the campaigner and engaged citizen needs to understand about the African poverty agenda in 2005. Its central argument – that the number one obstacle to eradicating poverty in Africa is the nature of the state – will not be universally popular; but the evidence assembled in the book leaves little room for doubt. What we need now is a robust and imaginative policy debate matching the historic proportions of the challenge Lockwood describes.'
David Booth, Overseas Development Institute

'In this extraordinarily rich and valuable book, Matthew Lockwood explores the gulf between international development narratives on aid, trade and debt, and the political and economic realities of Africa. The resulting reality check and proposals for how to bridge the divide, are essential reading for anyone interested in Africa's future.'
Duncan Green, Head of Research, Oxfam

'A thought provoking thesis that questions the basic assumptions underpinning the approach of much of the NGO community in the North to development. Essential reading for anyone who wants to understand the deep rooted difficulties in tackling global poverty.'
Shriti Vadera, Adviser to the Chancellor, HM Treasury

'This is an important book. Matthew Lockwood argues that the answer to Africa's problems is political reform to bring about effective states. Everybody who is interested in the future of Africa should read it.'
Larry Elliott, The Guardian

Viewpoints Series

Doing the Rights Thing
Rights-based Development and Latin American NGOs
Maxine Molyneux and Sian Lazar

Industrial Competitiveness in Africa
Lessons from East Asia
Sanjaya Lall with Erika Kraemer-Mbula

Social Progress and Sustainable Development
Neil Thin

The State They're In
An Agenda for International Action on Poverty in Africa
Matthew Lockwood

The State
They're In

An Agenda for
International Action
on Poverty in Africa

Matthew Lockwood

ITDG
PUBLISHING

Published by ITDG Publishing
Schumacher Centre for Technology and Development
Bourton Hall, Bourton-on-Dunsmore,
Warwickshire CV23 9QZ, UK
www.itdgpublishing.org.uk

First published in 2005

ISBN 1 85339 617 6

A catalogue record for this book is available from the British Library.

ITDG Publishing is the publishing arm of the Intermediate Technology
Development Group Ltd. Our mission is to build the skills and capacity of
people in developing countries through the dissemination of information in
all forms, enabling them to improve the quality of their lives and that of
future generations.

Typeset by RefineCatch Limited, Bungay, Suffolk
Printed in Great Britain by Antony Rowe Ltd., Chippenham, Wiltshire

Contents

Preface

I grew up with images of African poverty in the UK media in the 1960s and 1970s – principally of the war in Biafra and the Ethiopian famine of 1974. I first travelled to Africa in 1984. Perhaps naively, I always assumed that over the following twenty years a serious dent would be made in the extent and depth of hunger, disease and illiteracy that I saw. Over that twenty years I went into 'development', like many of my contemporaries, first in academia and then in the NGO world. But as time has gone on, it became clear that the development was all in our careers, and not in Africa itself.

Thus in writing this short book one motivation has been wanting to get to the bottom of why Africa's problems have been so persistent, even through changes of policy and donor fashion, from 'structural adjustment' through to 'Poverty Reduction Strategy Papers'. It has become clear to me that beneath the ebb and flow of donor enthusiasms, the 'business-as-usual' aid approach, along with its panoply of well-resourced bilateral and multi-lateral agencies, has failed the people of Africa on a massive scale.

The second motivation was a frustration arising out of six years spent working on NGO campaigns for debt relief, more aid with less conditionality, and changed trade rules.

Campaigning organizations always have to simplify to be effective, and, as I was reminded by my colleagues on frequent occasions, NGOs are not think tanks. Equally, all the people I worked with were motivated by the most admirable aims, and worked with quite astonishing energy to try to make the world a better place. But my experience of working on these issues was one of always having to sweep inconvenient facts under the campaign carpet. With debt relief there were what I judged to be serious concerns about corruption – concerns often voiced more strongly by our African partner NGOs than by us in the UK. On trade there was the inescapable if inconvenient finding that Africa's trade malaise was in many cases more to do with very small and weak export capacity than to do with trade barriers. What frustrated me the most was the lack of space to properly debate these issues within an NGO setting. However, I also knew from a brief experience of working for the Department for International Development that the space for thinking through these issues inside government was, if anything, even smaller.

So in the end I took the step of leaving and writing this book entirely unsupported by any organization or institution. My acknowledgements are to those individuals who have given comments on the manuscript – Duncan

Green, Henry Northover, Simon Maxwell and Jon Lunn – and to those who have helped with information – Robin Murray, Laura Kelly, Anne-Marie Goetz and Sophie Pongracz. I am particularly indebted to Susan Hawley not only for making me think through the arguments more clearly, but also for her moral support. I remain solely responsible for the content and any errors. I am grateful to David Lewis for introducing me to ITDG Publishing, and to Toby Milner for handling the publication process with efficiency and speed. Apologies are due to the author and commentator Will Hutton for stealing and adapting the title of his modern classic, *The State We're In*. But I'm not too sorry, as I think the adaptation is entirely apposite.

There are many people, too numerous to mention by name, who have, in ways I did not always comprehend or appreciate at the time, informed my understanding of Africa. My views have perhaps been unduly shaped by experiences of a particular aspect of the African story – Tanzania in mid-crisis in the 1980s, Nigeria under military rule in the early 1990s, Zimbabwe in terminal decline in the late 1990s and early 2000s. Uganda under 'Museveni 1', Rwanda since the genocide, or indeed Tanzania more recently might have led me to a more optimistic view. However, I remain convinced that the story I lay out here is basically fairly widely applicable, and that the political dynamics I describe are fairly persistent.

Finally, this book is dedicated to those – from Patrice Lumumba, to Edward Sokoine, to John Githongo, and countless others – who have fought with great courage for a different kind of politics in Africa, in the hope that their vision will one day be realized.

Matthew Lockwood
London
March 2005

Acronyms

ACP	Africa, Caribbean, Pacific
ADB	Asian Development Bank
AGOA	African Growth and Opportunity Act
AoA	Agreement on Agriculture
APRM	African Peer Review Mechanism
ART	Anti-Retroviral Therapy
AU	African Union
DBS	Direct Budget Support
DfID	Department for International Development
DRC	Democratic Republic of Congo
DTI	Department for Trade and Industry
EBA	Everything But Arms
EPAs	Economic Partnership Agreements
FDI	Foreign Direct Investment
GDP	Gross Domestic Product
GNP	Gross National Product
GSP	Generalized System of Preferences
HIPC Initiative	Heavily Indebted Poor Countries Initiative
IDA	International Development Association
IFI	International Financial Institution
IMF	International Monetary Fund
LDC	Least Developed Country
LICUS	Low Income Countries Under Stress
MCA	Millennium Challenge Account
MDGs	Millennium Development Goals
MFN	Most Favoured Nation
NAMA	Non-Agricultural Market Access
NEPAD	New Partnership for Africa's Development
NIC	Newly Industrializing Country
NTB	Non-Tariff Barrier
OAU	Organization of African Unity
OECD	Organization for Economic Co-operation and Development
OED	Operations Evaluation Department
PRGF	Poverty Reduction and Growth Facility
PRSC	Poverty Reduction Structural Credit
PRSP	Poverty Reduction Strategy Paper

R&D	Research and Development
S&DT	Special and Differential Treatment
SME	Small and Medium-sized Enterprises
SOE	State-Owned Enterprise
SWAP	Sector-Wide Approach
TNC	Trans-National Corporation
TRCB	Trade-Related Capacity Building
TRIMS	Trade-Related Investment Measures
UNAIDS	Joint United Nations Programme on HIV/AIDS
UNCTAD	United Nations Conference on Trade and Development
UNDP	United Nations Development Programme
UNECA	United Nations Economic Commission for Africa
UNICEF	United Nations Children's Fund
UNIDO	United Nations Industrial Development Organization
VER	Voluntary Export Restraint
WDM	World Development Movement
WTO	World Trade Organization

1 Introduction

DEEPENING POVERTY in Africa has become an apparently permanent feature of the modern world. International initiatives to solve Africa's problems are announced with regularity every few years. In the UK, 2005 marks a particularly intensive phase of activity. In March the Commission for Africa reported on its inquiry into the causes of stalled development on the continent. The report has raised expectations of action from the G8 at the leader's summit in July. The UK government has signalled firmly that it will use its presidencies of the G8 and the EU to tackle the problem of poverty in Africa. Meanwhile campaigners have marked the year as the one to 'Make Poverty History', with much of the focus on Africa.

The current round of activity follows literally decades of official inquiries, reports and initiatives.[1] However, there is considerable optimism[2] around that 2005 can mark, in the words of the Chancellor of the Exchequer Gordon Brown, 'a new beginning for Africa' (Brown 2004 p 131). A significant increase in aid to Africa is potentially on the table. Tony Blair's call to heal the 'scar on the conscience of the world' still resounds fairly loudly. Assessments of Africa's problems and potential solutions are therefore timely.

In this book I argue that much thinking on Africa – from both official donors and from international NGOs alike – is flawed, because that thinking either does not recognize or does not draw out the implications of the central role of politics and the state in Africa's development problems. There are reasons – some good, some bad – why this is the case. However, serious attention to these issues yields a somewhat different policy agenda from that of current debates. I argue that if the failures of the last forty years are not to be repeated over the next forty, it is key that these difficult issues are faced up to. This is especially so for those with a progressive political agenda. For years, many on the left have focused their attention on Africa's external economic relationships – debt, unfair trade rules, declining commodity prices, aid conditionality – and has largely abandoned thinking about domestic politics and the state to the right. In my view this is a serious mistake, and urgently needs to be addressed.

I should first emphasize that I am making a set of arguments specifically about Africa, not about developing countries in general. The political dynamics and relationships with the international environment are very different in other regions and countries. It is also the case that none of what I am saying is new or original. Essentially similar arguments were made – far more eloquently – twenty years ago by Richard Sandbrook in his book *The Politics of Africa's Economic Stagnation*. During the 1990s there were various attempts to draw lessons (more about policy than about politics) from the contrast between East and South-east Asia on the one hand, and Africa on the other (Lindauer and Roemer 1994, Stein 1995, Roemer 1996, Harrold et al 1996, Aryeety and Nissanke 1998). More recently, Alice Sindzingre (2004) and Mkandawire and Soludo (2004) have again made many of the same arguments.

In this book I focus on the economic stagnation that underlies poverty in Africa (Killick and White 2001 ch 5) rather than on the symptoms of poverty in the form of illiteracy, ill-health and malnutrition. I am of course assuming that the Millennium Development Goals are an important set of preliminary targets to be met on the road to poverty eradication, but I am working on the basis that none of them will be met without broad-based economic growth in Africa. Thus I focus mainly on how productivity can be raised and especially how industry and exports can be expanded, rather than on improvements in the delivery of services such as health and education.[3] My argument is that African countries lack effective states. I focus mainly on the inability of African states to foster investment and broad-based growth. However, this argument can be extended to the delivery of services, as collapse and inequity in service delivery can also be explained by the workings of the neo-patrimonial state.

I am also arguing that the quickest route out of poverty for African countries will be provided by a disciplined and socialized capitalism. That is, I am arguing for developmental states that foster accumulation through capitalist investment in raising productivity, but with a share of the resulting resources being recycled through the state into public goods and services. These phenomena have been very weak in Africa.[4] However, the argument for a capitalist developmental state is not a neo-liberal argument. On the contrary, central to the argument is the point that successful capitalist development requires substantial state intervention.

Perhaps the most controversial aspect of my thesis is the focus on factors *within* Africa, rather than on the external environment of trade, aid and debt. There is some of the standard NGO critique that I agree with, especially on the poor quality of aid. However, I argue that, while less tied, better coordinated aid would be a good thing, this is not the main issue.

Many UK commentators on the right have made arguments about Africa which might sound similar; it is frequently asserted that Africa is 'mired in corruption', or that Africa's problems are all down to 'poor leadership' or 'culture', or that all aid is wasted. There is often a veiled racism in these variants of Afro-pessimism; an implication that there is something uniquely and inevitably problematic about Africa—that the prognosis is, literally, hopeless. My approach here is quite different. First, my analysis is political, historical and comparative, not based on the idea that there is something 'essentially' wrong with Africa. Consequently, my prognosis is not a counsel of despair, but rather one of political realism. Second, although I argue that the conventional NGO and government perspective on aid, debt relief and the role of TNCs is mistaken, my view is that relationships between aspects of the external environment and the nature of politics in Africa are very important.

A final preliminary is to delineate the target of my critique. Although I believe what I say is of broader application, it is aimed at a UK audience; principally government and UK-based development NGOs. I distinguish clearly between the UK-based policy units of these latter organizations, and the Africa-based country offices or partners, since these two groups often have a different set of views and priorities. It is the former group that is the primary audience here.

A summary of the argument

Africa's deep poverty, economic stagnation and AIDS crisis are well known. Poverty is chronic; average incomes have remained stagnant since the mid-1970s. Africa's small share in world trade and investment flows has got even smaller. What was already a considerable development challenge by the early 1980s has become much more serious with the immense burden of AIDS. As a result, Africa has now become the most aid-dependent region in human history, with aid reaching well over half of GDP in some countries. Investment in physical infrastructure and in education trails all other regions, including South Asia. More widely, there are stark contrasts with a group of countries in East and South-east Asia that were as poor as African nations in the 1960s, but have since undergone rapid transformations in economic growth and human development terms.

The current policy debates between the UK government and NGOs over OECD agricultural subsidies, doubling aid, and conditionality are failing to engage with the central role played by the state in development, and the failure of states in Africa in particular. Eliminating rich world support to agriculture will be of only marginal help to African countries; their real problem is how to diversify out of primary commodity exports as a route to industrialization, especially in competition from the likes of China. Donors advise trade liberalization and privatization, but NGOs rightly point to the record of East Asian states such as Korea and Taiwan, showing that rapid growth only comes with state intervention in trade, industry, and finance, along with heavy investment in education. NGOs therefore criticize the World Bank, IMF and WTO for closing down the 'policy space' for African countries to try similar interventions. This is a real fear, but it glosses over the fact that when African states have actually had policy space, their actions have largely been *anti-developmental*, and the quality of their interventions abysmal. Neither liberalization nor *dirigisme* is guaranteed to lead to industrialization and sustainable economic growth – what counts is the quality of intervention, and therefore the nature of the state.

Related conclusions come out of the debates on aid and debt relief. Donors defend aid conditionality, while NGOs attack it, but neither side has fully engaged with the evidence showing that African countries have often not complied with donor conditions. Only partial economic reforms have actually taken place. This experience shows the importance of domestic political dynamics in African countries for what policies are actually implemented, a fact that NGOs have again largely ignored, and that donors do not know how to respond to. The decisive nature of political commitment also emerges very clearly from a review of the often failing attempts by donors to introduce governance reforms in Africa.

If politics and the state are so important, what has shaped these in Africa? Political historians emphasize the inheritance of Indirect Rule during colonial period, in which local chiefs ruled through a mixture of repression and patronage. The transition to Independence was so rapid that nationalist political parties, hastily assembled at the end of the 1950s, had to call on such local 'big men', and a reliance on buying the support of these 'clients' became an entrenched feature of post-colonial politics. Some national leaders tried to contain this clientelism, attaining political stability through one-party states. In other countries competition to 'eat' from the state descended into a 'spoils politics' and ultimately into state collapse.

Clientelist politics has had a corrosive effect on almost all African states. Behind a formal façade of sovereign government, informal patronage relations have undermined the capacity of states to plan and deliver development projects and, most crucially, to restructure economies away from commodity dependence. As a result, countries were hit hard by the 1970s oil shocks and the global recession of the 1980s. A downward spiral into corruption has been the result. In the 1960s a well-paid government job was a good reward for a political client; by the 1980s the real value of salaries had evaporated, meaning that such posts were only valuable for extracting 'rents' in the form of bribes, as a way of surviving amidst shortages and crisis.

Donors have compounded the problems by attempting to micro-manage solutions, taking over the developmental functions of the state. With economic decline, the aid relationship has become more and more central. On the one hand, aid resources have become a source of patronage. On the other, at least since the end of the Cold War, donors have been pressing more seriously for liberalizing reforms that would reduce the opportunities for rent-seeking. Regimes have responded both by undermining and distorting reform programmes, and by looking for new opportunities for patronage (for example in privatization deals).

Has this picture changed in recent years? Africa's recent history is full of false dawns. However, it is worth looking at some of the donor favourites for signs of change in political dynamics. A review of four 'good performers' – Uganda, Ghana, Tanzania and Mozambique – leads to a rather pessimistic assessment. Of these four, only Tanzania is showing some signs of a more developmental leadership, one that might be interested in rooting out clientelism in favour of a more effective state. Even here, decentralization and a change of leadership may yet derail such a political project. These case studies also make it clear that it will be difficult to second-guess the political shape of developmental states in Africa when they do emerge, except that they will not be clientelist in nature.

What does this account mean for the policy debates of 2005? A change in the *nature* of politics (in distinction to governance reforms, or changes in the form of politics) is central to more rapid progress, but this will come only from within Africa itself. However, the international community can play a (minor) supporting role. Donors have to align aid, trade, debt relief and corporate responsibility policies behind this role. Conditionality should be abandoned, and aid used to create incentives for political change, while trade policies should focus on assisting diversification of African exports. Finally, rhetoric on cleaning up offshore banking, corporate bribery and the extractive industries should be matched by action. This presents a series of challenges for the UK government and a clear campaigning agenda for NGOs in the UK.

In the next chapter, I take a long view of the record on Africa's development problems. The following three chapters look at donor and NGO explanations of why Africa is still so poor, and their recommendations for change. I focus particularly on trade, the aid conditionality debate, and the governance agenda. I argue that these explanations lack clarity because they do not give enough recognition and weight to the role of the state and politics in development.

Chapters 6 and 7 go on to lay out an alternative account, first focusing on African politics, and then on the implications for the nature of the state in Africa. This account covers the entire period from the late colonial years, through the stage of high state intervention in the 1970s, to liberalization in the 1990s. I argue that despite surface changes in policies, many states have been consistently 'anti-developmental' (or at best, 'non-developmental'), in contrast with the developmental states in parts of East and South-east Asia. I also look at the role of donors in perpetuating neo-patrimonial states in Africa.

In chapter 8, I raise the question, given the arguments of optimists that things are beginning to change for the better in Africa, of whether politics and state characteristics are being transformed in some countries. I focus in particular on four countries that have often been picked out as 'good performers' by donors: Ghana, Uganda, Tanzania and Mozambique, and ask whether these are becoming developmental states. Chapter 9 draws out some more general conclusions about what the political characteristics of African developmental states are likely to be.

Finally, in chapter 10, I return to policy agendas, and particularly to those for the UK within the context of the G8 countries. I lay out some principles for approaches to policy, and implications both for the government and for UK-based NGOs.

2 Africa in 2005: the long view

AFRICA'S CURRENT STATE is parlous. While official data can of course be criticized on grounds of accuracy and completeness, they do give an indication of the scale of the problem. Equally, while Africa-wide statements are criticized for overlooking important variations and being too sweeping, and while some countries are doing somewhat better than others, only two small countries out of the 48 in Sub-Saharan Africa – Mauritius and Botswana – have a consistently strong growth and poverty reduction record.

In 2002, the latest year for which data are available, average Sub-Saharan African per capita GDP at purchasing power parity was $1,790, or $469 using exchange rates. This is significantly lower than in any other region, including South Asia. Of the 50 countries at the bottom of the UNDP's Human Development Index, 37 are in Africa: 34 of the 49 Least Developed Countries are in Africa.

The $1-a-day headcount measure of poverty used by the World Bank and in the Millennium Development Goals has actually risen in Africa since 1990 from around 47 per cent of the population, to 49 per cent in 2000. Almost 75 million *more* people in Africa were living in poverty at the end of the 1990s than a decade earlier (World Bank 2001). Poverty in Africa is also deeper than in any other region, in the sense that people are further below the poverty line than in other regions (Chen and Ravallion 2001). Other methodologies, such as those developed by UNCTAD (2002a) suggest even more widespread poverty in the region. Widespread poverty means hunger on a huge scale; UNICEF estimates that in 2000, 27 per cent of children under five in the region were underweight, hardly changed since 1990.

The distribution of incomes within Africa is also very unequal. It vies with Latin America as the most inequitable region in the world. A majority of countries have a Gini coefficient of over 40. In 1998 just over half the population was living on less than one third of average national consumption, as compared with less than 20 per cent of the population in East Asia.

Many African countries also continue to suffer high debt burdens. Of the 42 countries eligible for debt relief under the HIPC Initiative, 34 are in Africa. While debt ratios have come down under the HIPC Initiative, a number of countries still have debt service to government revenue ratios of over 20 per cent (see Table 2.1).

Table 2.1   Debt service ratios, Sub-Saharan Africa HIPCs, 2003 (%)

Country	Debt service to exports ratio	Debt service to revenue ratio
Benin	6.3	4.9
Burkina Faso	11.4	8.1
Cameroon	8.8	12.8
Chad	6.8	14.9
DRC	8.5	21.0
Ethiopia	7.3	6.4
Gambia	11.4	21.1
Ghana	5.2	17.1
Guinea	8.5	18.1
Guinea-Bissau	6.4	12.8
Madagascar	4.2	9.3
Malawi	22.2	28.8
Mali	5.6	8.1
Mauritania	14.0	15.6
Mozambique	5.3	11.6
Niger	6.4	9.3
Rwanda	11.1	5.5
Sao Tome and Principe	24.4	36.6
Senegal	12.0	17.7
Sierra Leone	0.2	0.4
Tanzania	4.8	6.8
Uganda	7.8	8.5
Zambia	15.0	24.1

Source: World Bank and IMF (2005).

UNAIDS estimates that between 25 and 28 million people in Africa are living with HIV, with over 3 million new infections in 2003 (UNAIDS 2003a). AIDS killed over 2 million people in Sub-Saharan Africa in 2003, and cumulative deaths from the disease in Africa are thought to have reached over 15 million (UNAIDS 2003b) – over twice the number of people who died in the Holocaust. Prevalence reaches 40 per cent in some Southern African countries, but is high across East and West Africa too. Other health indicators are also poor; according to World Bank data less than 60 per cent of children in 2000 were immunized against measles.

In education, Africa's average net primary enrolment rate in 2000 was 63 per cent, scarcely higher than in 1990. UNICEF estimates that at current trends universal primary education will not be reached until after 2100. Secondary enrolment is much lower.

More generally, Africa is the region least likely to meet the Millennium

Development Goals, and on current trends no countries in Sub-Saharan Africa will reach them by 2015 (UNICEF and UNDP 2002). In fact, the goals of cutting child mortality by two thirds and halving the $1 a day poverty headcount will not be met on current trends until well into the next century.

Finally, in the last few years, there are signs that some of the major conflicts plaguing the continent for decades are coming to an end, notably in Angola, the DRC and Southern Sudan. However, in 2004 instability remained in eastern DRC, Cote d'Ivoire and on the Ethiopian–Eritrean border, and there is a major humanitarian crisis going on in Darfur. War continues in northern Uganda, with an estimated one million internally displaced people. Severe political repression continues in Zimbabwe. Levels of crime remain high across most countries, especially in the cities.

Five dimensions of Africa's problems

The picture of Africa given by current development indicators is fairly well known. Indeed, if it weren't for deep poverty currently, there would be no Commission for Africa in 2005. Beyond this general picture, however, I want to bring out some key contextual patterns and trends, important for understanding the nature of Africa's current problems.

African poverty is chronic

The first is that poverty is a chronic, long-term problem for Africa. A personal story shows the meaning of this for me. In 1986, I was living in a small village in coastal Tanzania, doing research for a Ph.D. '*Mwalimu*' Julius Nyerere was just retiring from his role as the country's President after 20 years in power. Early hopes for prosperity in Tanzania had given way to resignation. Stalled economic growth, droughts in the 1970s, commodity price crashes in the 1980s, unsuccessful government interventions in industry and agriculture, and a short war with Uganda had all taken their toll. By the time I arrived the shops were empty, many basic goods were not available in Dar es Salaam, let alone in the villages, clinics were largely empty of drugs, roads were in a poor state, power cuts in the city were common, corruption was pervasive and the country had less than six days of foreign exchange reserves. I remember asking a farmer in the village whether his expectations of Independence – some twenty years previously – had been met and, if not, when he thought they might be. Not for me, he replied, but maybe for my children. Another twenty years on, those children are now adults, and some of them will already have children of their own. Following substantial World Bank/IMF-led liberalization in the second half of the 1990s, soap and cigarettes are back in the shops, there has been a construction boom in parts of Dar es Salaam, and gold mining in the west of the country is thriving. However, Tanzania remains extremely poor. Progress on reducing poverty has called been 'painstakingly slow' (Sen 2002 p 1), with little progress over the 1990s. Per capita income in Tanzania today is scarcely higher than it was in the 1970s. AIDS, which was just appearing when I left the country, is now a major killer. The majority of people now, as then, grow food and cash crops in villages without electricity, water, roads, and clinics.

The wider picture is, of anything, even worse. At independence, African countries inherited a legacy of deep poverty and very low levels of health and education provision. After some expansion in the 1960s and early 1970s, African economies stopped growing above the population growth rate for any sustained period. Excluding South Africa, average real GDP growth rates in Sub-Saharan Africa were 1.9 per cent from 1975 to 1984, 3.3 per cent from 1985 to 1989, and 2.8 per cent from 1990 to 2000 (World Bank 2002). With population growth at around 2.8 per cent throughout the period, this means African income levels are essentially unchanged in the last thirty years.[5]

Indeed, average real GDP per capita in 2000 was roughly the same as it was in 1975 – around US$950 at 1995 prices (World Bank Africa database 2002 CD ROM cited in Herbst and Mills 2003). If this country average is weighted by population, the picture is even worse. The three largest countries in Africa – Nigeria, Ethiopia and DRC, with just under 40 per cent of total population – have had a per capita income of well under $500 at 1995 prices since the beginning of the 1980s, and have seen per capita incomes fall over that period (Herbst and Mills pp 17–18). Pervasive poverty and a lack of economic growth have been surprisingly consistent patterns across different policy regimes and across countries with different resource bases.

Strikingly, African countries with oil and mineral resources can be even poorer than those without (UNDP 2004).[6] Against an average per capita income in 2002 of $1,790 for Africa in PPP terms, oil exporters Nigeria and Congo have per capita incomes of $860 and $980 respectively. Angola is not far above the average at $2,130, and has some of the worst human development indicators. The figure for mineral rich DRC is $650. These per capita figures of course hide the fact that the substantial revenues from oil and minerals are highly unequally distributed. Most of these countries do not have official data on income distribution. Nigeria is one of the few that does, with a Gini coefficient[7] of 50.6, and a $1-a-day poverty head count of 70 per cent. Thus these African countries have suffered the 'resource curse'[8] strongly (Sachs and Warner 1995). Angola and DRC have seen civil war and instability almost continuously since Independence. Congo and Nigeria have also seen coups, civil war and simmering violence over long periods of time. The impact on neighbouring countries has been considerable. Instead of realizing their potential as large regional markets, oil and mineral producers have had a destabilizing effect.

It is also true that poverty has persisted through changes of policy and external environment. Most newly independent African countries inherited systems of considerable state intervention in the economy, especially in agriculture. Marketing boards were very common. Such intervention deepened in some countries in the 1970s, with the nationalization of manufacturing and commercial enterprises. Fixed exchange rates were the order of the day. By the end of the 1970s, these systems were buckling under the strain of economic crisis, international commodity price trends, oil shocks and their own internal contradictions. By the end of the 1980s, most countries had adopted reforms in macro-economic management (especially devaluations), and by the end of the 1990s there had also been some liberalization of internal and external markets, along with less comprehensive moves towards privatization of enterprises. Equally, with the fall in the Berlin Wall in 1989, many African countries made the transition from one-party states to formal multi-party democracies. Much of this policy change was of course made under pressure from donors, especially via the IMF and the World Bank. I will argue below that such change has not been as rapid and sweeping as is sometimes made out. But change there nevertheless has been, and it is possible to see a broad move towards economic and political liberalization in Africa from the 1970s to the 2000s. However, while there have been some periods of moderately higher growth than others, usually tracking boom and slump in global demand for commodities, this thirty year trend in policy change has not produced any significant sustained impact on poverty.

Africa is economically marginalized

Chronic poverty at home has gone along with a sustained marginalization from the world economy (from a position that was already fairly marginal for most countries at Independence). It is important to be clear that this does not mean that Africa is in any sense de-linked from global trade. Merchandise trade[9] as a share of GDP for Sub-Saharan Africa (excluding Nigeria and South Africa) in 2000–01 was over 50 per cent, significantly higher than the global average. This does not include non-merchandise items like tourism.

Thus trade is very important for African economies. However, Africa's trade is very unimportant for world markets. Sub-Saharan Africa's share in world merchandise exports has declined from 3.7 per cent in 1980 to 1.5 per cent in 2002 (Table 2.2). Its share of imports has declined similarly.

The main reason why this marginalization from world trade has happened is that Africa has not shared in the global boom in higher value trade, especially high-value manufactures, that has happened over the last 25 years (UNCTAD 2003b, Subramanian and Tamirisa 2001). Instead, exports from most African countries have remained heavily concentrated in a few items, mostly primary commodities (see Table 2.3 for African LDCs).[10] What is extraordinary, looking at Table 2.3, is how many countries have totally failed to diversify since the early 1980s. Many had become even *more* concentrated

Table 2.2 Shares in world merchandise exports 1980–2002 (%)

Region/Year	1980	1985	1990	1995	2000	2002
Sub-Saharan Africa	3.7	2.5	1.9	1.5	1.5	1.5
Developing Asia	17.9	15.6	16.9	21.6	24.3	23.3
Developing America	5.5	5.6	4.2	4.4	5.5	5.9

Source: UNCTAD (2003a p 3).
Figures for 2002 are estimates.

on a few commodities by the end of the 1990s. This is another reminder that while most African countries have stabilized their economies, virtually none has adjusted to external changes. Only a handful of countries have maintained or developed significant manufacturing or non-traditional agricultural export profiles – Ghana, Kenya, Zimbabwe, Senegal and more recently Madagascar, Tanzania and Lesotho. None of these are exporting high-value products. As a result, exports per head from Africa are far lower than those in East Asia and Latin America (Table 2.4).

Even within a continuing dependence on a few primary commodities for a significant amount of export earnings, African countries have lost market share to Latin America and Asia. Low levels of investment and high transport costs have eaten into productivity. Thus, while non-fuel primary commodity exports from Latin America grew at an annual average rate of 2.9 per cent over 1980–2000, and those from Asia a full 5 per cent, Africa's exports grew only 0.6 per cent (UNCTAD 2003a Table 3 p 6). East African coffee growers have, for example, lost ground to Brazilian and Vietnamese producers.

As a result, most African economies remain exposed to terms of trade shocks and export prices in long-term decline, with well-known consequences (UNCTAD 2003a pp 19–22, Page and Hewitt 2001). The World Bank estimates that cumulative losses from adverse movements in terms of trade for African non-oil exporters (minus South Africa) for the period 1970–97 amounted to 119 per cent of combined 1997 GDP, or 68 per cent of net resource transfers to the region (World Bank 2000 pp 21–22).

Africa also remains largely marginalized from foreign investment, obtaining about 1 per cent of world flows. By comparison, developing countries as a group receive 20–30 per cent of global FDI (Table 2.5). Within Africa, most investment flows to oil and mineral exporters, and is heavily concentrated in enclave developments such as mines and refineries (Commission for Africa 2005 pp 293–94).

Marginalization from trade and investment has meant that Africa has become progressively more dependent on official development finance for external resources. The combination of dependence on non-fuel commodity exports, the oil shocks of the 1970s and the global recession of the 1980s has

Table 2.3   Share of three leading export products in total merchandise trade of selected African LDCs 1981–83 and 1997–99 (%)

	1981–83	1997–99	Items
Angola	96.5	97.6	Petroleum and diamonds
Benin	52.9	86.1	Cotton, palm oil and cashew nuts
Burkina Faso	77.5	81.8	Cotton, sugar and meat products
Burundi	81.4	98.0	Coffee tea and gold.
Cape Verde	82.2	76.0	Fish and garments
Central African Rep.	74.4	79.5	Diamonds, tropical wood and coffee
Chad	95.6	97.0	Cotton, gum arabic and livestock
Comoros	93.0	93.2	Vanilla beans and cloves
DRC	68.4	79.6	Diamonds, petroleum, cobalt, wood, coffee
Ethiopia	80.2	81.1	Coffee, sesame seeds and leather
Equatorial Guinea	84.9	93.0	Oil and wood
Gambia	74.4	69.1	Fish and groundnuts
Guinea	96.9	80.1	Aluminium, bauxite and diamonds
Guinea-Bissau	58.5	79.8	Cashew nuts and fish products
Liberia	84.6	92.2	Diamonds, rubber and timber
Madagascar	70.7	40.5	Garments, shellfish and coffee
Malawi	82.9	78.8	Tobacco, sugar, tea and coffee
Mali	81.6	92.9	Diamonds, gold, cotton and livestock
Mauritania	93.3	89.7	Fish products and iron ore
Mozambique	55.6	59.8	Prawns and cotton
Niger	94.7	83.3	Uranium and live animals
Rwanda	91.2	84.4	Tea and coffee
Senegal	52.2	49.5	Fish and fertilizers
Sierra Leone	63.2	75.3	Diamonds, footwear, cocoa beans
Somalia	94.8	79.4	Live animals
Sudan	59.0	52.6	Oil, cotton, sesame seeds
Tanzania	54.9	51.3	Coffee and cashew nuts
Togo	70.8	76.5	Calcium phosphates and cotton
Uganda	97.5	69.9	Coffee and fish
Tanzania	54.9	51.3	Coffee and cashew nuts
Zambia	93.8	89.3	Copper and cobalt

Source: UNCTAD (2002 p 109 Table 28).

Table 2.4   Exports per capita 2002 (US$)

Latin America and Caribbean	648.8
East Asia and Pacific	632.2
China	253.3
Sub-Saharan Africa	139.8
SSA excluding Nigeria and South Africa	103.1
South Asia	47.8

Calculated from UNCTAD (2003a) and UNDP (2004).

meant recurring balance of payments problems for many countries, which has been the principal cause of much of the IMF's and Bank's programme lending in the region. Chronic debt problems have led to multiple rescheduling and eventually the HIPC Initiative to relieve the debt burden, supposed to be a 'sustainable exit' from debt. However, the close link between commodity dependence and debt has come back to haunt the HIPC Initiative, as falling prices threaten to prevent countries reaching 'debt sustainability' thresholds at completion point.[11] Indeed, as long as the underlying commodity trade problems remain unsolved, African countries will simply not be able to successfully manage their debt for any length of time.

Africa is highly aid-dependent

As many African countries are Least Developed Countries, with deep and generalized poverty, most people living in them cannot earn enough to maintain their existing assets, let along save to generate growth or effectively fund public services (UNCTAD 2002a p 80). Not only have savings rates in Africa declined since 1970, they are also now the lowest of any region (Table 2.6). At the same time, a significant proportion of what savings there are leaves Africa and is not invested there. Collier et al (1999) estimated that up to 40 per cent of capital in private hands leaves Africa in capital flight, a far higher proportion than in any other region.

This leaves Africa unusually dependent on external financing. Table 2.5 shows that Africa receives a relatively small share of global foreign direct investment. However, since domestic investment is so low, foreign investment is actually still relatively important for Africa. Moreover, per capita foreign investment in Africa (excluding South Africa), at $4.61 in 1997, was slightly higher than in South Asia ($3.40). However, both are dwarfed by per capita inflows into East Asia ($35.7) and Latin America ($120) (Collier and Gunning 1999a).

As a result of low domestic resources and low investment, accumulation has been very limited. In 1990, private capital stock per worker in Sub-Saharan Africa (excluding South Africa) was $1,069. This compares with

Table 2.5 Foreign direct investment ($ billion)

Region/Year	1998	%	1999	%	2000	%	2001	%
Total World	694.46	100.0	1,088.26	100.0	1,491.93	100.0	735.15	100.0
SSA	6.23	0.9	7.92	0.7	5.79	0.4	11.84	1.6
LDCs	3.95	0.6	5.43	0.5	3.70	0.2	3.84	0.5
Developing Countries	187.61	27.0	225.14	20.7	237.89	15.9	204.80	27.9
Developing Countries (excluding China)	143.86	21.1	184.82	17.0	197.12	13.2	157.96	21.4

Source: UNCTAD (2002b).

Table 2.6   Savings as a percentage of GDP (%)

	1970	1997
Africa (including South Africa)	20.7	16.6
South Asia	17.2	20.0
East Asia	22.3	37.5
Latin America	27.0	24.0

Source: World Bank (2000).

$2,425 in South Asia, $9,711 in East Asia (including China) and $17,424 in Latin America (Collier and Gunning 1999a). As noted above, investment in human capital – for example in secondary education – is at very low levels.

Lack of investment, accumulation and growth has meant that much consumption – and indeed much of the maintenance of health and education systems – has become dependent on aid flows. Per capita real aid flows to Africa in the 1960s were roughly on a par with those to Latin America, higher than those to East Asia, but lower than those to South Asia. By the 1970s and 1980s, however, they had mushroomed about ten-fold, peaking in the mid-1990s (Herbst and Mills 2003 p 16). In 2002, ODA per head to Africa was $27, compared with $10 for Latin America and $6 for Asia.[12] Overall, between 1960 and 2002 Africa (including South Africa) has received some $479 billion in aid, at 2002 prices.[13]

It is often said that Africa requires a 'Marshall Plan', offering much higher levels of aid than are currently on offer. The context is of course very different from that of Europe recovering from war. But in quantitative terms, at the height of the original Marshall Plan, aid to France and Germany was in the region of 2.5–3 per cent of GDP. In contrast, aid as a percentage of GDP in 2002 for almost all African countries was far above Marshall Plan levels (Table 2.7). Only some of the oil exporters had lower levels. Even donor 'pariahs' such as Sudan and Zimbabwe are receiving aid to the same proportion as the Marshall Plan. At the other extreme, in countries such as Mozambique and Sierra Leone over half the national income is aid. In many countries, aid makes up a majority of the resources available for government spending. In this sense, Africa has already received many Marshall Plans. Since African countries are very much poorer than European ones were at the end of World War II, a more appropriate way of looking at the comparison might be to look at absolute levels of aid. The Marshall Plan involved $13 billion of US aid over three and a half years, or $76 billion in 2004 prices.[14] This amounts to just over $20 billion a year. By comparison Sub-Saharan Africa received $23.7 billion in official aid in 2003.[15] Since Africa has a much larger population than Western Europe did at the time of the Marshall Plan, this means only $37 per head for Africa, as opposed to $293 per head in Western Europe (both at 2004 prices). On the

Table 2.7   Aid as a percentage of GDP 2002 (%)

Mozambique	57.2
Sierra Leone	54.1
Mauritania	36.7
Eritrea	35.9
Guinea-Bissau	29.2
Burundi	23.9
Ethiopia	21.6
Rwanda	20.6
Malawi	19.8
Zambia	17.3
Gambia	17.0
Burkina Faso	15.1
DRC	14.1
Mali	14.0
Congo	13.9
Niger	13.7
Tanzania	13.1
Chad	11.6
Uganda	11.0
Lesotho	10.7
Ghana	10.6
Cote d'Ivoire	9.1
Senegal	8.9
Madagascar	8.5
Benin	8.2
Guinea	7.8
Cameroon	7.0
Central African Republic	5.7
Togo	3.7
Angola	3.7
Kenya	3.2
Sudan	2.6
Zimbabwe	2.4
Swaziland	2.1
Gabon	1.4
Nigeria	0.7

Source: UNDP (2004).

other hand, Africa has received aid over a much longer period of time than three and a half years.

Africa contrasts with Asia

By contrast with Africa's chronic problems of poverty, low economic growth, and commodity dependence in trade, since the 1960s a group of countries in East and South-east Asia have demonstrated the fastest falls in poverty ever witnessed over the same period. This group includes the leader (Japan), the 'Asian Tigers' (Taiwan, South Korea, Singapore and Hong Kong) and a second wave of newly industrializing economies (Malaysia, Indonesia, and Thailand). For this group of countries, average GNP per capita over the period 1965 to 1990 grew by 5.5 per cent every year (World Bank 1993 p 2), and until the 1990s, distributions of income remained relatively equal. Since the 1970s, Taiwan and South Korea have effectively eliminated $1-a-day poverty. During the 1970s and 1980s Indonesia, Malaysia, and Thailand also achieved large reductions in poverty rates, although there are still poor areas within these countries (World Bank 1993 p 33). The 'Asian miracle' has most recently been joined by China, which has produced double-digit economic growth in most years since 1990, and has halved its poverty rate.

In the 1960s, incomes in Asia were substantially lower than those in Africa – on average less than half. But the contrasting growth pictures meant that per capita incomes in the East Asia and Pacific region overtook those in Africa by 1990, and are now about three times higher (Herbst and Mills 2003 p 13).[16] Tables 2.8 and 2.9 show how, from similar starting points, African and East and South-east Asian paths have diverged. China was one of Asia's poorest countries in the 1970s, with income per capita comparable with Malawi or Chad at the time. While per capita income in China has now grown six-fold, it has stagnated in these African countries. The collapse of incomes in the DRC can also be clearly seen.

The contrast between two oil giants is also interesting. Nigeria and Indonesia are both large, populous oil exporters. Initially poorer than Nigeria in 1975, Indonesia had seen per capita incomes triple by the late 1990s, whereas in Nigeria they are actually lower than they were in 1975. Kenya, from a similar initial level, has done little better. There are similar contrasts at higher initial income levels; Thailand and Senegal, or Malaysia and Cote d'Ivoire all show similar divergence.

In East and South-east Asia, economic growth has also been translated very effectively into human development, with rapid improvements in mortality rates, health, and education across the region (World Bank 1993 pp 43–45). Even in the 1970s these countries tended to have a high human development index for their level of income. But again, African countries starting from similar initial levels have not kept pace (Table 2.9).

Table 2.8   GDP pre capita trends for SSA and East and South-east Asia
countries (GDP at 1987 US$ prices)

	1975	1980	1985	1990	1997
SSA	671	661	550	542	518
South-east Asia and Pacific	481	616	673	849	1,183
China	109	138	210	285	564
Malawi	155	167	159	154	166
DRC	307	241	225	190	97
Indonesia	265	349	417	537	785
Nigeria	349	373	277	311	315
Kenya	332	370	354	392	372
Thailand	557	718	854	1,291	1,870
CAR	523	480	472	418	387
Senegal	716	661	664	676	674
Malaysia	1,253	1,688	1,902	2,262	3,387
South Korea	1,461	1,929	2,677	4,132	6,251
Cote d'Ivoire	1,169	1,181	992	893	899
Sudan	1,065	1,026	943	891	–

Source: UNDP (1999, 2004).

Table 2.9   Human Development Index trends for selected SSA and East and
South-east Asia countries

	1975	1980	1985	1990	1995	2001
China	0.521	0.554	0.588	0.624	0.679	0.721
Zimbabwe	0.544	0.570	0.626	0.614	0.567	0.496
Indonesia	0.464	0.526	0.578	0.619	0.659	0.682
Congo	0.462	0.506	0.553	0.538	0.517	0.502

Source: UNDP (2003).

Finally, the East and South-east Asian countries have transformed their
production and trade over the last thirty years. For the small countries, such
as Singapore and Taiwan, trade has been a key part of their development
strategy. For larger ones, and especially China, internal markets have proven
large enough for a more domestically focused approach.

It is clear from Table 2.2 (p 11) that Asian countries have managed to
capture an increasing share of world trade over the last 25 years. In fact, for
the original Asian Tigers the expansion started from the mid-1960s. Between

1965 and 1980, these countries managed to increase their share of world trade from 1.5 per cent to 3.8 per cent, and their share in exports of manufactures from 1.5 per cent to 5.3 per cent (World Bank 1993 Table 1.5 p 38). The other South-east Asian countries started later, from lower levels, but have still managed to significantly increase their shares.

As noted, East and South-east Asia have competed successfully with Africa even in the core traditional area of commodities. However, all these countries have also demonstrated the ability to diversify from low-value agricultural commodities into higher-value manufacturing and services. China and the four original Asian Tigers especially have moved very successfully into the highest value, high-technology products, including electronics, computers and components, and communications technology. Table 2.10 shows that this group of countries has achieved double-digit growth in high-tech exports and production on average *every year* between 1985 and 1997. China's high-tech exports grew at an astonishing 30 per cent per year.

There are obviously all sorts of initial differences between Africa and the East and South-east Asia regions, and explanations for their divergence are discussed below. Nor is this comparison necessarily an argument that Africa could or should emulate the particular path that the Asian Tigers have taken. However, this stark divergence in income, human development and productive terms since the 1960s is very real, and I will argue, of central importance to thinking about Africa's current problems.

AIDS is a massive burden

By the mid-1980s, most non-oil exporting African countries were in trouble. The trend towards falling commodity prices had been masked by the short-lived boom of the 1970s, unravelling much of the post-Independence growth.

Table 2.10   Rates of growth of high technology and other manufacturing 1985–97 (%)

	All production	All exports	High-tech production	High-tech exports
China	11.7	20.5	14.9	30.2
South Korea	10.2	10.6	15.4	18.7
Taiwan	4.7	12.0	11.6	18.9
Singapore	8.0	15.0	13.1	21.7
Hong Kong	−0.20	13.5	3.5	18.1

Source: Lall (2003 p 6 Table 1).
'High tech' consists of 18 products in the SIC classification, and includes information communications technology products. This group typically has a high R&D element.

Countries such as Zambia, which saw copper revenues plummet, were hit very hard. School enrolment rates stopped improving and health systems had started to collapse. The complex and difficult task of trying to diversify out of commodities and lead investment to improve productivity in a competitive world economy was a big enough challenge on its own.

However, it was precisely in the mid-1980s that the AIDS epidemic in Africa began to unfold. From a few isolated cases, estimated HIV prevalence rates have climbed to above 35 per cent in some Southern African countries. As already mentioned, AIDS is established across the continent. The burden of AIDS on society and economy makes the development challenge much more daunting. AIDS is having an impact at virtually every level (see UNAIDS 2004 ch 3 for a recent review).

In spite of economic crisis and prolonged stagnation from the mid-1970s onwards, many countries managed to maintain progress on some health indicators, including falling and child mortality rates into the 1980s (eg Hill 1992). However, by the late 1980s, these gains were starting to be reversed in countries such as Zambia, and excess adult mortality was beginning to appear as a result of the growing epidemic (Timaeus 1998). With both adults and children dying from AIDS, progress on life expectancy at birth has been reversed. In Botswana life expectancy has plummeted from around 65 in 1990 to below 35. In Swaziland life expectancy was still increasing in the 1980s towards 55, but has also now collapsed to little over 30. Due to the nature of AIDS, the life expectancy of adults has been affected particularly hard; in some countries 60 per cent of 15 years olds cannot expect to live to 60 (UNAIDS 2004).

The impacts of illness and deaths on this scale are pervasive and deep. At the household level, illness will mean the loss of income and labour of patient (who are frequently adults), increased household expenditures on medicines, and other household members missing school or work to care for the patient. Some studies in Southern Africa show income falling by 60–80 per cent. Death means the permanent loss of income, substantial expenditures on funerals and mourning, and frequently the removal of children from school to save on costs and provide labour on farms. In some cases people change what they are growing, reducing the variety of crops. Death of mothers or both parents frequently leads to households breaking up and orphaned children living alone or relying on relatives (UNAIDS 2004 ch 3, Barnett and Whiteside 2002, Bollinger and Stover 1999).[17] The additional burden of AIDS on rural households has meant that many have, over time, sold off any assets they may have, leaving them much more vulnerable to drought or other shocks (eg Koestle 2002). As adults die, old skills are lost. A 'new variant' of famine linked to the impact of AIDS may be emerging in Southern Africa (De Waal and Tumushabe 2003).[18]

There has also been a huge impact on public services. This is firstly because of the loss of skilled staff through illness and death, including teachers in education and doctors and nurses in the health sector. Secondly the additional burden on the health sector in many countries has been enormous, with a larger number of patients seeking care, and also because, even with the cost of ART coming down, AIDS care is more expensive than that for many other diseases.

For African firms, AIDS adds costs not only in terms of absenteeism due to illness and workers attending funerals, high turnover and loss of workers through death, but also increasingly in a direct burden of higher pension and health care costs. One study in South Africa estimated that the costs of benefits – disability pension, spouses pension, and lump sum at death – would rise from 7 per cent of salaries in 1995 to 19 per cent in 2005 (cited in Bollinger and Stover 1999 p 5; see also Aventin and Huard 2000).

Overall, the impact of AIDS will also be evident at the macro-economic level. In the early 1990s it was estimated that in the most severely affected countries, AIDS could lower the rate of growth by about 0.3 per cent per year (Over 1992). Another review paper cites an impact of up to 25 per cent over a 20 year period (Bollinger and Stover 1999 p 7).

In summary, Africa's current situation is rooted in a long history of low growth and failed development, spanning different policy regimes and fashions. Levels of income in the 1960s were not that different from many countries in East and South-east Asia that have since left Africa far behind, economically and in human development terms. Crucially, most African countries have failed to diversify their exports away from a narrow range of commodities whose prices are falling and volatile. Africa has not played any role in the global boom in high value manufactures trade. A combination of low savings, capital flight and low levels of FDI have meant that Africa has developed an extraordinary dependence on aid for physical and human investment. Finally, an already challenging situation by the 1980s has since got a lot worse with the impact of AIDS.

Any account of why Africa faces the current situation it does must fit with these broad facts. Any policy proposals for the way forward must also recognize them. In the next three chapters I look at explanations, policies and recommendations coming from two important sources – donors and international NGOs.

NGOs and donors produce analyses of Africa only periodically, the former usually in response to the latter. These analyses are in any case based on the general approaches to development taken by protagonists. Much of the debate in the UK has been dominated by a few themes: trade, aid and debt relief, and to a lesser extent, governance and corruption. NGOs have tended to argue that unfair trade rules, a paucity of aid and debt relief, and invasive conditionality attached to development finance have been responsible for poverty in developing countries, and by extension, in Africa. Donors have been more selectively critical of the current trading system, promoting a more general liberalization both North and South as the route to growth and poverty reduction, along with trade capacity building. They have also been much keener on conditionality, and much more concerned with the domestic governance of developing countries, and maybe Africa in particular. Running through these debates, one of the critical issues has been 'policy space' – how much can and should donors and international agreements constrain the freedom of developing country governments to choose their own policies. In the next three chapters I attempt to summarize these positions and see how far they can take us in understanding the African situation.

3 The truth about trade

I START WITH TRADE. Trade matters for Africa because African economies are small. The entire Sub-Saharan African economy is about the same size as that of France or Italy.[19] Even Nigeria, with a national income of $102 billion in 2001 at purchasing power parity, is smaller than Portugal and only about two-thirds the size of London's regional economy.[20] Ghana is about the economic size of Liverpool. As a result, internal demand within any one country is too weak and unstable to maintain high growth levels (Easterly and Kraay 2000). Even if African economies were to receive a massive inflow of aid, and this aid were well used to kick-start an accumulation process, a sustainable path of economic growth and escape from poverty would still mean accessing external markets through increased export earnings (Fafchamps, Teal and Toye 2001 p 1).

This does not of course mean that increased trade will lead directly or automatically to poverty reduction. Indeed African countries are already very open in the sense that trade makes up a relatively large proportion of GDP. As UNCTAD (2004) explains, for expanded trade to lead to poverty reduction, states need to manage the process, ensuring linkages between export production and the wider economy, enhancing broad-based learning, productivity gains and investment in infrastructure to enable more people to take part, and managing the growth in imports that typically accompany export growth in poor countries.

However, while certainly not sufficient, expanding trade is necessary for economic growth and poverty reduction in Africa. It will also become clear that states that can lead an economy to increase the value of the exports in a sustainable way, can also usually manage the sufficient conditions outlined above. Equally, Africa's poor trade record, and the limited impact of export earnings on poverty (especially in oil and mineral exporters) are intimately related.

Trade policy debates

Given the need for African countries to expand their trade, what are the policy issues? Current debates on trade policy between donors and NGOs have focused largely on the World Trade Organization, so this is a good place to start. What are the implications of WTO negotiations for Africa? Do they touch on the critical needs of countries, and if not, then what are these?

Agricultural subsidies

The issue that has seen the widest public debate is also the one on which there is the widest agreement (within the UK at least) – eliminating trade-distorting agricultural subsidies in the rich world.[21] This is part of the proposed agenda for the Agreement on Agriculture (AoA) within the current Doha Round of negotiations. The current system, in which something of the order of US $200–300 billion a year goes to support farmers in OECD countries, in a variety of means, is condemned by NGOs,[22] (including the Trade Justice Movement network of over fifty organizations and the Make Poverty History Coalition), by the UK government[23] and by the World Bank (2003) alike. NGOs have focused on examples of how particular developing countries or communities in them would benefit from higher world prices for their produce and better access to EU and US agricultural markets.

But how important would the removal of subsidies in the EU and US actually be for Africa? Very large figures for potential gains from agricultural liberalization have been given. For example, using a model that incorporates both static and dynamic gains, the World Bank (2003) gives a global figure of $358 billion annually at 1997 prices. It calculates gains to low and middle-income countries from agricultural liberalization in high-income countries of some $75 billion annually at 1995 prices.

However, a closer examination of the situation shows that Africa's share of this is likely to be fairly small. A good recent review is to be found in Sachs et al (2004 pp 31–34). First, in all the models, the majority of the total gains (for example two-thirds in the World Bank case) come from dynamic effects, whereby initial gains from greater export earnings are invested in the economy and produce multiplier effects. However, such gains assume that complementary policies to ensure efficient investment and growth are in place. It will be shown below that this is not the case in most African economies, so the net impact including dynamic effects is likely to be smaller than that given by models.

Second, African countries vary by whether they are net exporters or importers of different agricultural products, including foods. Net importers (which include many countries) would be hit by increases in world prices, unless it is assumed that they would be fully compensated under the Marrakech Agreement.

Third, the impact of liberalization is highly commodity and country-specific. In the case of sugar, as NGOs themselves note (eg CAFOD, Actionaid and Oxfam 2004), many African producing countries enjoy preferential access to EU markets, and so could actually lose from a liberalized

EU regime. Low cost sugar producers such as Australia and Brazil would stand the most to gain from an anticipated rise in prices. The net impact on African producing countries, such as Malawi, Mozambique and others in Southern Africa is 'unclear, and if positive, likely to be extremely small' (Sachs et al 2004 p 33, Borrell 1999). The impact on net importing countries could be negative, as mentioned above.

One of the most important and indeed most discussed commodities is cotton, with production subsidized most heavily by the USA, up to $2 billion a year (Achterbosch et al 2004 p 19). This is an issue for West African producing nations, as price falls have had an impact in the region of 1– 3 per cent of GDP (eg Achterbosch et al p 19, UNCTAD 2003c p 7). Production in Mali and Benin in the year 2000/01 was 9 per cent and 5.3 per cent of GDP respectively, and much more of merchandise exports (Sachs et al 2004 p 32). One estimate is that global elimination of support to cotton farmers would lead to a 10–12 per cent rise in world prices (Baffes 2004). This would mean a 13 per cent boost to exports, but translate into a welfare gain of only 1–2 per cent increase in GDP (Sachs et al 2004 p 32). Gillson (2004 p 3) predicts price increases in the range 12–28 per cent, and gains to West Africa producers between $94 million and $360 million.

What does this mean on the ground? According to Oxfam, around 10 million people depend directly on cotton production in Central and West Africa (Oxfam 2002c p 2). Taking the upper of the two figures above for impact – $360 million – this translates into a figure of $36 per dependent person per year in static gains. For people living in countries with per capita incomes of under $500 a year, this is a significant sum. However, it shows that cotton production in a liberalized world, by itself, will offer only a relatively small step away from deep poverty. Furthermore, the total population of producing countries is of course much larger. If Nigeria is excluded, it is of the order of 50 million people, giving a broader per capita impact of only around $7. Dynamic effects would bring this up to $21 per head per year, but it is unlikely that these would be fully realized, given the absence of factors and policies encouraging investment. Thus although they would be welcome, and the income would at least largely reach small farmers directly, these benefits will be relatively modest. The removal of cotton subsidies will not make a serious dent in broader West African poverty.

More generally, taking into account varying impacts on countries, a range of studies give Africa as a whole a net benefit from global agricultural liberalization of $2–5 billion per year, or up to 2 per cent of GDP at most (see Sachs et al 2004 pp 33–34 for a review). It is important to remember that this is not a growth rate, but a step up in income level. Achterbosch et al (2004) estimate static gains for Africa of 0.7 per cent of income, but also warn that partial reform (ie modest reductions in export subsidies and domestic support) would lead to net losses for Africa, a finding echoed by the UNECA (2004 p 67). Again, dynamic effects in models might increase the impact of global agricultural liberalization to an income gain of the order of 5–6 per cent of GDP per year, although actual effects in Africa would almost certainly be much smaller. And again it is important to remember that this is not a growth rate, but rather a percentage change in income flows. I am not arguing against the elimination of rich world agricultural subsidies. It is clear that there may be some gains for Africa from such liberalization. However, while they would be welcome, it is clear that these modest gains do not represent the transformation that Africa needs.

African producers of agricultural commodities will fail to benefit more deeply from the removal of agricultural subsidies in the EU and US partly because, for some commodities like sugar (although not cotton), they are less efficient than producers elsewhere. As noted in chapter 2 above, even in primary commodities, they have tended to lose market share across a range of products (although cotton is an exception). With investment in production and especially in transport infrastructure, this could of course change. The recent experience of sugar in Kenya shows that simply with improved accountability and corporate governance, the domestic industry can improve competitiveness substantially.[24] However, the question of how African producers can become more competitive, and therefore capture increased benefits from the elimination of rich world subsidies, is a much broader one, to which we return below.

Commodity dependence

The underlying reason why eradicating rich world subsidies will not address Africa's poverty problem is that already noted in chapter 2 above – African exports are highly concentrated on primary commodities, and for most countries, the concentration of merchandise exports has also remained unchanged for the last two decades. To escape the chronic poverty trap in the long term, African economies desperately need to *diversify* away from low-value primary commodities. Table 2.3 (p 12) reminds us that the value of exports for each person in East Asia is more than six times that of the per capita value for each African. This is of an order of magnitude higher than the gains from liberalizing world trade in agricultural commodities.

Despite the fact that this is Africa's most fundamental long-term external problem, NGOs in the UK have recently largely ignored the commodity concentration problem (they share this blind spot with the WTO). Oxfam (2002a ch 6) is one exception, with an overall analysis and a campaign on coffee (2002d). Their analysis is that low and volatile prices are caused by 'structural oversupply', and that producers suffer because an increasingly small proportion of the value added of the final product (ground or instant coffee in the shops in the North) goes to the farmer. Their recommendations follow from this analysis – essentially to resuscitate international commodity agreements, and to require the roasting and processing multinationals to adopt some form of fair trade pricing. A similar range of proposals has also been recently discussed by DfID (2004a).

The fair trade campaign has had some success in its immediate aims, even if the actual trade gains so far are modest. In the UK, supermarket own brands, and some multinationals, such as Kraft and Nestlé, appear to be developing 'fairer trade' products that will pay a premium to farmers, although less than the guaranteed price that Fair Trade Foundation certified products give.[25] Even the latter represents only a small increase in income, relative to the depth of poverty that farmers face. What is probably much more important is the institutional support to cooperatives, enabling them to access markets more effectively and ultimately to diversify their products.[26] And fair trade products still currently occupy a small niche (for example 'Divine' fairly traded chocolate achieved sales of £5.7 million in 2004 in a UK chocolate market worth almost £4 billion, a market share of just over 0.1 per cent).

The revival of international commodity agreements is far less likely to work. The difficulties of commodity markets run very deep, beyond the well-known problems of low income-elasticity of demand. The underlying reason is that increasing productivity in primary commodities can only really come from increasing the supply of the commodity per unit of land or labour. This contrasts with manufacturing, where increased productivity arises at least partly out of technical change and innovation, where new products can command higher prices. In the words of Gilbert and ter Wengel (2000 p 28): 'a year 2000 automobile is qualitatively superior to its 1980 counterpart. By contrast, a bag of year 2000 coffee beans will, broadly, be indistinguishable from beans from the same origin in 1980'. As a result, the terms of trade between commodities and manufactures will always tend to be in long-term decline.

In these circumstances, international commodity agreements aimed at price support are almost impossible to sustain for any length of time, as they become enormously expensive. Those (consuming) countries that have the resources to fund them also have no incentive for doing so (Gilbert 1996, Page and Hewitt 2001 pp 24–25, Deaton 1999 p 39).[27] The only alternative would be the much more radical one of entirely suspending global markets in commodities, replacing them with a centrally determined allocation and pricing system, hard to imagine in the current political climate.

This contrast between primary commodities and manufactures is also part of the explanation for the striking divergence between the price for the primary tropical agricultural commodities (say, green coffee beans) and the price for the finished product (roasted, ground and packaged coffee in the shops), meaning that over time the primary commodity has made up a lower proportion of the cost of the final product. Thus, whereas in 1984, 64 per cent of the retail price of a cup of coffee in the US was the cost of the green beans, this had fallen to 18 per cent by 2001 (Oxfam 2002d p 20). This trend is partly due to the decreasing market power of producers relative to the large corporations dominating processing, shipping and retailing. However, it is also due to the fact that final products involving primary commodities have value added in, and are sold in industrialized economies where both costs and incomes are linked closely to rising productivity in manufactures and services. Thus the largest profits in products made from commodities are to be found at the downstream end of the value chain, towards wholesaling and retailing especially. This is clearest in the few areas where there is innovation, such as with specialty products at the consumer end (for example with 'single estate' teas and coffees). The higher prices for these products are captured by processors and retailers, not by producing countries. The key problem for producers, or producing countries, is that these markets are very difficult to enter. Thus, for example, for the Ghanaian or Cote d'Ivorian chocolate manufacturer the biggest challenge is how to break into US and EU markets, dominated by very large firms such as Nestlé or Hershey that are able to spend very large amounts of money on advertising. Brand establishment in these circumstances is extremely difficult.[28]

This leaves commodity producing countries with the prospect of trying to increase export earnings simply by raising the productivity sufficiently to out-compete producers in other regions. In fact, this has been a successful strategy in coffee for Vietnam and Brazil, and in copper for Chile, all of whom have gained market share at the expense of Africa producers (see previous chapter).[29] African countries would benefit from winning back some of that ground, but it is clear that with low price elasticities of demand, this is close to a zero sum game, and higher productivity from any one region will lower world prices still further. Indeed, for some commodities Africa has been particularly hurt by the fact that, while productivity increases in primary commodity production have been seen in countries not highly dependent on those commodities for export earnings, Africa has been both commodity dependent *and* uncompetitive.

There are steps that can be taken *within* the constraints of commodity production, including better domestic and international competition authorities to counter the growing market power of the few large corporations that increasingly dominate one or more of the marketing and processing stages of different commodities (Gilbert and ter Wengel 2000, DfID 2004a). Equally, there are cases for support to producer organizations, and for the provision of some of the functions of the now defunct marketing boards, such as extension and input packages. However, as long as primary commodities continue to be traded within world markets, these measures offer producers only a higher proportion of a small and shrinking price.

A major danger, then, of seeking solutions to the 'commodity problem' is that, much like EU banana and sugar regimes, it inadvertently becomes a way of encouraging African economies to continue relying on commodity exports (Page and Hewitt 2001 pp 17–19).[30] It seeks to compensate producers for not moving up the value chain, rather than encouraging them to do so. It works against what Africa really needs to do to address its chronic poverty problem, which is to diversify production and exports.

Diversification

The first question about Africa diversifying its trade is diversification into what? The standard assumed 'ladder' of diversification in exports is from commodities into labour-intensive light industrial products such as shoes and garments. The next step is into intermediate goods – heavy manufacturing inputs (steel, or chemicals, say) and components within global product chains, such as electronic equipment or automobiles. The final step is into high-value finished manufactured goods, including consumer electronics, and high technology products such as silicon chips. Along the way service exports may also be developed. This is the path taken by many of the highly successful East Asian economies, with several South-east Asian economies coming up behind them. Mauritius has also moved from sugar to garments and tourism as its major export earners.

However, there are some reasons why most African countries may not take this route (Wood 2002, Arrighi 2002, Deaton 1999). The argument is that Africa's production and trade path will be determined by its relative factor endowments. Because it is more land and mineral abundant than Asia, Africa will always have larger agricultural and extractive sectors and a smaller manufacturing sector than Asia does. In this sense, Wood argues, Africa will end up looking much more like America (North and South), which has a lot more primary products in its export mix. Asia's comparative advantage lies in lots of (cheap) labour, which is why Asian countries have done so well at exporting labour intensive manufactures. Others have made a similar argument that, within the Asian context, Africa's path is likely to be more like the relatively natural resource abundant South-east Asian countries such as Malaysia, Indonesia and the Philippines, rather than the land scarce East Asian countries of Japan, Taiwan and Korea (Lindauer and Roemer 1994).

This would mean African countries face a tough challenge. Wood's analysis implies that movement into manufactures to the same degree that East Asia would be extremely difficult, working against Africa's factor endowments. At the same time, diversification out of commodity exports by moving up the value chain of agricultural products (ie from cocoa to cocoa butter or chocolate, or from green coffee beans to instant coffee) has almost never worked as a development strategy (Page and Hewitt 2001 p 15). One problem is that tariff escalation in Northern markets works against this strategy, although I will argue below that this is not a decisive factor; the more fundamental problem is market entry, as explained above.

However, the argument from factor endowments is based on a static notion of comparative advantage. While factor endowments do exert an influence on how easy or hard it is to compete in a product on world markets, experience shows immediately that they are not determinant. The experience of East Asia has been that comparative advantage can be dynamically shaped, and South-east Asian countries, with similar factor endowments as many African countries, have succeeded in expanding their manufacturing exports (World Bank 1993 pp 37–38). Thus, in practice, if Africa is more likely to follow the paths of Latin America or South-east Asia rather than that of East Asia, export growth will come from a combination of diversification into manufactures (probably including some intermediate processed agricultural and natural resource products), services and commodities, where growth in the latter will have to come from increased productivity (Fafchamps et al 2001 p 13). The essential step remains to move away from commodity *dependence*. The developmental challenge is substantial. What are the main elements of this challenge?

Market access

From both the NGO side and the donor side there is a broad agreement on the barriers to diversifying – market access problems, especially tariff escalation and tariff peaks, and supply-side problems. However, while NGOs tend to emphasize market access problems, donors tend to emphasize supply side problems. Here I examine the market access case, returning to supply side, or trade capacity issues, in chapter 5 below.

Oxfam (2002a ch 4) again has the fullest statement of the NGO position, drawing attention to Northern protection in areas where developing countries have comparative advantage, arguing that barriers against the developing world are four times higher than those against rich world competitors. This arises from the differences between tariff barriers to industrialized goods (under 3 per cent on average in 1999), labour-intensive manufactures typically exported from developing countries (around 8 per cent) and agricultural goods (14 per cent) (Oxfam 2002a p 100). They also deal specifically with tariff escalation (pp 102–03), arguing that: 'the removal of escalating tariffs would enable developing countries to capture locally a larger share of the final value of export earnings . . .' (p 102). The examples used are all from agricultural commodities and processed foods. The UK government has also recently criticized the use of tariff peaks and escalation (HM Treasury and DTI 2004 pp 47–48 and ch 6 specifically on Africa).[31] Again, the example used is a foodstuff (the frequently cited cocoa/chocolate contrast), but a wider range of data is also used. However, as with subsidies, what appears to be a simple powerful argument becomes less clear in the case of Africa.

First there is the issue of Africa's preferential access. Many of the statements about tariff escalation apply to the pattern of tariffs under the Most Favoured Nation (MFN) system, or sometimes, under Generalized Systems of Preferences (GSP).[32] However, African countries have enjoyed further preferential access to EU markets under the EU–ACP Lomé Convention (now Cotonou) since 1975, and African LDCs since 2001 under the Everything But Arms (EBA) agreement. Most African countries have also enjoyed preferential access (especially for apparel) to the US under the American Growth and Opportunities Act (AGOA), and there are also preferential access arrangements for LDCs into high-income Asian markets (Achterbosch et al 2004 p 38).

Even before the introduction of the EBA, it was estimated that for most African countries, 97–98 per cent of existing exports to the EU entered at a zero tariff (Amjadi et al 1996 p 15). Only Cote d'Ivoire and Kenya faced more than 10 non-zero MFN duty lines. The analysis of 19 commodity chains (covering agricultural non-food materials, oil seeds and ores and minerals) also shows that for this range of products, tariff escalation applied to only a few product chains, and mostly at levels below 10 per cent (Amjadi et al 1996 p 22). The updated and broader analysis by Achterbosch et al (2004) shows that Sub-Saharan African countries enjoy substantial preference margins over MFN tariffs particularly in textiles, clothing and footwear exports into the EU and into high-income Asia, and into all three major Northern trading areas for heavier industrial products (2004 p 39). The highest tariff barriers facing African countries exporting into OECD markets are in cereals and sugar (even with preferences). Tariff barriers to light and heavier industrial products are much lower (2004 p 41). Thus overall, Sub-Saharan African countries have enjoyed substantial preferential access over a range of goods, including those they might want to diversify into, over a number of years. The Commission for Africa (2005 p 268) concludes that tariff escalation is not the main problem in accessing markets, but rather non-tariff barriers such as product standards, rules of origin (see below) and reputational barriers.

However, in many cases these preferences have not been taken up fully. Sugar is one example, where only Mauritius and Swaziland (and to a lesser extent Malawi) have really taken advantage of preferential access to the EU. In the case of the AGOA, again only a few countries – notably Kenya and Lesotho – have effectively utilized improved access to US markets for garments. Indeed, the EU is currently seeking to eliminate ACP preferences in the new Economic Partnership Agreements under the Cotonou convention on the grounds that they have not been effective.

In practice, both the recent preference systems for Africa have problems (Stevens and Kennan 2003). One is that quota based systems such as the EU–ACP preferences impose heavy administrative demands and uncertainties on producers – often the devil is in the detail. Another is that the rules of origin are too restrictive, applying particularly to the EBA system (Brenton 2003) and early on to AGOA (Mattoo et al 2002). Another problem, specifically with AGOA, is that preferences on clothing exports have not been given to all African countries (Brenton and Ikezuki 2004). Yet another is the inappropriate and rapidly shifting application of non-tariff barriers, such as the EU's use of Sanitary and Phyto-sanitary (SPS) regulations (Stevens and Kennan 2003 pp 4–5) which African countries have had difficulty in meeting. All the preference systems have a limited life, which creates uncertainty about what will follow after they expire, which can deter investment in export capacity.

Perhaps most importantly, preferences for African countries are only worth a lot if they actually give a relative advantage over other developing countries: 'Often a preference is available effectively to all suppliers, in which case it is as if it did not exist' (Stevens and Kennan 2003 p 3). Thus, for example, although the EBA agreement gives African LDCs duty free access to the EU for almost all products, it also gives that access to other LDCs, such as Bangladesh. Since the latter has a mature garments industry, against which African countries would have no obvious competitive advantage, Africa's preferential access to the EU on garments under EBA is of little interest to potential investors. Only if an African country had offsetting attractions (perhaps efficient, low cost domestic cotton and textile industries) would this change. This is indeed one reason why preferential access quotas to the USA on garments under AGOA has led to investment in and a growth in exports from Lesotho and Kenya, ie precisely because other, especially Asian, developing countries do not have this access. The AGOA garment quota scheme has been perhaps the most effective and useful of the preference systems for Africa, because it has encouraged diversification away from commodities (even if the resulting export production has few backward linkages and is based in export processing zones close to ports). Unfortunately, this system has also now come to the end of its effectiveness, as the complete phase out of the Multi-Fibre Agreement (MFA) from the beginning of 2005 now means that African producers can only be offered some tariff preferences, unlikely to be enough to help them against competition from India and China.

Thus the market access picture for Africa is complex – many countries and especially LDCs have benefited from preferential (and often duty free) access to OECD markets, but at the same time, these preference schemes have had limitations and problems. However, the fact that some countries have been able to exploit some preferences, while others have completely failed to do so, means that the capacity to export and to market products abroad must be a key factor in determining trade performance.

In a broader sense, this can be clearly seen in the challenging market access conditions facing the newly industrializing countries (NICs) in East Asia at the time of their export drive at the start of the 1960s. These were far more severe than those faced by African countries in recent years (Amjadi et al 1996 Box 1 p 17). This export push pre-dated the creation of the GSP in the 1970s, so these East Asian countries were competing without preferences. They enjoyed no special preferences of the EU–ACP or AGOA type. Average tariffs on imports of manufactured goods from developing countries in the

1960s were 17.9 per cent in the USA, 19.5 per cent in the UK, 14.3 per cent in the European Community and 18.0 per cent in Japan. By comparison, OECD tariffs on African manufactures in the mid-1990s averaged 1 per cent. The Asian NICs also faced stiff non-tariff barriers (NTBs) in the form of 'Voluntary Export Restraints' (which were not really voluntary).

It is true that this export push came at a time of an expansionary phase of the world economy along with financial stability and predictability, which was over by the time of the late 1970s and early 1980s. The recession in the later period not only meant a shrinking market in the North, but also a rise in levels of protection that was discriminatory against developing countries (Wade 1990 pp 346–47), although preferential access for Africa meant that it escaped some of the worst of this. However, the end of the Uruguay Round, increasing FDI to developing countries and a recovery in global demand in the 1990s means that opportunities did improve again. Amjadi et al (1996) concluded that: 'the external environment for exports facing Africa today appears to be considerably more favourable than that which faced, and was overcome by, the Asian NICs'. They go on to infer that supply side problems are a more important cause of Africa's marginalization in world trade.

Before turning to this issue, there is one more external factor to consider. While OECD agricultural subsidies and market access barriers are not fundamental problems for African long-term export growth and diversification, one such problem does exist – China. As labour costs have risen in the original NICs, production of cheap manufactures has shifted to other countries with large pools of labour, including Vietnam and Bangladesh, and now China. In fact China now dominates developing country exports of all types, whether resource based, low-tech labour intensive manufactures or high-tech (Lall 2003 pp 24–25). China's exports of manufactured goods have exploded from around $5 billion in 1985, to almost $170 billion in 1998, and around $225 billion in 2000. Along with China, Africa will face increasing competition from India, which is beginning to crank up its export drive. As preferences erode, African countries risk losing the small advantages they currently hold. As noted, this will definitely be the case in apparel, where the ending of the MFA means that the likes of Kenya and Lesotho will no longer be protected from China and India by quotas. China has already substantially benefited from phase out of quotas in the last 3 years (HM Treasury and DTI 2004 p 81).[33] This is the real difference between the external environment facing the East Asian NICs in the mid-1960s and Africa now. The former were the only serious low-wage players on the block. Africa now faces competition from the most populous country in the world, with a highly developmental state, currently at the height of its export powers.

Liberalization

This then is the nature of Africa's real export challenge. To meet it will require a strong strategy for diversifying, increasing productivity and breaking into both OECD and expanding developing country markets against stiff competition and with shrinking preferences.

What will such a strategy look like? For donors (including the World Bank and the UK government), trade and investment will prosper through a combination of liberalization and an 'enabling state' – one that plays basic functions, such as providing public goods like infrastructure and education, and a business-friendly environment with predictable governance and administration (eg World Bank 1998b, DfID 2000, DTI 2004 pp 82–84, HM Treasury and DTI 2004 ch 5). While the UK government acknowledges there is a case for sequencing liberalizing reforms, compensating losers, and allowing poorer countries to open up more gradually, there is a firm view that this should not mean 'wholesale or long term exemptions' (DTI 2004 p 86). Infant industry arguments are not endorsed.

In policy terms, this means that the UK government basically supports much of the liberalizing mechanisms of IFI conditionality, and has been happy to agree to the EU pushing for developing countries to open up their markets under the AoA and NAMA negotiations in the World Trade Organization. The government also continues to be a supporter of the principle of investment agreements, for example in the current EU–ACP Economic Partnership Agreements (EPAs) negotiations. The UK did lobby the EU trade commissioner to back off on Singapore Issues at Cancun, but only really on the tactical grounds that this would risk bringing down the Ministerial, rather than on the grounds of substantive opposition to the proposed investment agreement.

By contrast, NGOs have argued consistently that developing countries should be allowed to chose their own trade and investment policies, and that protection can be good for them. All the major NGOs have supported calls for the principle of protection in agriculture (Green and Priyadarshi 2001) and more broadly (eg Oxfam 2002a ch 5, Melamed 2002 pp 6–8, Christian Aid 2004a, Actionaid et al 2002, Christian Aid and CAFOD 2000). Beyond trade liberalization, six of the major agencies also collaborated on a joint campaign in 2003 to oppose the proposed WTO investment agreement (Actionaid et al 2003).

The NGO case against liberalization for developing countries is based partly on the empirical debate on trade liberalization, economic growth and poverty reduction (eg Rodrik and Rodriguez 2001, Dollar and Kraay 2001), and the fact that liberalization has not led universally to growth and poverty reduction, particularly in LDCs (UNCTAD 2004) and in Africa. Despite a reduction in the percentage of Sub-Saharan Africa countries classified by the IMF as 'trade restrictive' from 75 per cent in 1990 to 14 per cent in 2001,

Africa's share in world merchandise exports has fallen over the same period (IMF 2001). It is also based on the observation that liberalization has decimated previously protected African industries (Lall and Wangwe 1998). For example, Melamed cites cases from Zambia in the early 1990s, Mozambican cashew nut processing, and Ghana in the period 1987–1993 (Melamed 2002 p 7).

This part of the case is accepted up to a point by the UK government (see eg HM Treasury and DTI 2004 p 69), and usually leads to arguments first about needing to compensate losers in trade liberalization, and secondly about liberalization not being sufficient by itself, but requiring complementary or 'flanking' policies to ensure that countries capture the benefits of liberalization.

The role of developmental states

Some of these flanking policies are measures that NGOs would not disagree with, such as ensuring a supply of healthy and well-educated workers, and providing good infrastructure. However, the sharper disagreement is over protection and government intervention as intrinsic elements of a successful model of development. NGO thinking has become much influenced by the role of the state in successful East Asian economies and indeed in the early history of development in Europe and the USA.

The evidence on East Asia (Aoki et al 1996, Kwon 1994, Stein 1995, Lall 1996), including Japan (Johnson 1982), Korea (Amsden 1989, Chang 1993, Kim 1995) and Taiwan (Wade 1990, Brautigan 1995, Amsden 1985) is now well known. These states have come to be known as 'developmental states' (White and Wade 1984, Johnson 1999, Woo-Cummings 1999). In the early 1980s, Chalmers Johnson laid out the characteristics of the East Asian 'capitalist developmental state', which included:

- Economic development (meaning growth, productivity and competitiveness rather than welfare) is a top priority for the state.
- The state is committed to private property and the market, but guides the market with instruments formulated by an elite economic bureaucracy.
- The state consults with and coordinates the private sector through numerous institutions, and this is an essential part of the policy making process.
- State bureaucrats rule, politicians reign, so that the latter provide political space for the former to act, but also require bureaucrats to respond to groups on which the stability of the system rests.
- There is heavy and consistent investment in education.

In these countries, while governments did play various aspects of the 'enabling state' well – including providing education, infrastructure and a predictable macro-economic framework – they also used trade and industry policies to actively and systematically intervene in markets. These were thoroughly *dirigiste* regimes. Korea, Taiwan and other countries intervened in labour markets, land markets, product markets, and financial markets, and engineered trade policy at times to protect certain industries and sectors, and at other times to promote exporting. Beyond 'picking winners', they 'created winners', encouraging the formation of banking and industry conglomerates. Interventions included price fixing, policies to encourage savings, selective taxation and subsidized credit to reward performance by particular firms, targeted allocations of foreign exchange, protection through tariffs, quotas and the use of 'voluntary' export restraints (VERs), draconian exchange controls, limitations on foreign shareholdings, promotion of training, direct investment in technology transfer, learning and R&D,[34] state ownership of industrial enterprises, land reform and ceilings on land holdings. These policies were largely directed from within strong, centralized states, often from smallish groups of bureaucrats well insulated from political pressures and not 'captured' by specific industrial interests.[35]

Certain themes guided the use of these mechanisms. Governments prioritized economic growth as an objective, and specifically growth through industrialization based on learning and continuous technological upgrading. Likewise a competitiveness strategy was based on subsidizing learning, rather than low wages (Amsden 1994). Finance was kept subordinate to this goal. Frequently, national capital was promoted over foreign capital, and developmental states have supported the emergence of corporations that can compete successfully both at home and abroad with multi-national corporations.[36] Policy was flexible to changing circumstances – when it became clear that the limits of import-substitution industrialization (ISI) had been reached, and US aid was to be withdrawn, both Korea and Taiwan switched to aggressive export-led growth strategies in the 1960s. Perhaps most importantly, while government strategies supported capitalist accumulation, they also 'disciplined' it (Khan 2002 p 166). While well-performing firms and industries were rewarded, inefficient ones were dropped. No firm or industry was able to 'capture' state resources on any scale.

The centrality of state intervention to development success in Asia also makes sense in theoretical terms. Simple economic theory, with assumptions of perfect information and diminishing returns to scale, produces relatively simple theories of growth and generally leads to recommendations to liberalize trade and domestic markets. However, the 'information revolution' in economics, and more recent work incorporating increasing returns to scale, provide theoretical foundations underlying justification for strategic interventions in trade, in industry and in the labour market (eg Stiglitz 1989, 2001, Murphy et al 1989, Roemer 1986, 1990, Krugman 1986).

Stiglitz (1996) has argued that East Asian developmental states were so successful because they correctly identified and addressed various types of market failures in their policies, including: weak and non-existent markets; positive technological and marketing externalities that would otherwise go unharnessed; infant industry problems arising from capital market imperfections combined with increasing returns to scale; coordination failures, (in which upstream and downstream industries both rely on the existence of the other to be profitable, and so neither is formed without intervention[37]), and unbalanced competition in strategic negotiations over technology. Lall (2000) focuses on market failures specifically related to learning processes and acquisition of technological capabilities, arguing that government intervention has been crucial for accelerating and deepening R&D and skills acquisition, which free markets would undersupply.

Other candidates for developmental states have also arisen outside of East Asia, including some South-east Asian states such as Thailand and Malaysia and more recently Vietnam. Ha-Joon Chang has also shown that, contrary to myths of *laissez-faire*, America, the UK and other European countries pursued active management of their economies through interventionist trade, industry and technology policies during successful development in the 18th and 19th centuries (Chang 2002, Chang and Green 2003). Comparative studies also show that successful paths have not all been the same. Some countries, such as Japan and Korea, have based accumulation on domestic savings, others, such as Thailand, have relied more heavily on foreign investment. Rodrik describes heterodox strategies adopted by countries as varied as Mauritius and China (Rodrik 2000).

East Asian developmental states were not perfect – the example often used of their fallibility is Korea's unsuccessful attempts to foster a heavy chemical industry. It is also important to recognize that the East Asian 'Tigers' and South-east Asian followers were usually not democracies, but were often run in the early phases by military regimes, while Johnson characterized them as having tendency towards one-party systems. Initial comparative advantage was in part based on cheap labour underpinned by the brutal repression of trade unions. Accumulation and economic growth did mean rapidly rising living standards – for example, Korean (largely male) real wages increased by 10 per cent per year on average between 1967 and 1977 (Kim 1995 pp 116–17). However, especially since the late 1980s, as many East and South-east Asian countries have started to liberalize internal and external markets, growth has slowed and inequality has sharply increased (Ahuja et al 1997).

'Initial conditions' at Independence of course did differ between East Asian nations such as Taiwan and Korea, and African countries. However, in some areas the differences are not as stark as might be thought. We have already seen in chapter 2 above that levels of per capita income in East and South-east Asia were no higher than those in Africa in the 1950s and early 1960s. Certainly it is true that the colonial power in the cases of Taiwan and Korea – Japan – was itself a strong developmental state and developed the manufacturing industries and infrastructure of its colonies further than Britain and France, which were more interested in primary resource extraction, did in Africa. However, while manufacturing as a share of GDP in 1960 was 22 per cent in Taiwan and 14 per cent in Korea, it was over 15 per cent in Sub-Saharan Africa in the same year (Wade 1990 p 44, UNCTAD 2003d). Furthermore, South-east Asian states had no particular industrial head start over Africa in the 1960s (eg Edwards 1995). Equally, as long ago as 1981, a number of African countries had manufacturing shares of the same order, but have failed to achieve high growth since, including Burkina Faso (16.9 per cent), Chad (18.6 per cent), Cote d'Ivoire (19.6 per cent), Malawi (15.7 per cent), Rwanda (17.7 per cent), and Zimbabwe (22.1 per cent) (UNIDO 2004 ch 4).

The international environment was also in some ways favourable to the early East Asian developmental states – an expanding, managed world economy with low levels of financial volatility (Wade 1990 p 346). However, as discussed above, trade barriers were not insubstantial. African countries also benefited from the same international stability up until 1974. At the same time, South-east Asian 'followers' managed to take on a more difficult international economic environment successfully in the 1980s, and new entrants, such as Vietnam, have shown that rapid growth was possible from the early 1990s. The international environment is important, but not a decisive factor.

Aid volume comparisons also do not satisfactorily explain East Asia's faster growth. Taiwan and especially Korea did receive substantial US aid in the 1950s and 1960s, but on the whole Africa has received more. Between 1950 and 1965, US aid to Taiwan averaged 6 per cent of GNP, but had dipped to around 2 per cent by the end of the period. It ended altogether in 1968 (Brautigan 1995). Japanese aid then replaced US aid, but by 1970 this was less than 0.2 per cent of national income.[38] By comparison, aid to Sub-Saharan Africa was 8 per cent of GNP in 1987. South Korea received more aid than Taiwan in the immediate post-war period, much of it tied to the conflict with North Korea. Up to the mid-1970s was one of the largest global aid recipients. Until 1965, it received heavy aid from the US, probably in the region of 15 per cent of GNP or more, thereafter Japan played an increasingly important role.[39] During the 1966–74 period, foreign assistance constituted about 4.5 per cent of GNP. However, even the larger role of aid in Korea's development story is surpassed by African cases. Aid-to-GDP ratios for some African countries had reached much higher proportions through the 1980s, peaking at 30 per cent for Tanzania in 1990, 27 per cent for Kenya in 1993, 27 per cent for Uganda in 1992, and 36 per cent for Zambia in 1991 (Bigsten et al 1999 p 3). Probably much more important than the volume of aid were the type and origins of aid. Early post-war aid from the US went almost entirely on infrastructure. From the mid-1960s, as Japan became the main donor, East Asian nations drew heavily on its developmental model, receiving very different policy lessons than did Africa under European and multilateral aid. Throughout the 1960s and 1970s, Japan tied aid to FDI and specifically sought to help build up industrial capacity in recipient countries.

Explanations based on the 'ethnic Chinese' argument are also rather weak. Certainly, ethnic Chinese have been a dynamic commercial presence in parts of the region, but not others – they played no part in Korea's *chaebol*, for example. At the same time, African regions have played host to minorities concentrated in trade, such as Gujeratis in East Africa and Lebanese in West Africa. The contrast is not so much in the presence or absence of commercial minorities, but rather in how Asian and African states managed and treated them.

Some also insist that a decisive factor in explaining divergence between East and South-east Asia and Africa is the pervasive conflict that the latter region has seen. However, this argument is not as straightforward as it might appear. While some African countries – notably Ethiopia, Somalia, Mozambique and Angola – suffered from Cold War proxy conflicts in the 1970s and 1980s, so too did Vietnam, Cambodia and Laos. Indonesia saw major massacres in the 1970s, along with the long running East Timor conflict. It is true that the 'East Asian miracle' countries have largely been peaceful since the end of the Second World War, but the same is also true of many African countries that have not managed to achieve the same developmental progress, including Tanzania, Zambia, Kenya, Senegal, Cote d'Ivoire (until 2003), Malawi, and Ghana. Finally, conflicts in African countries did not appear of out nowhere. I argue below that they were first and foremost the result of political processes that led to state collapse. Certainly, conflict has a devastating and long-lasting developmental impact, but it cannot be an exogenous explanatory variable; rather it is a sign of differences in political institutions and organization.

It is in these factors that I believe the most decisive contrast lies in 'initial' regional situations. Korea before colonization was a long-standing political entity with centuries-old traditions of bureaucracy and centralized power. The post-war rulers of Taiwan, the defeated Nationalists fleeing Mao from mainland China, also brought with them the traditions of a strong, centralized state and a core of technically able planners. These histories contrast strongly with the immediate post-colonial situation in Africa, which is investigated in chapter 6 below.

'Policy space' and anti-developmental states

NGOs are therefore correct to argue that successful development in East Asia and elsewhere in rapid growth of productivity and exports has been based on *dirigiste*, non-Washington Consensus policies. Donors have failed to put forward convincing counter-arguments to explain East Asian success (eg DTI 2004 pp 83–85).[40] The NGO concern is then that rich countries are 'kicking away the ladder' (Chang 2002), using instruments such as

WTO agreements in market access (Oxfam 2002a ch5, Christian Aid 2004a, Hardstaff and Rice 2003), services (Hilary 2003, World Development Movement 2003a) and investment (Actionaid 2003, Chang and Green 2003) to impose neo-liberalism on poor countries at great cost. Melamed (2002) makes similar, if broader arguments.

How important is this concern for Africa? In theory, it is substantial. My argument is that Africa's most serious trade problems are on the supply side, and that to tackle these, interventionist trade and industrial policies are needed of the type used by successful developmental states in the past. Dani Rodrik argues that although East Asian states did face tariff and non-tariff barriers, they managed to prosper in an environment where they had considerable 'policy space':

> These countries were free to do their own thing, and did so, combining trade reliance with unorthodox policies – export subsidies, domestic content requirements, import-export linkages, patent and copyright infringements, restrictions on capital flows (including FDI), directed credit and so on – that are largely precluded by today's rules. In fact, such policies were part of the arsenal of today's advanced industrial countries until quite recently ... The environment for today's globalizers is significantly more restrictive. (Rodrik 2000 p 28)

In practice, how far the WTO actually 'bites' on African countries' policy space currently is a little less clear. First, there is the issue of how much space there actually is within WTO rules. Contrary to Rodrik's view, Amsden (2000 pp 3–6) argues that despite concerns about WTO restrictions, 'there is no shortage of methods that can be used by less industrialized countries even under new WTO laws.' She points to flexibility on the use of tariffs and non-tariff barriers, continuing use of local content requirements even under TRIMS, up to eight years of infant industry protection available under various safeguards, permissible subsidies on R&D and regional development and export subsidies for countries with per capita incomes up to $1,000 (most of Sub-Saharan Africa, including non-LDCs Kenya and Ghana). Export processing zones, used for example by Mauritius, are allowed. She concludes that: 'All in all, the liberal bark of the WTO appears to be worse than its bite, and "neo-developmental states" ... have taken advantage of this, where necessary.' Second, most African countries are LDCs, and under the special and differential treatment (S&DT) provisions of WTO agreements are sometimes excluded from requirements made of developing countries (for example, on market access under the 2004 framework paper). However, S&DT provisions are often not binding, which is a problem (Melamed 2003). Clear binding S&DT for LDCs – a process that has gone virtually nowhere within the Doha Round – would be a priority for Africa on this view.

Against this view is some evidence that countries are in practice making less frequent use of what policy space there is under S&DT rules, while some, such as article XVIII allowing protection of infant industries have rarely been used. (Page and Kleen 2004 pp 32–33). This may be because of pressure from the World Bank not to do so (see below), and it may also be due to a degree of self-censorship by developing country governments themselves. Here it is worth noting that international campaigning NGOs have tended to dramatize the degree to which the WTO closes down policy space. It is an open question as to whether this has led some of the smaller LDCs to believe that they are more constrained than they actually are.

WTO agreements may indeed be a problem for African countries in the longer run. However, other international agreements and institutions probably represent more immediate constraints on 'policy space', including bilateral investment treaties, of which Africa had signed 428 up to 2001, some of which include investor-state mechanisms, and the proposed EU–ACP Economic Partnership Agreements, under which the EU is seeking reciprocal free trade with African countries on 90 per cent of products within 10–12 years (Actionaid 2004a). And over the last two decades the main pressure on LDCs in Africa to liberalize trade, investment, industrial and agricultural policies has come not from the WTO but from the IMF and the World Bank, in the form of conditionalities attached to soft loans, backed up to some extent by bilateral donors. I examine this relationship in the next chapter.

But the biggest problem with the 'policy space' argument in relation to Africa is the very obvious observation that African states were not 'developmental' (Sandbrook 1985 pp 31–36, Stein 1995, Sindzingre 2004). With the exception of Mauritius, these states evidently failed to lead processes of successful ISI leading to sustained industrialization and export growth in the 20 years following Independence. As Richard Sandbrook wrote in 1985: 'Neither consistency nor efficiency characterize the public sector of most African countries. In fact, most regimes actively *discourage* the mobilization and productive investment of resources' (Sandbrook 1985 p 35). Chronic poverty and low levels of human development have their roots in these failures.

In general, the *quality* of intervention in markets by African states was terrible. The overtaxation of agriculture through price-setting by parastatals was an early target for neo-liberals (eg Bates 1981, World Bank 1981) as well as from those on the left (eg Bernstein 1981). While there may have been exceptions,[41] the general picture was fairly extreme; in the 1970s and 1980s, African agriculture was being taxed at an estimated 23 per cent, compared with 2.5 per cent in Asia and 6.4 per cent in Latin America (Rodrik 1998 p 25). Parastatals,[42] such as marketing boards, were also frequently loss-making, drawing off scarce public resources from other possible uses. Exchange rates were overvalued, in contrast with East Asian states. While the latter did try to maintain exchange rate stability, they did so at levels that did not punish exporters.

Meanwhile in industry, Sanjaya Lall describes the results of African government intervention as 'abysmal' (Lall 2000 p 31). Poor performance in African manufacturing is partly explained by conflict, political instability, debt and bad macroeconomic management, but flawed industrial policy is a considerable part of the story. The challenge for governments was considerable, including small and fragmented local markets, poor infrastructure, a small entrepreneurial base, and weak human capital. However, rather than trying to overcome these barriers, governments generally compounded their problems. Lall cites the following: a lack of clear industrial policy objectives; excessive and prolonged protection not offset with export promotion measures or incentives for learning or upgrading technology; lack of coherence between product and labour market policies, including training and technology support; weak or non-existent institutional structures for developing capabilities, including R&D, SME extension services, effective quality and standards bodies, and training institutions; lack of monitoring of the effects of industrial policy; lack of flexibility in adapting policies to changing market and technological conditions; weak legal structures to protect property rights; 'widespread and constant' political intervention, and lastly, a lack of commitment by both bureaucrats and leaders (Lall 2000 p 32, see also UNECA 2004 ch 2).[43]

Despite considerable increases in aid in real terms over the 1970s, African economies and industries nose-dived. Macro-economic stability was badly hit by the oil shock of 1974 and commodity price falls at the end of the decade. Only countries with oil or mineral rents could avoid crisis. Policies and interventions were having the opposite effect to the outcome in East and South-east Asia. Not only was agriculture and manufacturing failing to thrive, African economies were in considerable trouble. It is important to remember the depth of the crises that preceded any structural adjustment programmes. For example, in Tanzania by 1985 'virtually all basic household goods including clothing, soap, edible oils, sugar, salt, batteries, kerosene, corrugated iron sheets, soft drinks, beer and cigarettes were scarce or non-existent' (Sharpley, quoted in Temu and Due 2000). The situation in Ghana deteriorated faster and even more dramatically: 'The crisis had become so bad in Ghana that the group benefiting from administrative allocation of foreign exchange was extremely limited. Indeed by the early 1980s the economy had deteriorated to such an extent that even senior government officials, who normally benefit from access to imported goods even in times of shortage, reported that they were growing hungry and were concerned that they could not find food for their families' (Herbst, quoted in Rodrik 1998 p 22).

Conversely to the use of the concept of market failures to understand how interventions in East Asia succeeded in fostering development, neo-liberal analysts have used the idea of 'government failures' to explain unsuccessful interventions[44] (eg Lal 1983, Krueger 1990). The argument is that governments fail to do better than markets in allocating resources partly because they are not as good at coordinating information as markets are, but also because government bureaucrats are also self-interested, and will seek to use any government control over the economy to extract a 'rent' (Krueger 1974), in the form of bribes and favours. The neo-liberal position is that government failures are almost always deeper and more pervasive than market failures, so that even though the latter may exist, attempts to correct them by government intervention will almost always tend to make things worse. In this view, it is a *good* thing to close down 'policy space', because when governments are allowed to use it, they ruin economic growth. International institutions like the IFIs and WTO that pressurize or lock governments into liberalization are needed precisely because they are 'agencies of restraint' (Collier 1999, Collier and Gunning 1999b) that prevent bad interventions.

Clearly, given the history of highly successful interventions in East and South-east Asia, it is simply not true that governments always fail. External agencies pushing liberalization often get it wrong, as in the case of the IMF leading up to the Asian financial crisis of the late 1990s. On the other hand, as the African record shows, severe government failure is a very real possibility. Neither liberalization nor intervention is guaranteed to lead to industrialization and sustainable economic growth – what counts is the quality of intervention (Stiglitz 1996).[45] While NGOs have focused on defending 'policy space', they have spent far less time trying to understand why intervention has failed when it has, and what could be done about this, which for Africa is the central question for trade and industrial policy. There is a tendency to underplay the seriousness of government failures at intervention in the past, and to overestimate the likelihood of effective intervention now. Rather, it is donors who have been preoccupied with this issue, usually under the rubric of 'good governance'. I examine the governance agenda in chapter 5 below.

Summing up

At this stage, it may be useful to summarize the argument. Trade policy is a major component of current NGO–government debates about development, and trade is also a key issue for African growth. However, much of the current debate focuses on issues of minor importance for Africa, and fails to grapple with the fundamental problems. Other parts of the debate offer an abstract dichotomy between liberalization and intervention.

NGOs, government and the media are preoccupied with the removal of agricultural subsidies in the rich world. However, elimination of subsidies would have a relatively small impact on Africa's poverty. A major reason for this is that subsidy removal will not address Africa's major long-run trade problem – commodity dependence. Rather than palliative measures of uncertain effectiveness, such as international commodity agreements, the only long run solution to this is diversification of exports. Africa's challenges here are substantial, since its factor endowments are not favourable for the development of labour-intensive manufacturing. At the same time, despite NGO and government preoccupations with tariff escalation and peaks, the market access environment facing Africa is fairly good, certainly a lot better than that facing East Asian NICs in the 1960s. Preferences could be improved, certainly, but the major problems in diversifying lie ultimately in supply side issues, an issue we return to below in chapter 5.

Donors have also recommended that developing countries, including those in Africa, open up their own markets. However, it is clear that liberalization has not worked so far. According to donors, this is because of the absence of 'flanking' policies that one would normally expect from governments interested in supporting trade and investment. Commitment and capacity are again the problems.

The NGO view is that policies need to be a lot more interventionist than donors accept. They point to the outstanding trade and investment performance of the East Asian NICs, arguing that this was the result not of liberalization and a minimalist, 'enabling' state, but rather of extensive 'developmental' state intervention in the economy, adding that the UK and USA themselves followed these policies in earlier eras. On this view, the main problem for late industrializers such as African countries is precisely that WTO rules threaten to close down the 'policy space' needed to use developmental state-type policies. For many African countries, especially LDCs, World Bank and IMF conditionality may have actually been more constraining in practice than WTO agreements. However, a more fundamental issue, that NGOs tend to gloss over, is the severe failure of African interventions in the 1970s and 1980s, including in trade and industrial policies. It is the poor *quality* of interventions by African states that is the underlying problem to understand and engage with.

Overall, the conclusion of this chapter is that the political commitment and state capacity to deliver good quality interventions in the economy are of central importance to Africa's trade performance, and to its economic growth; much more central than NGOs think. Of course, some will say that it is ridiculous to compare Sub-Saharan Africa with East and South-east Asia, because there are too many differences between them, and the latter region had too many initial advantages, and the former has many additional disadvantages.[46] In fact, I have argued at various points that initial economic differences were not that large. But even if they were, this would not invalidate the underlying argument – that African countries would have been better off with developmental states (if not as well off as Korea or Taiwan), whereas in fact they had states that were largely *anti-developmental*. Some of these themes are revisited in the next chapter, on aid, debt relief and conditionality. Donors have been much more willing to engage with government failures in Africa, and have done so mainly within a 'governance' framework. I will turn to those issues in chapter 5.

4 Aid, debt relief and conditionality

The case for (more) aid

AS WITH THE TRADE AGENDA, there is an issue on which both NGOs and the UK government (and some other donors) agree – that there should be more aid[47] and debt relief. Both the Chancellor and campaigning NGOs in the 'Make Poverty History' campaign are calling for a sharp increase in aid and debt relief generally, and to Africa in particular.

'More and better aid' and 'Drop the debt' are two of the three Make Poverty History slogans, along with 'Trade Justice'. NGOs have frequently called for the UK and other countries to meet the UN target for aid of 0.7 per cent of national income, and also have often used the figure of an additional $50 billion in development financing needed each year until 2015 to meet the Millennium Development Goals (MDGs), a figure developed for the Financing for Development conference at Monterrey in 2002. Oxfam has used a figure of $25–35 billion needed additionally to meet the Millennium Development Goals in Africa, again citing the Monterrey Consensus (Oxfam 2003).

The UK government, meanwhile, has increased its allocation to aid, pledging specifically to raise assistance to Sub-Saharan Africa to £1 billion per year. Beyond this, the Treasury has shown its commitment to accelerating the delivery of aid resources through the proposed International Financing Facility. It has also given a 100 per cent write-off of bilateral debt, and most recently, also of its share of multilateral debt. Meanwhile Jeffrey Sachs has called for a 'big push' for Africa, financed by aid, in order to meet the MDGs. He estimates that aid of the order of 20–30 per cent of GDP (around $60–90 billion) will be required every year until 2015 (Sachs et al 2004 p 26). The Commission for Africa (2005 p 292), for its part, calls for a doubling of aid to Africa in the next 3–5 years, with a further increase to $75 billion a year by 2015.

It is almost self-evident that Africa will need a lot more aid to achieve sustainable growth. Almost all African countries lack access to capital markets, and there are clearly huge existing needs in infrastructure and investment.

However, it is worth bearing in mind that African countries are already the most aid-dependent in history, and that almost $500 billion of aid and debt relief at 2002 prices has been absorbed over the last 45 years into a continent that now has record levels of poverty (see ch 2 above). It is also true that there is significant capital held by Africans outside of Africa. One recent estimate puts total capital flight, including accrued interest, in the mid-1990s at $285 billion (Boyce and Ndikumana 2000). Finally, oil and minerals have provided some countries with large revenues over the years. In Nigeria, for example, net oil export revenues in 2004 were estimated to be $27 billion: $212 per head of the population if it were distributed equally, as against a per capita income in 2002 of $328.[48] However, in 2000 distribution was highly unequal, with the top 2 per cent of the population receiving the same proportion of income as the bottom 55 per cent (Sala-i-Martin and Subramanian 2003 p 4). According to these authors the IMF recently estimated that Nigeria's cumulative net government revenues from oil since 1965 were around $350 billion at 1995 prices. Similar stories can be told for Angola and DRC.

At the same time, aid to Africa has been an expensive business. One study, looking at the number of people raised above the poverty line for each dollar of aid found that the cost of raising each beneficiary by $365 per year was $9,523 in 1990 and $3,521 in 2000 (Herbst and Mills 2003 p 66). Donor aid has been tied to home commercial interests, and has been poorly targeted and badly coordinated, while a lack of harmonization has meant duplication and an unnecessary burden on recipients. As a result, aid has been massively less effective than it could be (eg Tarp 2000, Commission for Africa 2005 ch 9). As described in chapter 7 below, donors have contributed substantially to the erosion of state capacity in Africa. NGOs have justifiably criticized donors on all these points. While some donor fora, such as the OECD's Development Assistance Committee, perennially try to address poor performance by donors, success seems as chronically elusive as it does for Africa's developmental project.

Some conclude that aid and debt relief in Africa is therefore wasted. However, despite the rather gloomy picture painted above, there is evidence at the macro-economic level that aid does, in fact, bring growth. This debate was much influenced by Burnside and Dollar's (2000) argument that aid only has a positive impact on growth in the presence of 'good' (ie Washington Consensus) policies. However, their findings have not been widely replicated (see Addison et al 2004 for a review), and their approach has been questioned on methodological grounds (Hansen and Tarp 2000). The majority of studies find that aid has a positive and statistically significant impact on growth regardless of policies.[49] There is evidence that aid has the strongest effect in the poorest countries and where there are low levels of human capital (Gonamee et al 2003).

For Africa, there is fairly robust evidence that aid over the period 1970–97 contributed to growth through increasing investment (Gonamee et al 2002 p 20):

Despite large aid inflows, SSA countries on average experienced only 0.6 per cent growth in real per capita GDP per annum over the period. On the face of it, this may appear to be a case of aid ineffectiveness. Our econometric results, which are robust regarding outliers, endogeneity, and country-specific effects, consistently show that aid has had a positive effect on growth, largely through aid-financed investment. On average, each one percentage point increase in the aid/GDP ratio adds one-third of a percentage point to the growth rate. Africa's poor growth rate should not therefore be attributed to aid ineffectiveness.

The Commission for Africa (2005 pp 298–302) also makes an argument for aid at a less aggregated level, citing positive impacts in the educational and health sectors, on investment and on capital flight.

Thus aid does seem play a role in very poor economies, basically by providing capital. While growth has been low in Africa over the past 30 years, it would have been even lower had large amounts of aid not been provided. There is a logic to this; even if aid is somewhat inefficient, a poorly designed road building project, for example, in circumstances where infrastructure is very minimal, is better than no road at all.[50]

However, it is equally clear that, while aid may have a positive effect in Africa, and despite very high ratios of aid-to-GDP, it has not been enough to produce rapid growth rates of the type seen in East and South-east Asia. The findings of Gonamee et al 2002 show an association between aid and growth *within* Africa, but since growth has been low and aid high, the overall relationship for Africa will be weaker than elsewhere.[51]

More aid will help, but volume alone will not make African poverty history. Somewhat like the issue of eliminating agricultural subsidies in OECD countries, more aid in the business-as-usual context will have a small, if welcome impact. But if low growth in Africa is not due to the ineffectiveness of aid, then it must be due to something else, and we should look elsewhere for routes to transforming growth. Thus the real debate on aid to Africa is about the nature of aid, and the context in which it works. The two most frequently discussed issues are governance and policy conditionality. Donors have tended to emphasize the importance of the former, while NGOs have focused campaigning on the latter. These factors are seen as having a determining influence on growth or poverty reduction, either cutting across the impact of aid, or interacting with it. Even those who argue that aid works see economic policies and the governance context as key for growth (Addison et al 2004 p 3, Sachs et al 2004).

The conditionality debate

Indeed, many of the biggest battles to do with aid and debt relief have not been about whether aid itself works, but rather about the policy conditions attached to it. The origins of conditionality lie in the expansion of programme lending (as opposed to project lending) by the IMF and the World Bank at the end of the 1970s. The crisis of the 1980s led many governments to turn to the IFIs for support, leading to what Tony Killick calls a 'veritable explosion' in the use of policy conditionality (Killick 2004 p 12). Between 1988 and 1993 alone there were 99 IMF loan agreements in developing countries (Killick 1995 p 4), of which a great many were in Africa. Programme lending has continued through the 1990s and up to the present: in 2004 there were 28 IMF programmes in Africa, making up more than half the total global number (Independent Evaluation Office, IMF 2004 p 16). Bank lending is similarly Africa focused, with almost half of IDA going to the region. Over the 1990s Bank programmes were focused increasingly on particular sectors. Between 1980 and 1996 the Bank disbursed $15 billion in 163 adjustment operations in 37 countries (OED 1997). The share of adjustment lending within total lending grew to 61 per cent by 2002 (Killick 2004 p 14).

Along with associated bilateral support, estimates are that of aid going to Africa in 1990s, a third to a half was explicitly tied to policy reform (van de Walle 2001 p 7). Conditions attached to early loans focused on macroeconomic stabilization policies, including devaluation, auctioning of foreign exchange and reductions in government spending to contract the money supply. However, as it quickly became clear that growth was not following, the Fund pushed for a 'second generation' of reforms, including structural reforms in agriculture, trade, the banking sector, public expenditure and governance. In more recent years divestment of state owned enterprises has been added to the list. The number of conditions attached to each loan increased sharply, to a peak of 58 per World Bank loan in the period 1988–92. Meanwhile the IMF's drift into structural conditions escalated from an average of 2 per programme in 1987 to 14 in 1997–99 (Killick 2004 p 14).

NGOs have been long-standing and trenchant critics of conditionality and structural adjustment. From campaigning by Christian Aid on Zimbabwe's ESAP in the early 1990s, through denunciations of IMF programmes by Oxfam's Kevin Watkins (1999), to WDM's current 'Colludo' campaign and a report on Zambia (World Development Movement 2004b), there has been consistent opposition to both the content and the politics of conditionality. The 2005 'Make Poverty History' campaign explicitly calls for an end to economic conditionality.[52] The target of much current NGO activity in particular is donor pressure on developing countries to privatize SOEs and utilities (eg Actionaid 2004b, War on Want 2004).

The critique is on two broad fronts. One is that adjustment policies have hurt the poor, and have failed to produce growth. These criticisms built on similar analyses by some academics[53] and also on UNICEF's landmark study in the late 1980s (Cornia et al 1988). NGOs highlighted cases where particular groups had lost out from trade liberalization, and especially pointed to falling expenditures on health and education and the introduction of user fees for basic services. The IFIs have consistently defended their programmes. However, they did respond to criticism, especially the World Bank under Wolfensohn, by developing 'transitional' aid programmes supposedly compensating losers under adjustment, and by the mid-1990s, coming out for the protection of social spending and against user fees. This criticism also hastened the renewal of a 'poverty focus' by the leading donors, with the Bank and the Fund adopting the International Development Targets as their central objectives to great fanfare at the end of the 1990s.

The poverty debate obscured the fact that the 'adjustment' experience has not helped economies adjust to the fall in prices of commodities on which they were dependent for foreign exchange, by diversifying exports, as described above. This is a particularly telling indictment of the Bretton Woods institutions, as it was this express purpose that they were originally established for.

The second criticism was on political, or process grounds; that the IMF and World Bank, as unelected, external, shareholder-dominated institutions, should not have the right to impose policies on countries. Conditionality has undermined normal democratic politics, by making governments upwardly accountable to donors, rather than to their own people. From the mid-1990s there were increasing calls for the narrow IFI–government relationship to be opened up to 'civil society' in developing countries.[54] 'Partnership' became the new buzz word.[55] With the expansion of the HIPC Initiative under the pressure of debt campaigning, these concepts were crystallized in the creation of the Poverty Reduction Strategy Paper process, in which donors, government and civil society were to collectively set poverty reduction goals for the use of debt relief and aid, and monitor progress. Under Clare Short, DfID gave particularly strong support to the PRSPs, and remains firmly wedded to making them work. Ironically, the PRSPs have added further process conditionality to the donor–recipient relationship.

NGOs have found it much harder to articulate what they would like to see instead of conditionality. Should aid come with any strings attached at all? Often this question has not been answered directly. In other cases, there are calls for aid to be dependent upon a process involving civil society in policy-making. At the same time, it is clear that many NGOs have become disillusioned with the PRSP process (Actionaid USA 2004). One reason is that it has become clear that conditionality has survived the Poverty Reduction Strategy Paper 'revolution' intact, through PRGF and PRSC programmes, and with bilateral donors also still exercising conditionality through their grant programmes (Wood 2004). While some conditions in loans and grant agreements are linked to PRSPs, conditions on key policy areas such as macro-economic and trade policy are often set outside the PRSP framework (eg Christian Aid 2003). Even within the PRSP process, NGOs have also seen that the content of PRSPs is still heavily influenced by donors (Action-aid USA/Actionaid Uganda 2004), with civil society input being fairly limited in some countries (McGee 2002). In some cases, NGOs have with-drawn from PRSP processes in protest.

More recently, Actionaid has proposed the concept of 'fiduciary account-ability', meaning that: 'Conditionality must be restricted to what is necessary to ensure that aid is spent on its intended beneficiaries . . .' (Actionaid 2004b p 25). However, for such accountability to have real meaning, there would have to be a radical transformation in transparency and auditing practices in most countries, especially for programme aid, in the form of sector-wide approaches (SWAPs) and especially direct budget support. Currently, there are cases where budget support is given where there could not possibly be such assurances of fiduciary accountability. For example, DfID gives direct budget support to Malawi, but the budget process there has been recently described as: 'a theatre that masks the real distribution and spending' (Rakner et al 2004 p iv). It is difficult it see how fiduciary conditionality will be easily operationalized under these circumstances, circumstances that are likely to be common across Africa, without a profound change in the gov-ernance of budgets. I argue below that this will, in turn, require profound political changes.

Both poverty and process debates have been inconclusive. The Bank and other donors have made palliative changes to their conditionality packages, but still remain committed to the underlying ideas, while NGOs continue to attack them.

Methodological complexities and a selective use of data on both sides help keep things going. Likewise, the NGO criticism of the World Bank and IMF as wielding fundamentally undemocratic influence remains in place, despite the PRSP experiment. At the same time, NGOs are uncertain and sometimes divided about what degree and kind of conditionality there should be, who should set it, in some cases whether there should be any conditionality at all, or what should replace it.

A major reason for the confusion on both sides is that NGOs and donors have failed to engage fully with the one clear body of evidence we have about conditionality, namely that it hasn't actually work very well. NGOs have mostly ignored this evidence.[56] Donors have acknowledged it, but then carried on acting as if it didn't exist.

Early evidence that IFI programmes with conditionality were not actually being completed came from Tony Killick's 1995 survey of IMF programmes. He found that 53 per cent of 305 IMF programmes over the period 1979–93 were not completed (50 per cent for Sub-Saharan Africa), in the sense that 20 per cent or more of the credit remained undrawn, largely meaning that the final tranche of a two- or three-year programme was not reached (Killick

1995 p 61). This proportion rose over time. Similar evidence was presented by other studies of both Bank and Fund programmes in the mid-to-late 1990s (Killick 1998, Mosley et al 1995, Collier et al 1997). This was followed by a number of donor-sponsored studies showing that developing country governments were not fully complying with aid conditionalities. The Bank's Operations Evaluation Department assessment of adjustment lending in 35 African countries showed 'good' compliance in only 10 countries, and 'weak' or 'poor' compliance in the remaining 25 (OED 1997). An independent review of the IMF's ESAF programmes, commissioned by the IMF, found that 75 per cent of programmes broke down or experienced lengthy interruptions, two-thirds of which were caused by delays in implementing IMF policy conditions (IMF 1998). An evaluation of the Special Programme for Africa found that only 8 of the 28 reform programmes in the period 1992–96 remained on track (OED 1998 p 98). This evidence on IFI programme breakdown was supported by a number of statistical studies showing no link between aid and policy change, supporting the idea that donors cannot 'buy' policy change with aid (see World Bank 1998a). Revisiting the issue in 2004, Killick (2004 pp 12–18) reviews the recent evidence and judges that it is too mixed and incomplete to say definitively whether compliance has improved in recent years. However, he does find plenty of support for the view that 'Fund conditionality is ineffectual, perhaps increasingly so (Killick 2004 p 17).

At the very least, the findings of these studies amount to clear evidence that governments do not always do what donors tell them to (and indeed suggests that on average they don't). The evidence on the poor effectiveness of conditionality has implications for both of the aid debates.

On the *impact* of adjustment, it means that observed outcomes for growth and poverty are often the result not of policy reform as donors specified, but rather of partial reforms, reforms over a much longer time frame than conditionality would imply, and sometimes policy reversals (van de Walle 2001 ch 2). What has actually happened in Africa since 1980 is not a straightforward roll out of neo-liberalism, but rather a compromise between donors and recipient governments.

In many cases, policy change started only after countries were in economic crisis, so that even though the IMF began pushing for macro-economic reforms from around 1980, most were not implemented until the late 1980s (van de Walle 2001 p 69, Devarajan 2001 p 7–9). For Ghana, crisis came early, in 1983, for Tanzania and Uganda a little later in 1986. Since foreign exchange availability was closely tied to commodity export earnings, the timing of crisis was often delayed or hastened by shifts in commodity prices.

Although pressure started around 1980, it was only by the early to mid-1990s that almost all African countries had undertaken some of the 'first generation' stabilization reforms, including devaluation, elimination of parallel exchange rates and liberalization of foreign exchange, and reducing fiscal deficits (van de Walle 2001 p 68). However, while stabilization measures are easy to introduce, requiring just a 'stroke of the pen' rather than complex institutional change, they are for the same reason easy to reverse. Rodrik cites the example given by Collier of Nigeria in the 1990s: 'In the past decade Nigerian trade policy has swung from intense foreign exchange rationing, indicated by a parallel market premium of over 300 per cent, to a completely free market, back to even more intense rationing' (Rodrik 1998 p 12). In the same decade, Ghana, Kenya and Gabon all saw ballooning deficits as Presidents increased spending ahead of elections (van de Walle 2001 p 70). Even in the late 1990s and into the 2000s, it is not clear that deficits are as low as they might appear, as governments have found ways to spend more than donors want them to. Governments have often run up arrears on civil service salaries,[57] or sold oil forward (against IMF rules) to make deficits appear smaller than they are. Donor insistence on cash budgets seems only to encourage the accumulation of arrears and use of promissory notes. In 1997, the Zambian Ministry of Finance admitted to arrears equivalent to 1.5 per cent of GDP (van de Walle 2001 p 72). Finally, the amount of government revenue raised through tax as a proportion of GDP has not systematically increased since the 1980s. It is highest for oil and mineral producers, as one might expect. However, there are wide variations in revenue ratios between countries with similar economic structures (van de Walle 2001 p 74).

For more structural reforms, van de Walle (2001 p 85) argues that up to the end of the 1990s, the record is 'even more ambiguous and uneven'. Banking deregulation has been almost universal, and while there has also been some liberalization of agricultural pricing and marketing, in some countries key crops and prices are still controlled or managed. Again, most change happened in the 1990s rather than the 1980s. van de Walle emphasizes how long it has taken for reforms to happen, giving the example of Ghana where Rawlings came to power in 1981, turned to the IFIs in 1983, but where import licensing was not abolished until 1989, exchange rates liberalized only in 1992–93, and Ashanti Gold Fields privatized only in 1994 (van de Walle 2001 p 76). Divestment of SOEs generally happened mainly in the 1990s, especially from the mid-1990s onwards (Bennell 1997), but in many countries is still far from complete. Trade reform – despite being proposed by donors from the early 1980s onwards – was almost non-existent up until the mid-1990s (van de Walle p 81 Table 2.2). Some tariffication and declines in applied tariffs have happened since then. Average tariffs declined by less than a quarter between 1990 and 2002 (UNECA 2004 Annex 6.1) and bound tariffs remain quite high, but the majority of African countries are now seen as quite open in trade policy terms (IMF 2001).

Finally, civil service reform, where donors put a premium on reducing numbers of employees (despite a relatively low ratio of civil servants to population in Africa), has been slow or non-existent with a few exceptions. van de Walle (2001 pp 64–65) gives the example of Zambia, where an initial statement of government commitment to civil service reform led to at least three separate packages over 15 years, but with no discernible impact on numbers. By the late 1990s donors saw retrenchments on any scale only in Ghana, Guinea, and Uganda, subsequently reversed in two cases. Tanzania subsequently joined this group in the 2000s (Kjaer 2004).

Clearly, some policy change has happened in Africa since the early 1980s. However, reform happened in fits and starts. The typical initial reaction of governments was first to resist implementation as specified by donors, work to understand how far a reform threatened their political position and how far not reforming threatened the flow of aid from the donors, and then implement some elements of reform in varying degrees of completion. Where easily reversible, policy changes have sometimes been reversed when these calculations changed. In Ghana early macro-economic reforms were embraced because they were administratively easy and reasserted central control over revenue that had been lost during the crisis to smugglers and parallel currency markets (Hutchful 1995 pp 305–08). However, structural reforms such as privatization were resisted. Resistance to certain reforms was very long lasting, especially those eliminating trade barriers, and above civil service reforms aimed at cutting numbers.

I should make it clear at this point that, unlike van de Walle, Collier, Gunning, Dollar, Killick and others who have pointed to the ineffectiveness of conditionality, I am not in favour of the usual package of donor policies. While the 'developmental state' model suggests that some of these policies are sensible, such as not maintaining an overvalued exchange rate, I believe that the evidence shows that many others, especially liberalizing structural reforms, will not produce rapid diversification, industrialization, accumulation and growth.[58] As will be clear from the previous chapter, I believe that Africa in fact desperately needs interventions – of the right design – in markets, and an effective public sector. However, while I do not endorse the standard package of donor reforms, I *am* arguing that this package has not in fact been implemented in the way that has often been assumed by NGOs or as presented by donors.

The politics of conditionality

The most important implications of the evidence on non-compliance and partial reform are for the *process and politics* of conditionality. One lesson from the studies cited above was that a large number of detailed conditions attached to aid were not an effective way for donors to convince governments to change policies, and pointed to the need for governments to 'own' reforms themselves. When it came to a clash between what donors wanted governments to do on the one hand, and domestic political considerations on the other, domestic politics almost always won out (Devarajan et al 2001 p 5, Killick 2004).[59]

Various ways of reforming conditionality were proposed by academics, or experimented with by donors.[60] A more radical conclusion was that donors should abandon conditionality and instead selectively give aid to countries that already owned reforms that donors liked. This view was embraced by some parts of the donor community in principle, and is practised to varying extents by the Bank, the US and Dutch governments and DfID. Within the World Bank and DfID local 'ownership' of reforms became a key concept, and the Bank's research department in particular promoted the minimization of conditionality and the adoption of selectivity (World Bank 1998a, Collier and Dollar 1999, Devarajan et al 2001). DfID's 2000 White Paper also endorsed selectivity, albeit more cautiously (DfID 2000 p 92). However, it is worth noting that while many donors have embraced selectivity, they have *not* actually abandoned conditionality, but rather practise combinations of both.

As mentioned, NGOs have largely ignored this issue. They continue to criticize conditionality as if it were highly effective, and a major example of the IFI's closing down 'policy space', as discussed in the trade context above. In debate, donors are often described as 'forcing' or 'requiring' developing country governments to undertake reforms such as liberalization of trade, or privatization of utilities (eg Christian Aid 2004b p 3; World Development Movement 2004c; Actionaid, CAFOD and Oxfam 2004 p 9). Developing country governments themselves are presented sometimes as victims, sometimes as willing dupes, and sometimes are simply absent, transparent ciphers, with no agency of their own. This approach is unhelpful, not least to NGO proposals for what should replace conditionality, or understanding what developing country governments would do with increased policy space.

What actually happens in terms of policy change in African countries depends largely on the outcome of the dynamics between donors, government and domestic political processes.

On the one hand, donors are powerful, but not all-powerful. Certainly, they do command lots of money in an environment of scarce resources, and this does give them substantial bargaining power. On the other hand, donors are also under considerable pressure to make grants or loans. Up to 1990, Cold War geo-politics was a major factor in aid allocations, and developmental objectives often took a back seat. However, the pressure to disburse has continued since then, partly because of political and humanitarian pressures from the donor home country, and partly because lending volume has been linked to career progression in donor institutions.[61] This explains why donors have often continued to support governments that refused to implement conditions. Collier (1997) gives the example from Kenya in the 1980s and 1990s, where the government agreed and failed four times in a row to implement conditions linked to Bank loans, and four times the Bank approved new loans despite non-compliance. Ravi Kanbur, who was the World Bank resident representative in Ghana in the early 1990s, gives a vivid account of the pressures he came (many from within the donor community itself) under to disburse a tranche of lending, even though budgetary conditionality had been clearly breached (Kanbur 2000 pp 414–15). Thus, another way of looking at the relationship between donors and government is to say that donors tend to have power to define policy, but developing country governments have power over implementation.[62]

In some cases, the governments of even quite poor countries, without oil or mineral money, have walked away from the donors, such as Zambia in the 1980s, Tanzania in the 1990s or Kenya in the 2000s. Thus the motivations of developing country governments clearly do matter for understanding why certain policies are adopted or not. Equally clearly, NGO analysts do have some underlying uneasiness about the commitment of some developing country governments to poverty, and their integrity, which is why there is often a call for 'minimal' or 'fiduciary' conditionality. But without a deeper understanding of government objectives, there is no reason to assume that such minimal conditionality will be any more effective than the current IFI version.

Why have African governments sometimes resisted considerable donor pressure to reform? NGOs often implicitly present African governments as holding out for one or both of two reasons.

The first is that the reforms are wrong or badly designed, ie that they will not bring growth, poverty reduction, etc, and that governments are trying to implement much more sensible policies. However, while the first part of this account is plausible for some reforms (Mosley 1995, Mosley et al 2003), the second generally isn't. Until the mid-1980s, most African economies were still largely under the sole control of their governments, and the record on poverty and growth had been terrible for 10 years or more. Governments only agreed to IFI conditionality at all because their own attempts at economic management had driven them into acute foreign exchange crises. Since the 1980s, senior government officials and political leaders have received messages on policy that are consistently Washington Consensus in tone. The opportunities to define and develop a coherent alternative agenda have been far and few between. The occasional points at which governments have put forward coherent alternative policy packages, for example as with Museveni's debate with the Bank on roads vs schools in the mid-1990s, are conspicuous by their rarity.

The second reason sometimes given for governments resisting reform is that domestic interest groups make it politically too costly to implement them. The World Development Movement has kept a running tally of protests spawned by unpopular Bank-Fund backed reforms (see World Development Movement 2003b for the latest version). Trade liberalization is seen by some analysts as costly in political terms, the argument being that it hurts organized urban groups (eg workers in protected import substitution industries), while it benefits dispersed rural groups (eg producers of export crops) (Rodrik 1998). Likewise, it is easy to see why public sector reform involving large numbers of layoffs in capital cities would be politically sensitive. This approach has a lot of appeal, and it connects with the political point that conditionality does actually work against the democratic principle that governments should be accountable to their own people rather than external agencies. However, there is quite a lot of evidence that works against this interest group argument. High profile examples, such as the riots in Zambia in 1986 against the removal of subsidies on white maize meal, have masked that fact that the wider picture does not fit the model linking reforms to political instability (Bates and Krueger 1993). A recent review of public sector reform in East Africa concludes that: 'In all, broad or vocal resistance to public sector reform appears to have been lacking' (Kjaer 2004 p 394). The key reason why the interest group account does not work well for Africa is because sections of the population with economic interests are usually not actually formed into well-organized interest *groups* able to put substantial pressure on governments. In relation to population size, urban groups such as trade unions are often small, and were in many countries weakened or taken over by one-party states, or repressed by military regimes. van de Walle (2001 p 31) points to Zambia and Nigeria as having probably the most powerful trades union movements in Africa, movements that at times have contested policies forcefully. Yet, he argues, 'their power still appears ephemeral, with temporary episodes of prominence that are not sustained because of weak organization and the continuing power of the state to co-opt and manipulate the groups'. Street protests can in fact be a sign of organizational and political weakness, as they imply that negotiating power is not strong enough to work on its own. Rural populations, meanwhile, are almost never organized into sustained independent political structures. And civil society, including NGOs, while it has blossomed substantially since 1990, remains relatively weak and increasingly controlled by legislation. Thus, while African states are weak in some conventional senses, politically they are surrounded by an even weaker civil society:

> In Africa, the state projects upwards from its surroundings like a veritable Kilimanjaro, in large part because the open plains of domestic society appear to be thinly populated with alternative institutions . . . in this lilliputian environment, even a weak state can seem to be strong. (Bratton 1989 p 410)

If African governments have not resisted reforms because they have coherent alternatives or because of domestic pressure groups, then what is the reason? Here my central argument (and that of a range of analysts including van de Walle, Sindzingre, Chabal and Daloz, and Hibou) is that it is because the elites controlling African states have often seen their own personal and political interests threatened by these reforms, and have resisted them until they have found ways to secure those interests in other ways. As I will describe in detail in chapter 6, post-colonial African leaders secured their power through a system of patronage politics. The resources dispensed to supporters, or clients, came from the state, especially through access to public sector employment and subsidies. Later, as economies faltered and goods and services became scarce, control over any kind of state resource or service – such as access to scarce foreign exchange, subsidized credit or fertilizer or import licences – became a crucial source of livelihood for public servants in the form of bribes. At the same time, looked at from the point of view of government failure, these were also 'rents'. Opportunities to extract rents became the object of patronage, given in exchange for political allegiance. Reforms aimed at liberalizing controls over markets and trade, at cutting public sector employment or at selling off state owned firms threatened the whole system. Leaders have therefore been reluctant to carry out reforms until they can find ways to re-route or reshape patronage (van de Walle 2001). They have had to do this partly, or indeed mainly, because as African economies and budgets collapsed, aid itself became a major source of patronage resources.

The argument is therefore that the motivation of African governments in their relationship with donors has been political survival, not in the conventional sense of managing competing interest groups, but rather in trying to maintain a patronage system. It has not been protect the workings of a developmental state. Thus through the crisis and 'adjustment' period from 1980 onwards, while governments have largely protected both numbers in the public sector employment and public spending as a proportion of GDP (van de Walle pp 95–96), they have abandoned much of their developmental ambition. Where under pressure to cut or restrain expenditure, governments have tended to protect posts at the expense of developmental goods, and centrally located politically significant posts at the expense of front-line skilled staff. They have consistently skewed spending within health and education away from the rural poor, and towards the richer, urban dwellers (Castro-Leal et al 1999). They have particularly protected discretionary spending under the control of Presidents and cabinet ministers.[63] Finally, they have protected 'sovereignty' expenditures associated with elite consumption. This includes not just the excesses of Houphouet-Boigny's basilica in Yamoussoukrou, but wider spending on diplomatic and other facilities. Between 1984 and 1993, while the Zambian economy was in a drawn-out crisis, the government spent more on Zambian foreign services abroad than it did on primary school services (net of teachers salaries) in the entire country (van de Walle 2001 p 109).

If the elites running African states are motivated by maintaining political power through the use of state resources in patronage (and also sometimes in conspicuous consumption), then simply getting rid of conditionality – ie giving unconditional aid to patronage-based regimes – will not yield developmental outcomes of growth, poverty reduction, diversification and improvements in human welfare. It is more likely simply to lead to stagnant economies and politically unaccountable regimes, punctuated by foreign exchange crisis for the poorest countries. Some of the worst repression and mismanagement took place under regimes receiving largely unconditional aid driven by Cold War politics in the 1970s and 1980s.

One NGO counter-argument is that instead of the upward accountability of governments to donors that conditionality seeks to impose, what is needed is downward accountability to society; that donors should simply support processes that increase accountability, with possibly only some minimal political conditionality to back this up. But how realistic is this is the African context? I go into this issue more deeply in the following chapters, but here it should be noted that there are two major challenges for this project.

The first is that of capacity. As noted, in many cases nascent civil society was seriously weakened or destroyed by the state early after independence. Economic decline and stagnation has also hurt the emergence of civil society organizations. Indigenous NGOs in Africa are still politically weak, and largely urban based. Churches have stronger and wider roots, and were able to challenge Presidents attempting to change constitutions to give themselves a third term in several East and Southern African countries, including Zambia and Malawi. However, they often lack technical capacity. Trade unions, women's groups and professional associations in many cases were for many years subsumed into one-party state mechanisms, and severely weakened financially and organizationally. South Africa has exceptions, and there are signs – perhaps in the Kenyan elections of 2003, for example, or in Ghana – that civil society is beginning to have some kind of political impact, but elsewhere there are serious doubts about capacity to influence the policy and political debate more than marginally. Capacity to monitor Poverty Reduction Strategies systematically is even weaker (Lucas et al 2004 p 18). Even Parliaments often lack capacity on budget monitoring (Rakner et al 2004).

The second set of issues is political exclusion or cooption, as a result of patronage politics itself. The PRSP process is a good example of the former. While there has been some participation of civil society groups in the writing of PRSPs, many have been excluded from the process (Christian Aid 2002, Actionaid USA/Actionaid Uganda 2004). What happens in many cases is the establishment of a civil society elite, or at least a privileged circle who are invited where others are not. But even being in the PRSP process may not be enough. In most countries, mirroring the nature of politics whereby an informal patronage-based politics goes on behind the façade of formal structures, real political decisions do not get taken in PRSP workshops. Kelsall, writing about Tanzania, quotes a donor talking about a distinction between the 'shop-window' talk of good governance and PRSPs, and the 'smoke-filled rooms' where meetings of the ruling party really decide on priorities (Kelsall 2002 p 597). On the donor side the smoke-filled rooms are the consultative group meetings, and the Bank and fund missions that produce the PRGFs and PRSCs, IFI-controlled instruments that build macroeconomic and structural reforms into conditionalities outside the PRSP process. Civil society rarely gets a look in on either side. Finally, civil society groups themselves will not be immune to patronage politics. In most countries, genuine civil society members are easily able to identify 'briefcase' NGOs, set up solely to attract some of the funds put through non-state routes, which swelled considerably in the 1990s. Presidents and their families have also established NGOs. While these are usually widely known within countries, such members of 'civil society' can be very handy for voicing the views of members of the elite. Even at the local level, development associations or farmers' groups can often be linked to particular political patronage networks, and so may even seek to resist more accountable public services that threaten those networks.

Overall, NGOs display some ambivalence and confusion over conditionality in the aid relationship. Some Northern NGOs, like Oxfam during the debt campaign of the late 1990s, disagreed with the content of conditionality, but were in favour of alternative conditionalities. Others have tended to be firmly against almost all conditionality, although an awareness that corruption permeates African countries, and makes some uneasy about the idea of no conditionality at all. To their surprise (and sometimes dismay), their southern counterparts and partners can often be more in favour of conditionality (especially political conditionality), although they also (not surprisingly) chafe at the arrogance and lack of accountability of the donors.[64]

An impasse for NGOs and donors?

If NGOs are confused about what to do instead of IFI conditionality, donors are confused about what to do with it. A recent review by Tony Killick shows that, although the World Bank intellectually embraced the critique of conditionality, it continues to rely on it operationally (Killick 2004 p14). While there has been a reduction in the number of conditions per loan, these have been largely of 'non-binding' conditions, and the share of adjustment lending in the Bank's portfolio has actually risen in recent years. The IMF never really accepted the critique, and although it is taking steps to 'streamline' its conditionality, Killick (2004 p 15) argues on the basis of the available evidence that this is 'a fairly limited exercise'. Their notion of 'ownership' largely seems to be that governments accept policies devised by the IMF, even if they don't actually agree with them (Boughton, cited in Wood 2004).

A key issue here is that donors are often not clear *how* to streamline conditionality. While a loan with a large number of benchmarks and trigger points is self-evidently more likely to end off-track than one with a small number, simply reducing the number of conditions per se may not help. There is no clear evidence that streamlining leads to greater compliance (Killick 2004, Wood 2004). The account given above implies that what is needed is a proper understanding of the domestic political system and dynamics (Deverajan et al 2001). I return to this point below.

Many donors are now combining an element of selectivity in aid alloca-tion, together with an element of conditionality in aid disbursement. The US government, under its radically neo-conservative leadership, has taken the step of apparently abandoning conditionality and investing everything in selectivity. Its Millennium Challenge Account first round funding in Africa has gone to only 7 countries (Lucas and Radelet 2004). Of course, selectivity can be seen as post-hoc conditionality, and whether countries qualify for the next round of MCA depends on their continuing to perform well enough on a range of Washington Consensus–style governance and economic freedom criteria, along with efforts on the 'war on terror'.

The UK government, meanwhile, has recently produced a position paper on conditionality that rather fudges the issue (DfID, FCO and HM Treas-ury 2004). The paper accepts the argument that aid cannot be used to buy reform, and proposes to base aid on a 'partnership' linked to a country's 'own strategy for reducing poverty'. On the other hand, there will still be conditions, but ones that will be 'agreed by all parties, rather than being imposed on partner governments'. In practice, IFI conditionality will still be supported by the UK, and while there is a proposal to open up a debate, UK government policy apparently continues to be to follow the IMF on macro-economic benchmarking. Largely a restatement of the principles of 'owner-ship' and 'partnership' from the last decade, this approach invests much in the assumption that PRSPs are the genuine expression of a domestically formed poverty reduction agenda produced and embraced by government and civil society. As we have seen, this is likely to be the exception rather than the rule. Where there is no anti-poverty strategy, no acceptable PRSP and 'difficult environments' make a partnership impossible, the paper is not clear what should be done, but the provisional approach is to deliver aid through non-state actors. Where exactly the borderline falls between these different cases is not clear.

Donors have clearly come to an impasse with conditionality. They find it extremely hard to relinquish even the illusion of control over policy to governments who they see as reluctant and lacking capacity (see Wood 2004 p 49 on the IMF). It is also true that abandoning conditionality would probably mean retrenchments in the aid policy machine, especially at the World Bank, as the massed ranks of policy advisers and mission chiefs would become largely redundant. Yet they are under pressure from the cri-tiques of NGOs and academics. They are aware that conditionality is rarely effective in the face of domestic political opposition, and they are equally aware that it pulls accountability in the wrong way when they are trying to promote participation, partnership and local ownership.

Summing up

In this chapter I have argued that the donor–NGO debate on aid and conditionality is doomed to circular and rather sterile repetition. Many of the current debates have scarcely changed from those raging almost 10 years ago. This is because the full implications of the ineffectiveness of conditionality – specifically the very particular political nature of policy implementation and the uses of aid in Africa – have not been fully accepted by donors and NGOs. Rather unreal 'shop window' notions litter the landscape, including 'partnership', 'ownership', 'participation', and 'accountability'. Even the PRSPs themselves, while they have had some effect on the relationship between civil society and government in some countries, are a largely unreal exercise. Donor governments, and especially the World Bank, are somewhat constrained in the degree to which they can openly discuss and analyse the nature of politics in Africa. They are concerned largely with government-to-government aid, and must work on the basis of the supremacy of sovereignty. This is why the Commission for Africa is investing so much hope in the AU, NEPAD and the APRM. In some cases, it is also easy to understand the reluctance of NGOs to be more open about the nature of politics in Africa – in repressive situations such as contemporary Zimbabwe, it is safer for local NGOs and their international backers to avoid open political analysis. However, in the more general advocacy debates in the UK, its absence is surprising.[65]

5 The limits of 'governance'

AFRICA'S POVERTY IS CHRONIC, stands in sharp contrast to the East and South-east Asian experience, and is fundamentally rooted in a failure of economic accumulation through investment. The developmental challenge is becoming even more profound with AIDS and climate change. The main debates on development policies, especially trade and conditionality, point to the central role played by the state in development, a role that both NGOs and donors have had some difficulty in grappling with.

Typically, donors have thought about African states primarily in terms of 'governance', which can be broadly defined as the performance of the state. This approach is also taken by the Commission for Africa report, whose 'foundation' rests on the importance of strengthening states (Commission for Africa 2005 p 134). Following quite early donor recognition that there were problems with the way that states functioned, both for the economy and for human development, donors drew up a model of how the state should function, and embarked on reform programmes. However, the failure of these programmes soon revealed the limits of the models. The story of the 'governance' approach confirms De Waal's aphorism that governance is 'government minus politics'.[66] Indeed, it becomes clear that governance problems are but a symptom of deeper political troubles.

Africa's record on governance

Nevertheless, it is true that for African populations, there are multiple problems of governance. At the extreme end of the spectrum, the crisis of governance has spilled over into open conflict and the failure of states to provide even the most basic security. This is not just in the case of civil wars, often externally fuelled as in the proxy Cold War conflicts in Angola, Mozambique, Ethiopia, and Somalia in the 1980s, but also in cases of state collapse and warlordism, as in Sierra Leone, Liberia, DRC, Guinea-Bissau, Rwanda, Somalia and Sudan in the 1990s. Millions of people have died as a direct result. Lower level violence has also been widespread, either because of regional and social divisions, as in Nigeria or northern Uganda, or actually organized and manipulated by the state itself, such as in Zimbabwe and even in Kenya in the mid-1990s. Africa has been particularly prone to military coups and repression, especially West Africa.

At a more mundane level, corruption has emerged as a key aspect of government that affect everyday life in Africa. The African Union has recently estimated that corruption costs Africa $148 billion per year, increasing the costs of goods by up to 20 per cent and deterring investment. Similarly the World Bank states that corruption impedes growth by 0.5 per cent.[67] Out of the 145 countries in Transparency International's Corruptions Perceptions Index, 20 of the bottom 55 are African countries, and only Botswana and South Africa make it into the top 50. Because it is an index based largely on business perceptions, some African countries do not appear on it at all, because they are completely shunned by the business community. In many countries, corruption occurs at all levels, from Presidents and close associates right down the provision of basic state services at the local level. Corruption especially within the police and local courts was a recurrent theme raised by people in the World Bank's Participatory Poverty Assessments in the early and mid-1990s. Some writers go so far as to talk of the 'criminalization' of the state in Africa (Bayart et al 1999).

Perhaps the most important aspect of corruption is the widespread failure to apply sanctions on corrupt behaviour. In many countries people know that corruption goes on (especially with a more independent media)[68] but do not expect anything to happen as a result, because generally no sanctions are applied (see ch 8 below for the example of Mozambique).

There are also massive problems of state undercapacity. Civil servants make up only 1 per cent of the population in African countries on average, much lower than in other developing regions at 3 per cent, and also down from 1.3 per cent in 1991 (Lienert and Modi 1997). Despite the fact that most countries had only a handful of graduates at Independence, in 1996 the African Governors of the World Bank reported that: 'Almost every Africa country has witnessed a systematic regression of capacity in the last thirty years' (cited in van de Walle 2001 p 130). Citing a range of sources, van de Walle (2001 p 131) describes Africa civil services as characterized by 'pervasive absenteeism, endemic corruption, politicization, declining legitimacy and low morale'. There has been a widespread impact on public services, including in health and education, which has been an underlying cause of both poor services and of the failure of particular projects. There have also been consequences for African infrastructure, which, after three decades of inadequate investment and maintenance, is in a terrible state. In 1999 the African Development Bank estimated that one third of roads built in the 1980s and 1990s had eroded due to poor maintenance (ADB 1999). van de Walle (2001 p 87) cites the case of the main Nairobi–Mombassa highway being in such a poor state that a 300-mile journey took three days for a fully-laden lorry. This situation adds hugely to Africa's transport costs, which remain well above those of other regions (Sachs et al 2004).

Low-skilled positions tend to be overstaffed, whereas at skilled level there are typically many unfilled positions. Donors and NGOs have exacerbated an already existing brain drain which saw an estimated 50,000–60,000 middle and senior-level state managers leave Africa between 1986 and 1990 alone on one estimate. Poor capacity is often blamed by NGOs on poverty itself, and of course many of the aspects of civil service performance listed above are closely related to the collapse of wages. During the 1970s and 1980s civil services salaries in Anglophone Africa lost roughly 80 per cent of their value (van de Walle 2001 p 134, Lienert and Modi 1997). In the post-Independence period the size of the public service was expanded very quickly, and pressures to cut spending have almost always been responded to by allowing the value of wages to fall, rather than cutting numbers. But it should also be noted that the absolute level of resources is not necessarily related to state capacity in a direct way; oil-rich Nigeria has severe state capacity problems, and indeed oil and mineral exporting LDCs are on average poorer than other LDCs (UNCTAD 2003d).

Added to this record is the fact that African states did not manage their economies at all well, as discussed in chapter 3 above. It is this poor management and the resulting crisis and failed 'adjustment' that indeed underlies much of the poor record in delivery of services. Overall, in contrast with the 'developmental' states of East Asia, and indeed of Botswana and Mauritius closer by, African states have been mildly to severely 'anti-developmental', or at very best, 'non-developmental' (Sindzingre 2004).

The rise and fall of governance reform

The donor response to pervasive problems with the state was to frame the issue as a 'governance' problem. In taking this approach, donors have focused on the performance of the state and the immediate causes of poor performance, especially rent-seeking by bureaucrats. It is only very recently, as the limits of the approach and the failure of governance reforms have emerged, that donors have started to think about the political logic underlying the workings of the state, asking why the rent-seeking regime has emerged and why it is so stable, resisting donor pressure for reform. A major reason for this is that donors are reluctant to be seen to be visibly engaging in political analysis and manipulation.[69] Most aid is government-to-government, and sovereignty is still the foundation of the international aid system, which makes thinking about, let alone acting on, the nature of the state a tricky business. The World Bank cannot withdraw from a country on political or even human rights grounds. Thus there is an in-built inertia in donor thinking that made 'governance' – a much more neutral concept – the natural frame of analysis. That said, when the issue was first opened up by the Bank and other donors, it was still controversial.

Serious engagement with governance issues in Africa began in the 1980s. The first generation of reforms pushed by the IFIs focused on 'getting prices right' through deregulating agricultural markets and liberalizing trade and exchange rate regimes (World Bank 1981). Although much of this did not actually happen until the 1990s, early experience in countries such as Ghana, along with a growing realization that institutions do matter for the development process, led to a focus on governance as a major issue in Africa by the time of the World Bank's 1989 report *Sub-Saharan Africa: From Crisis to Sustainable Growth*. The Bank turned to the issue of states again in the 1997 World Development Report, and governance was also a major theme of the 2001 *Can Africa Claim the 21st Century?* (World Bank 2001).

These documents all provide a consistent set of messages about the ideal role of the state in Africa. Beyond the minimal function of providing peace, law and order, the state should provide or organize services, such as health, education and infrastructure, and it should also ensure an 'enabling' environment for investment, which includes macro-economic stability, secure property rights and the transparent adjudication of disputes (eg World Bank 2001 pp 50–51). A major part of the problem in Africa, according to this view, is that states are overambitious and involved in too many activities, giving too many opportunities for extracting rents.

Similar views have been expressed recently by analysts in or close to donors, especially in the area of the enabling state and economic growth. Killick and White (2001), Fafchamps et al (2001), Wood (2002), and Collier and Gunning (1999a) have all recently characterized Africa's long-term problems as a trap where poor 'institutions' or 'governance', poor export performance, and low investment and productivity all reinforce one another.[70] Wood (2002 p 1) argues that: 'What is mainly needed to raise Africa from poverty to prosperity are improvements in governance which will reduce the risks of investment and encourage the return of flight capital, physical and human.' Again, the agenda for the state is fairly close to that of the Bank, and include investing equitably in human capital through health, education and training, improving infrastructure,[71] and creating an environment for business growth through political and macro-economic stability, and through interventions that 'reduce coordination failure, favour institutional innovation and minimize commitment failure' (Fafchamps 2001 p 1, 17–20, Collier and Gunning 1999, Wood 2002 p 27).

Donors have tried to grapple with governance problems in various ways. In the 1980s and early 1990s, influenced heavily by the 'government failure' literature described in chapter 3 above, the emphasis was on scaling back the African state, removing regulation in markets and state ownership, and urging minimization of ambitions for what the state could achieve. More recently, there has been a shift from preoccupation over the size of the state towards concern about the quality of institutions and state performance. However, donor attempts to reform and improve governance have made re-markably little progress in the absence of an interest by senior political elites.

Certainly, by the mid-1990s many African states were hardly functioning in a normal way, and aid was a part of the problem. Because of low capacity, many donors had given up working through the main ministry budget and structure, and instead set up units and projects off-budget. Overall sectoral coordination and the capacity to plan and manage a sectoral budget had been largely lost. A response to this situation was the sector wide approach, or SWAP, which began appearing in the early 1990s (Andersen 2000). This was aimed at coordinating donor inputs to a sector – typically health or education – and strengthening the capacity of the sectoral ministry in planning, budgeting and implementation. However, whether SWAPs actually worked or not turned out to depend on the degree of political buy-in from the top. An authoritative study in 1999 (Foster et al 1999 p 47) concluded that: 'The conclusion of successive SWAP reviews that governments need a broad and high-level commitment to which donors can broadly agree, remains true.'

Similar considerations apply to attempts to reform the civil service in African countries directly. We already saw in the last chapter that public sector reform was the one area that conditionality worked least effectively in producing changes on the ground, and where domestic political considerations loomed large. In a review of the failure of reforms of public sector management, Berg concludes that although the inadequacies and impacts of the aid agencies themselves play a role, probably the most important reasons lay outside the programmes, largely in political factors (Berg 2000 p 297). Kjaer's (2004) review of public sector reforms in Uganda, Kenya and Tanzania makes it clear that the (changing) attitudes of Presidents have been the decisive factor in the nature and pace of reform.

A more recent OED review of the World Bank's anti-corruption programmes provides further similar findings. In September 1997, following endorsement from the Board, the Bank launched a major work programme on corruption. During the period 1998–2001, the Bank made 53 loans totalling $2.7 billion to 22 countries for governance work in the Africa region. The review concluded that while the activities undertaken by the Bank were highly relevant to the problem, working on state intervention, rule of law, transparency in public sector operations, capacity building for good government and a competent civil service, the programme has produced 'only modest success so far in achieving durable outcomes' (OED 2004 p ix). In the two African case studies, by now familiar reasons are given for a lack of impact. In Kenya political commitment was lacking (this was still the Moi era), while in Tanzania the study concludes that: 'Overall the long-term efficacy of the Bank's programme in Tanzania remains unevaluable due to lack of local ownership and uncertain policy regime' (OED p 94).

Meanwhile on the 'enabling' state side, the efficacy and especially the sustainability of donor interventions also seems to depend on political commitment. In chapter 3 above we saw that supply side problems are a central factor in explaining Africa's difficulties in diversifying away from commodity exports. A key element of the donor response has been 'trade-related capacity building' (TRCB), which has evolved out of previous trade related technical assistance. The 2004 DTI White Paper, *Making Globalisation a Force for Good* defines trade-related capacity building as being 'about supporting the ability of developing countries to produce and implement a trade development strategy, and then incorporate this strategy into their development or poverty reduction programmes' (DTI 2004 p 94). Such a strategy, according not only to the UK Government but also the EU and the World Bank, should consist of an 'enabling state' menu, combining trade and investment liberalization with 'flanking' or complementary policies, including measures to tackle poor infrastructure and the absence of a well-educated workforce, and institutions and regulations to support trade (DTI 2004 pp 82–84).

This is obviously a wide agenda, which again requires an improvement in the capacity and performance of the state in a broad way. But even the exercise of supporting the development of the supply side *strategy* itself has had limited success. Since 1998 the UK has given £174 million in TRCB (with over half of this focused on Africa including the Africa Trade and Poverty Programme (ATPP)), and contributed to the EU programme, which was worth $700 million in 2002 alone.[72] The World Bank has also launched TRCB pilot programmes involving up to 14 countries by 2002 (Powell 2002 p 12). Much of this support goes to research studies, training of government staff, advice to the private sector in developing countries, policy development and institution-building.

A recent review of TRCB work draws similar conclusions to that of PSR (North-South Institute 2004). Projects suffered from some of the usual design flaws, although they were generally well run. However, impact in the African cases has been rather limited.[73] In general, the projects working directly with the private sector have been more successful than those trying to change government thinking and action. In the Kenyan case, an attempt to support policy input on the business environment did not lead to government taking the suggestions up, because of 'attitudes of policymakers' and 'institutional barriers to change' (Blouin and Njoroge 2004 p 23) Governments have not been willing to commit funds to allow analytical work on trade capacity to continue after the end of the programmes (North-South Institute 2004 p 36). The Malawian case study strongly emphasizes the 'severe capacity problems' in the trade department and the Malawian Export Promotion Council, and their neglect by government (Weston and Tsoka 2004 pp 6–7). It is in Tanzania, where government commitment is strongest, that TRCB work seems to have been most effective in creating more sustainable capacity.[74]

Assessing the governance problem

There are recent claims that governance in Africa is improving. For example, the recent Commission for Africa (2005 pp 134, 300–01) cites the ECA's

African Governance Report as evidence of some progress towards 'good governance', in the functioning of democracy, systems of accountability and levels of economic management.

This may signal the emergence of political leaders more interested in effective states. In chapter 8 I assess some of the evidence for four of the countries often cited as 'good performers'.

However, it is also important not to mistake changes in the *form* of politics or institutions in Africa with changes in substantial *nature* of politics and governance. The presence of formal structures of accountability is not necessarily a guide to their actual functioning, as the case of the budget process in Malawi shows (Rakner et al 2002). Zimbabwe is, formally speaking, a multi-party democracy, with many of the offices of the Parliamentary system. This hybrid nature of the state in Africa is a theme taken up in more detail below in chapter 7.

The ECA survey also shows that African states still have along way to go. The Commission for Africa (2005 p 134) report goes on to note that: 'weaknesses remain in most countries in the efficiency of government services, the control of corruption, the transparency and accountability of the civil service, and the effective decentralisation of government structures.'

Certainly, the evidence is that, thus far, most externally-led governance reforms have failed (Poldiano 2001, Goetz 2005). In the words of one of the leading experts on anti-corruption reforms: 'The last ten years have been deeply disappointing. Much was done, but not much was accomplished. What we are doing is not working.'[75]

Nevertheless, the lure of governance reforms remains strong. The exhortation to African governments to tackle corruption and draw up 'comprehensive capacity-building strategies' is a central plank of the Commission for Africa (2005 p 136) report, without any analysis of what political incentives there are to do so. The World Bank is currently attempting public service reforms in the Central African Republic (CAR), which experienced a coup in 2003 and has a barely functioning state. But if such reforms have not been successful in eradicating corruption in Tanzania, there is no chance at all that they will work in CAR.

'Governance' remains an attractive proposition to donors because it is addressed to very real problems with how states act and work (or don't work) in Africa. However, we have seen in this chapter again and again that whether governance reforms have been taken up depends on political commitment from the most senior levels. At the same time, governance problems are symptoms of the politics that underlie African states. It is the reluctance and difficulty that donors have with engaging with politics that makes them turn again and again to governance reforms. However, without such engagement, it will be impossible to address the chronic governance failures seen across the continent. It is to politics in Africa that we now turn.

6 Politics in Africa

DONORS HAVE BEEN TRYING to change Africa for over 20 years. A recent commentator describes the decline of Zambia over the last quarter century, and goes on to say:

> For much of this period, Zambia received support from the international community. Yet almost every attempt to help made matters worse. Like a patient who baffles medical science, Zambia has been poked and prodded by experts from the IMF and the World Bank, who prescribed repeated doses of shock treatment. The result has been worsening poverty and a dramatic build up of foreign debt. (Adams 2004 p 11)

This compelling image applies to Sub-Saharan Africa more broadly. Initially donors focused on what they perceived, partly through an ideological filter, to be bad policies. Slow progress, and a dawning realisation that even 'good' policies were not producing investment and poverty reduction, led to a focus on the poor quality of institutions, which applied to the state meant an absence of 'good governance'. As we have seen, governance as a frame of analysis also quickly showed its limits, and governance reform programmes their failures.

Again and again, in understanding both Africa's predicaments, and also debates about policies for a solution, the role of the state has emerged as a decisive factor. Looking beyond the details of state performance to think about the function of states, African states appear to be largely anti-developmental, in stark contrast with the developmental states of East and South-east Asia. Many of the developmental problems of African states – including a tendency to exacerbate inequality, to run down capacity, to tolerate and even promote corruption – seem also to persist whatever donors try to do, as the quote above implies.

To understand, and possibly act upon, Africa's problems, the key question is therefore: if the state in Africa is not there to promote development, what function is it serving? How have such anti-developmental states emerged? What is the political logic holding these states together, and can it be changed?

The roots of clientelism

An essential starting point in answering these questions is the story of the evolution of the African state. Many accounts of Africa emphasize the material and human legacy of colonialism, including forced labour, heavy taxation, a skewed infrastructure, underdeveloped industry, and negligible health and education services. However, even more decisive has been the political inheritance.

The central political mode of both British and French colonialism was indirect rule. Rather than direct settlement by large numbers of Europeans, seizure of land from the original inhabitants and the conversion of these into slaves or workers, the indirect rule system kept a 'free' peasantry on the land, ruled by 'traditional authorities' (in fact, often invented or redefined[76]). While sections of land were appropriated in the 'settler colonies' of Kenya, Rhodesia and South Africa, even in these cases indirect rule applied to the mass of the population. This arrangement gave a very particular nature to political identity and leadership in colonial Africa. Indirect rule made a crucial distinction between the law and rule that applied to European colonizers, and that applying to the African population:

> The tribal leadership was either selectively reconstituted as the hier-
> archy of the local state or freshly imposed where none had existed, as
> in 'stateless societies'. Here, political inequality went alongside civil
> inequality. Both were grounded in a legal dualism. Alongside received
> law was implemented a customary law that regulated non-market rela-
> tions, in land, in personal (family) and in community affairs. For the
> subject population of natives, indirect rule signified a mediated –
> decentralized – despotism. (Mamdani 1996 p 17)

Indirect rule thus had a number of very important features that have resonance through to contemporary African politics.

First, African 'natives' were the subjects of tribal leaders, not citizens with rights of free association and political representation under civil law (Mamdani 1996 pp 18–19). Tribal subjects were ruled under a customary law by authorities pledging to enforce tradition, and not open to political debate and change. Tribal leaders, backed up ultimately by the threat of force from the colonizing power, ruled through a mixture of authoritarian coercion and patronage. Chiefs allocated government jobs, land, and exemption from tax-ation and communal labour. This form of rule accentuated 'tribal' or ethnic identity, and also meant that where there were uprisings, they were often ethnic in inspiration: 'Peasant insurrectionists organized around what they claimed were an untainted, uncompromised, and genuine customs, against a state-enforced and corrupted version of the customary.' (Mamdani 1996 p 24). Crucially, these revolts sought only to replace leadership, not to trans-form the system.

This was partly because the contrast between customary rule and civil rule was only really evident in colonial African cities. It was in the cities that it became clear to Africans that, although often skilled workers, they were excluded from the rights of citizenship, and it was in the cities that the nationalist struggle for these rights began.[77] In the cities too, markets operated in a more thorough-going way; in the countryside, precisely because land remained under customary control, the penetration of markets was always limited. Thus a second feature of the system was a 'bifurcated' state that operated rather differently in urban as opposed to rural areas.

A final aspect of indirect rule was that although it was a despotic system, it was also decentralized, unlike direct rule. It did not rely on a strong, centralized state apparatus with many representatives and service points across the territory. Indeed, because it did not do so, indirect rule was imperialism on the cheap, which was one of its attractions to the colonizing powers.

Thus, on the eve of the emergence of nationalist, anti-colonial movements and parties in the 1950s, political life was characterized on the one hand by a relatively small group of urban workers and emerging intellectuals, aware of their exclusion from full civil rights, and on the other, the much larger rural population, ruled as subjects under customary law by an semi-autonomous authoritarian class of ethnically defined local chiefs, through a mixture of coercion and patronage.

At this stage, both Britain and France were moving towards a post-war strategy that accepted decolonisation as inevitable. They initially planned a gradual, long-term handover to the more conservative wing of the nationalist movements. However, the experience of being confronted by Nkrumah in the Gold Coast in the late 1940s led the British to a new strategy of trying to hand over power to the conservatives quickly before the more radical elements could take control of the process. The French followed suit. With this switch:

> decolonisation was now to occur in a matter of years not decades, and to be achieved through a series of elections with mass . . . suffrage, allowing African governments to be formed with successively more extensive powers. These elections were introduced with little notice, sometimes only a few months, requiring nationalist organisations to mobilise huge electorates in a very short time. (Allen 1995 p 304)

This was to prove a decisive political moment. The need to throw together political alliances at very short notice with minimal resources, and the absence of party organization outside of a few urban areas, meant that the nationalist leaders – typically urban-based teachers, union leaders or administrators – had to rely on the existing political structures. This meant finding individuals – often chiefs or other prominent notables – who had local followers, and using patronage to bind these individuals to the party, and local voters to the candidates:

In essence, voters were offered collective material benefits (roads, schools, clinics, water, etc) for their votes, while candidates and not-ables were offered individual benefits (cash, access to licences, credit and land, etc) as well as being portrayed as responsible for the arrival of the collective benefits. (Allen 1995 p 304)

The result in most countries, by the end of the era of Independence in the early 1960s, was a set of locally based MPs, responsive to local demands, only loosely knitted in to the ruling party, whose leader now had access to public (or in a few cases private) resources. The access to public resources became key. Once parties were in power, they could use ministry funds to consolidate and extend their support. Allen gives the example of the Sierra Leone Peoples' Party, which used control over rural credit to favour key supporters, who never had to repay the loans.

Thus the circumstances of late colonial rule and the rapidity of the nationalist moment led to the birth of a politics based on political patron-age. This system has become known by a variety of terms, including clien-telism, neo-patrimonialism and pre-bendalism.[78] Clientelist politics involves an exchange between political patrons, dispensing 'privileged access to state resources, rationed by state leaders following a strict political logic'[79] and clients offering political support and allegiance:

For those within the clientelist network, loyalty to the party or its leaders was rewarded by access to valued resources. These could be passed on to more minor supporters, and to voters to reinforce their loyalty – or they could be retained for personal enrichment. (Allen 1995 pp 304–05)

In the first few years of African independent states, it soon became clear that clientelism had a certain logic, which gave the neo-patrimonial state distinct characteristics.

First, it produced a politics that was not based on issues or particular social classes, but rather a politics that revolved around personalities. It is difficult to understand, say, Nigerian party politics in terms of issues or social class.

Second, it gave elections, or indeed any kind of political competition, a particular edge, since in this system the winner would take all. This was because access to power gave rulers access to public resources, which as described above could be used to reinforce power through further allocation to supporters: '. . . to have power was to have the means to reproduce it; to lose power, however, was to risk never having the means to regain it.' (Allen 1995 p 304). Not surprisingly, political conflict became increasingly violent, with harassment of opposition parties, vote rigging, bannings and banishments, beatings, jailings and killings.[80]

At the same time, ruling parties also attempted to co-opt those who were willing, a feature that continues today (eg Rakner et al 2004 on Malawi). One of the tendencies of neo-patrimonial regimes is to have a large cabinet with a high turnover (both to accommodate the elite and to prevent the emergence of a rival to the President). van de Walle (2001 pp 103–06) has assembled data on size of cabinets over the period 1979–96. These climbed from 19.1 to 22.6 over the period. Bearing in mind the small size of African economies, these are strikingly large numbers.[81] He also finds a positive relationship between cabinet size and ethnic diversity. Those in opposition, meanwhile, fell back on the only political resource available under the old colonial regime – the use of ethnic, regional or religious identity – to threaten the new state. It is this dynamic that has sometimes given African politics a 'tribal' character.

As well as producing political instability, clientelism also introduced a tendency towards economic instability arising from corruption. Ensuring or rewarding loyalty to the party, or helping one's extended kin group, could be achieved by allocating state offices to clients. At first the rewards came in the form of employment. Certainly new African states needed expanded public services, and there was a shortage of skills. However, the massive rate of growth in the early years of Independence[82] was also driven by the need to allocate opportunities to clients, and the resulting appointments were not made on the basis of merit. The expanding state payroll, the lack of a merit-based civil service and the need to maintain or extend controls over the economy weakened the capability of countries to respond to external economic shocks, in the form of oil price rises, commodity price falls, and increasing indebtedness. Slowdown in growth in the 1970s led to crisis by the 1980s. As the real value of civil service salaries fell, the rewards shifted from the employment itself to the possibilities of extracting rents. Clientelism therefore bred corruption (Allen 1995 p 305).

Some have argued that clientelism has acted as a crucial social 'glue' holding African societies together. Others have even argued that it represents a form of redistribution from the wealthy to the poor, and that African societies are successfully functioning, just in a different way (eg Chabal and Daloz 1999). However, the material and human costs of this form of politics have been enormous. Furthermore, the patron-client relationship is actually highly unequal; patrons can and do dispense with their clients, and not much real wealth trickles down. Although clientelism and petty corruption run right through African societies, van de Walle (2001 pp 123–25) emphasizes the narrowness of the elites that really benefit: several hundred to a thousand individuals and their families, with the President at the apex.

The years immediately following Independence were therefore ones of intense political competition and growing potential or actual instability, which leaders responded to in different ways. In the words of political scientist Claude Ake 'The struggle for power was so absorbing that everything else, including development, was marginalized.' (Ake 1996 p 116).

Managing instability (or not)

Chris Allen makes a useful distinction between two variants of the post-colonial state, going beyond the simple neo-patrimonial description. It helps explain some of the variation in the degrees of corruption and disintegration in state capacity across Africa, with important implications for prospects for developmental states, and also for donor interventions.

He argues that the response of regimes to the instability of clientelism in some states, including Kenya, Tanzania, Zambia, Senegal and Cote d'Ivoire, was to centralize and bureaucratize power. Most of these changes happened in the 1960s.[83] A wide range of powers were taken into the office of an executive President (Allen 1995 p 305). Allen cites the example of Kaunda in Zambia after 1970, who had control of the executive, wide-ranging powers of appointment to public service positions, control of the parastatal sector, emergency powers and the presidency of the ruling single party. The positions of Kenyatta, Nyerere, Banda and Houphouet-Boigny were similar.[84] Political parties were displaced as the main distributors of clientelist resources by a bureaucracy answerable to the President (in Tanzania the party itself was changed into a bureaucracy). Other institutions, including political parties, independent trade unions, local traditional structures, cooperatives, etc, were either abolished or marginalized. All of these changes meant that clientelism was brought under central control, working through an institution controlled by the President. There was also a political continuity with the authoritarianism of indirect rule. Clientelism as a mechanism for holding national politics together did not disappear, but now mixed with coercion that made it clear that the authority of the central state was not to be questioned, it did become much less destabilizing. Indeed, until the 1980s in these countries we see a great deal of political stability with leaders remaining in power without civil war or coups for up to 20 years, and able to handle political succession without chaos.

In other states, including Nigeria, Sierra Leone, Liberia, Uganda, Ghana and Somalia, the incipient crisis of clientelism was not resolved, leaders did not bureaucratize and centrally control clientelism, and the system as a result became more and more unstable. Political competition and the extent of looting were magnified in cases where countries had oil or mineral resources. Here oil and mining multinationals have played a key role, at best asking no questions and at worst being deeply involved in facilitating the fraudulent use of state resources, often in the midst of state collapse. Perhaps the most grievous example is the role of European and US companies in the looting of gold, coltan, diamonds and timber and the perpetuation of the war in the Democratic Republic of Congo, in which an estimated 3 million people lost their lives.[85] It is only with international campaigns in recent years that calls have been heard for transparency and accountability by corporations.

These regimes, which Allen (1995 p 307) characterizes as having 'spoils politics' continued to display 'winner takes all' electoral politics, increasingly extreme corruption leading to a looting of the economy, more rapid moves to economic crisis, and a lack of political institutions and mediation. Leaders tried to maintain their positions through repression and violence, which contributed to the endemic instability of regimes, with coups and communal ethnic or religious-based political challenges common. It is these regimes that gave full expression to Jean Francois Bayart's expression 'the politics of the belly', where it has become the aim of all to 'eat' from the resources of the state (Bayart 1993).

Politics in these regimes has only occasionally been about changing the system. Rather, 'spoils politics results and is shown especially in the creation and collapse of a series of essentially similar regimes.' (Allen 1995 p 309). Thus as in uprisings against chiefs in the colonial era, as Mamdani describes, the political challenges have tended to be *within* the political idiom.

In some cases, especially where there were cunning leaders, windfall gains from oil or diamonds, external aid and a good internal security system, leaders have managed to hold on to power. Mobutu in Zaire would be the classic example, or Stevens in Sierra Leone for many years. However, in probably more cases, terminal spoils politics led to economic collapse, debt default, state collapse and violence (Allen 1995 pp 313–14). A first wave of implosions came in the 1970s, in Uganda, Chad and Ghana. A second wave came in the early 1990s, including Liberia, Somalia, Rwanda, Sierra Leone and arguably Nigeria under Abacha.

In the 'centralized-bureaucratic' systems, things unravelled in a slower and more controlled fashion. Undoubtedly some nationalist leaders did have developmental intentions, and many of these states did attempt to rapidly expand services to their African populations who had largely been ignored under the colonial regime. However, unlike as in the East Asian case, where political leaders saw stability coming from the collective benefits of economic growth driven by increasing productivity and investment (Wade 1990 pp 246–48), these African states attempted to manage stability by providing services, and offering particularistic[86] benefits through state employment. The political imperative was 'to fund elite consumption, public sector salaries and clientelist distribution to local networks and their citizens' (Allen 1995 p 322). States did not fundamentally change the structure of their economies, which remained constructed as they had been under colonial rule.

The weakness of the system only became fully apparent as the 1970s unfolded (Ndulu and O'Connell 1999 pp 44–45). There were two major oil shocks, and commodity prices became more volatile before slumping in the early 1980s. The World Bank gave consistently overoptimistic and misleading predictions of commodity price recovery from the early 1970s through to the mid-1980s, encouraging a false sense of security in governments (Deaton 1999 pp 32–33). However, falling export earnings and mounting debt led to economic crisis into the 1980s, and it became increasingly difficult to keep the system going and stable. Legitimacy began to be undermined. States became less able to pay salaries. While they were reluctant to risk political reaction by sacking civil servants in the face of mounting deficits, since this would signal a challenge to clientelism, they did allow the value of salaries to be eroded. Rent seeking rose rapidly as a result, and the population generally came to rely more and more on informal networks and the parallel economy. Those in power became more visibly corrupt (see eg Szeftel 1982 for Zambia).

The clientelist analysis raises the question of what, ultimately, is motivating political leaders, since this mode of politics is incompatible with a developmental project, or indeed any kind of project that requires an effective state. Of course, it is a common phenomenon that power is its own reward, and politicians in office can become solely focused on staying there, largely forgetting what they were trying to achieve in the first place. However, Chabal and Daloz (1999 pp 158–59) argue that African leaders essentially seek power to establish status: 'the aim of political elites is not just to gather power. It is much more fundamentally to use that power, and the resources which it can generate, to purchase, as it were, the "affection" of their people.' Thus part of the purpose of clientelism is to buy political support, but the other part is to impress. In the extreme cases of 'Presidents for Life', or figures such as 'Emperor' Bokassa, this is very clear, as is the use of fear mixed in with munificence. It is much more difficult to make this case for other leaders, such as Nyerere, who clearly did have some ideological projects in mind at least initially. However, no one who witnessed the party leaders and businessmen who queued for hours to lavish gifts and praise on Nyerere on his retirement in 1985 can have failed to see this dynamic at work even in Tanzania.

It also follows that the apparent ideological stance of African regimes in the 1970s and 1980s is not as significant as one might think. At the time, contrasts between Tanzania's 'African socialism' and variants of Marxist-Leninism in Mozambique, Angola and Zimbabwe on the one hand, and the apparently capitalist road of Kenya, Cote d'Ivoire and others seemed important. However, while ideological stance did somewhat colour the regime's stance towards investors and the private sector, policies and practices were often more similar than this contrast would lead one to believe. Kenya, like Tanzania, had many state-owned enterprises, and heavily controlled agricultural marketing. But more significantly, clientelist politics ran through states of all apparent ideological hue, undermining the coherence of both socialist and capitalist projects.

The case of Tanzania

The case of Tanzania is instructive.[87] Seen by many in Europe in the 1970s and 80s as a pioneer socialist experiment, with attempts to follow Chinese health care models and a developmental model of 'self-determination' under a wise leader ('Mwalimu' Nyerere) with charisma and integrity, undermined by global markets and the IFIs, the reality was more complex.

Nyerere came to power as head of TANU, a classically cobbled-together nationalist party with many constituencies and factions including the trade unions, the cooperatives, and many local leaders. TANU was formed in 1954, and it was only five years before the British agreed to leave the then-Tanganyika. The only other political party was the UTP, formed by the British and supported by conservative chiefs and white settlers. In the first elections in 1960 TANU won 70 out of 71 seats in the new Parliament. In 1962 TANU moved to consolidate its power within the transitional cabinet, and crucially, local chiefs – the Native Authorities – were removed, and their powers assumed by Regional and District Commissioners appointed by the party. Candidates for MP had to be approved centrally by the Party. There was also a new constitution, creating the post of President with a full range of powers, which Nyerere became at the end of 1962, as well as the declaration of one-party rule. Throughout the 1960s and 1970s the office of President dominated the political system. Nyerere maintained an inner circle of the political elite, but outside this group constantly reshuffled junior ministers and especially potential political opponents, from position to position within government (van Donge and Liviga 1986). Meanwhile, his lieutenant Rashidi Kawawa, previously head of the independent trade union movement, took steps to suppress the labour movement through a series of legal steps in 1962 and 1963. Key union leaders were detained without trial. In 1964 the final challenge to the control of the regime was overcome. An army mutiny was put down with the help of British troops at Lugalo barracks outside Dar es Salaam.

For the first years of Independence, contrary to Nyerere's later reputation, health services were largely curative and urban-based, and education policy focused on expanding secondary and tertiary places. Primary education grew, but only at the pace of population growth. It was only after the Arusha Declaration (see below) and in the 1970s that there was a change in strategy. This involved radically increasing the supply of services to the rural population, but, crucially, with lowered expectations. Primary education was not to be seen as a route to salaried employment, and most school leavers were expected to go into farming. Health services were to be rudimentary. In practice, the attempt to expand low-grade services rapidly on the base of a failing economy led to poor quality provision and disillusionment. By the 1980s it was a common complaint that dispensaries were empty of medicines and schools empty of teachers (who were off pursuing second jobs).

A series of crises in the 1960s led Nyerere towards a radical step at the beginning of 1967, the Arusha Declaration. One crisis arose from the expectations of those coming through the education system that they would get jobs, whereas import-substitution industrial growth in the 1960s had mainly been in capital-intensive sectors. At the same time, ministers and civil servants were beginning to abuse their allowances and take up private business activities on the side. A further problem was a breakdown in relations with some bilateral donors by 1966 over aspects of Cold War politics.

The Arusha Declaration was undoubtedly in part a result of Nyerere's personal ideology. He was concerned about the corrosive effect of patronage, and its unequalizing tendencies. However, he could not ignore the expectations of elites and the wider population, and the combination of coercion and state patronage remains a familiar one. The Declaration was intended as a warning to the regional and national elites not to go too far, as a mechanism to lower expectations amongst the general population, an opportunity to deepen political control in rural areas, to increase state control over the economy and over patronage resources especially employment, and finally, to further dismantle the other independent axis of support for nationalist politics, the cooperatives. To a great degree, it worked: 'Political quiescence among the . . . population owed a great deal to the fact that government, an expanded parastatal sector and [by the 1980s] a revamped co-operative sector, offered employment to national and local elites.' (Kelsall 2002 p 608). At the same time, regional imbalances were addressed through the use of cabinet posts (van Donge and Liviga 1986 p 628).

At the local level, the party extended its reach through local representatives for every 10 households, and district councils were abolished. The Arusha Declaration paved the way for the state take-over of key institutions that had previously been an independent form of patronage. Cooperatives, whose senior officers had become increasingly corrupt, were largely replaced by marketing boards. More widely, the number of parastatal government corporations more than doubled to 139 in the seven years following the Arusha Declaration. Import–export companies were taken over and merged to form the State Trading Corporation, and finance was similarly taken into government control, as well as the docks and various industrial companies. These moves helped address the employment problem; employment in parastatals and public service increased from 118,000 to 262,500 within five years, while private sector employment fell. However, unlike in the East Asian systems, the state was not supporting capitalist investment. Domestic investment in the mid-1960s, especially by the small Asian community, was beginning to grow, but following the Arusha Declaration the state became extremely hostile to capitalist investors. Equally, the state was not able or willing to impose discipline on the industrial and commercial enterprises it had taken over. There was an explosion of managerial positions, and initially at least, salaries were attractive. However, the performance and financial management of the parastatals was generally poor. Capacity and production in industrial parastatals often bore little relation to staffing levels; for example, the Wazo Hill cement factory saw a decline in production from 1973 go hand in hand with a 40 per cent increase in the number of workers employed. A series of poor decisions on investment projects led to a major misallocation of resources and a growing unserviceable debt burden, balance of payments crises and the beginning of exchange controls. Again, by the 1980s, corruption and theft from the workplace was widespread. Parastatals became a major fiscal drain on the state.

In the countryside, Nyerere's vision of '*ujamaa*' collective agriculture failed to appeal to the rural population, and the authoritarian tendency came to the fore in attempts to force people into collective farming through 'villagization' (von Freyhold 1979). Large numbers of peasants were moved by the army at gunpoint. However, they largely resisted the collective farming that was central to the original vision. There was sporadic pressure from the local state and party representatives to maintain cash crop production, but with poorly performing marketing boards increasingly paying late or not at all, and with shortage of basic goods by the 1980s, many peasant farmers couldn't see the point. The state could effectively use coercion to counter political unrest, but it didn't have the capacity to impose collective cash crop production, and the peasants remained, in Goran Hyden's words, 'uncaptured'.

Nyerere was probably the most explicitly socialist leader of the original nationalist generation, but this ideology only emerged after an initial period in which he consolidated power and patronage in a manner very similar to others. These considerations remained central even during the Arusha Declaration period, which was not so much socialist as one of state-managed industry and attempted state management of agriculture. Key differences between this state led process and those in East Asia is that the need to maintain clientelist-driven employment expansion and an inability to discipline industry meant that accumulation failed, while in education and health the approach was to manage popular expectations, rather than focusing on investment in human capital.

The multi-party variant of clientelism

Towards the end of the 1980s, in most of these countries, demands for more accountability and political openness began to increase. The declining ability of the state to provide clientelist resources meant that important constituencies, especially what remained of the urban middle classes and some regional leaders, felt increasingly excluded from the pot. Chabal and Daloz (1999 pp 34–35) argue, for example, that it was this process that underlay the movement that led Chiluba to replace Kaunda in Zambia. Other leaders handled the situation more skilfully, and maintained control over the situation, as in Tanzania, Kenya and Zimbabwe.

Nevertheless, this crisis, coinciding with the end of the Cold War, the fall of the Berlin Wall and a collapse in the legitimacy of the one-party state, together with some pressure from donors, did lead to the wave of 'democratization' or re-introduction of multi-party systems across the region in 1990.

Discerning the impact of multi-party politics in Africa is complex, and the full impact is still working itself through. One central theme, however, is the persistence of clientelist politics. The crises of the 1980s did not end the system. Chabal and Daloz (1999 p 37) are not alone in arguing that 'it is the decline in the resources available for patronage rather than dissatisfaction with the patrimonial order per se which has undermined the legitimacy of political elites on the continent'. What the political reforms have done, in those cases where political competition has emerged, is to reassert political parties, and ethnic and regional lobbies as routes for patronage:

> The vote in not primarily a token of individual choice but part of a calculus of patrimonial reciprocity based on ties of solidarity. Elections thus provide opportunities for instrumental political competition. Multi-party elections do not in this respect change the fundamental rules of the game. Admittedly they tend to make more visible and more vocal the rivalry between various challengers, which was previously obscured and muffled within the single-party political machine. Nevertheless, the process of legitimation which elections engender remains essentially the same. (Chabal and Daloz 1999 p 39)

As the case of Zambia reminds us, the new multi-party politics can resemble the old politics, whereby all that changes is the make-up of the leadership trying to 'eat' form the state pot; Chiluba turned out to be as corrupt as Kaunda, if not more so. If anything, reforms have increased political instability in some countries as a result (Malawi would be a good example). In cases where no party has gained a clear majority, factional in-fighting has paralysed decision making (eg Benin in the early 1990s), or there have been military coups (Congo, Niger).

However, in most countries that re-introduced multi-party politics, the transition has been handled more carefully by leaders, and real party political competition has been limited. The dominance of the single party has survived and strengthened in subsequent elections (van de Walle 2001 p 262). Furthermore, in virtually no country has the power of the executive (President) been significantly weakened and Parliament given greater powers. The capacity of Parliaments to act as a check and scrutineer of the executive remains notoriously weak, and in many cases the office of MP is mainly seen as an opportunity for access to patronage resources.

van de Walle also finds that democratization has had little impact on economic management and investment (2001 p 255–56), echoing the broader common finding that democracy is not statistically linked to developmental indicators (eg Moore et al 2000).

Finally, running through all of these systems – spoils politics and centralized bureaucratic, one-party and multi-party – are the historical inheritances of indirect rule. Key to these are not only the continuing tendency towards a combination of authoritarianism (or repression in spoils politics) and patronage, but also the urban–rural split. Rural people in many African countries still have a particular view of their relationship with their political leaders.

They expect their leaders to work to deliver some local benefits on their behalf, as well as expecting those leaders to collect their own personal rewards. However, Mamdani's point about the bifurcated state and the subject–citizen distinction remain true – rural people generally do not see the provision of services in terms of individual citizen's rights, but rather in terms of the bonds of kin, ethnic group and region requiring patrons to play their part. Thus a recent survey in Uganda finds that 59 per cent of respondents think that 'people are like children and the government should take care of them like children' (Moncrieffe 2004 p 30). Equally, civil society in Africa remains largely urban based, and engaged in urban debates, with the possible exception of the churches. For many years, authoritarian governments have controlled the media. With the reforms of the early 1990s, some began to allow independent newspapers to open. However, with widely scattered and often illiterate rural populations, newspapers in Africa have typically had urban readerships, and so have not been a threat to the rural mass constituency of ruling parties. Until relatively recently, even where independent newspapers were allowed, radio – the key rural medium – has been kept under state control. Moves to allow independent radio stations are therefore an important development, and a sign of the deepening of political liberalization (Amaoko 2004). Now, with the exception of Eritrea and Zimbabwe, all countries have allowed independent radio stations to open – partly because of the advent of technology that makes broadcasting much easier, so that it would become increasingly difficult for governments to maintain a state monopoly. However, even here, most radios have a local 'footprint' that is mainly urban.[88]

7 The state they're in

THE FORMAL FEATURES of states vary little across the world, each having an executive, a legislature and a judiciary. However, the real feel and performance of states is heavily dependent upon the nature of politics in a country. In the previous chapter, I provided an account of post-colonial African politics that identified clientelism as its major dynamic. In this chapter I argue that clientelist politics has been the key factor determining the nature of state actions, the absence of a developmental project and the relationship with donors. I lay out the characteristics of states associated with varying degrees of clientelist politics, and examine the relationship between those characteristics and the nature of Africa's developmental problems as laid out above.

A common observation is that African states are hybrid in nature. Budgets, laws, bureaucracy, cabinet and Parliament are all features of modern African states, but they coexist with personal rule and patronage – what anthropologist Emmanuel Terray called the 'politics of the veranda' (Kelsall 2002 p 598). For Chabal and Daloz (1999 p 95), 'the state in Sub-Saharan Africa is nothing other than a relatively empty shell. For socially and culturally instrumental reasons, the real business of politics is conducted informally and, more stealthily, outside the official political realm.' Kelsall, writing about contemporary Tanzania, also makes a distinction between the formal and informal faces of the state, quoting an anonymous donor representative who says:

> the Permanent Secretaries, those people who speak the language of 'good governance', those who can talk the talk even if they don't walk the walk, are like a shop-window – what is put on public display. But of course the real decisions are made behind the shop windows, in the 'smoke filled rooms' of the [ruling party]. (Kelsall 2002 p 597)

Van de Walle (2001 p 128) argues persuasively that both formal (rational-legal) and informal (patrimonial) politics are bound together: 'the two tendencies coexist, overlap and struggle for control of the state in most countries'. Crucially, and as shown by the political history in the previous chapter, the neo-patrimonial state is not some vestige of an African 'tradition', but rather a product of modernization. It has also become a product of aspects of globalization. Post-partial adjustment neo-patrimonial states have apparently embraced much of the 'globalization' policy package. Elites in resource rich countries have always had a close relationship with oil and mining multinational corporations. Elites in all countries have made extensive use of globalized banking systems to hedge against risk, and have offered international travel as patronage to clients.

van de Walle also characterizes patrimonial politics as a 'free-rider' on the formal state. The possibility of rent-seeking depends upon the ability of the state to make rules that are generally followed. Thus getting a bribe by allowing an importer to evade paying duties does require the existence of a state that would normally require duties to be paid. Pushed too far, excessive rent-seeking can lead to a break down of the credibility of the formal state, and a consequent decline in the profitability of rent-seeking itself. This is what underlies the instability caused by clientelism: 'State elites are constantly subverting the rational-legal order, but in the end need it to maintain their own positions' (van de Walle 2001 p 128).[89] In the terminal spoils politics of a Sierra Leone, 'the descent to state collapse is mostly the unintentional result of increasingly desperate leaders who have progressively sawn off the state branch on which they based their neo-patrimonial rule' (van de Walle 2001 p 185).

Indeed, the need for the state as a resource is what keeps countries such as DRC from disintegrating altogether. It is striking that despite the constant refrain about the weakness of nationalism in Africa, and an ethnic or regional character to politics in many countries, only two countries in Africa – Somalia and Ethiopia – have actually been broken up by secessionist wars since Independence. Englebert (2003) not only makes the point that it is surprising that DRC has not long ago fallen apart, but also notes that all the various regionally based rebel movements seek to maintain the territorial integrity of the DRC. His explanation for this is that the international recognition of DRC's sovereignty (and therefore the international aid and mineral taxes that flow from that sovereignty) is a resource that all parties wish to capture for themselves:

> the government's capacity to act as a sovereign ruler confers the seal of legality to robbery and persecution and contributes thereby to the elites' strategies of accumulation. Whether in the case of Zaireanization, or the Banyaranda or the exploitation of Congo's natural reserves, the instruments of predation are policy instruments which are reserved to states. (Englebert 2003 p 11)

Explaining weak states

The erosion of state capacity in Africa, (despite many capacity-building programmes) is clear – some of the evidence was discussed above in chapter 5. This erosion started well before adjustment programmes squeezed spending in the late 1980s and early 1990s. van de Walle (2001 pp 133–37) argues that this erosion is 'the direct consequence of the formal policies and informal practices of governments for which a developmental state apparatus is not a priority'.

The first aspect was an 'excessively' rapid expansion of civil service and parastatal jobs. Newly independent African countries did desperately need enlarged public services, but at the same time the local skill pool was very small. Despite this, expansion of employment was very rapid, essentially to accommodate clientelist demands. Jobs were guaranteed to all graduates, short-circuiting meritocratic employment practices. Independent civil service commissions, where they existed, were put under the President's office and authority, and effectively neutered. In some cases, such as Kenya, rules preventing civil servants from having business interests were also removed. The policy of maintaining and increasing civil service employment as patronage also led inevitably to the slump in real wages – by 90 per cent in Tanzania between 1964 and 1984 – which played a major role in decimating capacity. The effect overall has been to produce a government machine that has, at best, highly variable capacity, with staff motivated largely by opportunities for rent seeking.

Beyond this, neo-patrimonial states have a logic that discourages effective decision making, planning and above all implementation, since the actual use of resources tends to become hijacked to a greater or lesser extent by considerations of patronage networks. Thus, for example, it is a common finding that of the funds for, say health and education, voted from the centre for particular final purposes, a significant proportion 'leak' to other purposes.[90]

Capacity problems were also severely exacerbated by donors. The 1960s and 1970s saw the proliferation of donor projects in a growing number of countries, with both presence and activities increasingly haphazard and uncoordinated (van de Walle 2001 pp 191–209 has a good account). Ministries with weak capacity for strategic planning would have struggled even without the fragmentation of decision-making that came with this proliferation, but with it there was little chance for the emergence of an effective bureaucracy responsive to domestic priorities. Donor, and later NGO projects began to actually replace government structures in places; they certainly encouraged the disengagement of governments from developmental tasks, as donor project staff had more resources and were better organized. As civil service salaries began to nosedive in value, the drift of skilled staff away from government to donor institutions began. van de Walle (2001 p 204) cites an example from Kenya where a World Bank project was offering packages worth 10–20 times what a senior government economist would expect to earn. It is estimated that $4 billion a year is spent on some 100,000 expatriates (Commission for Africa 2005 p 139).

Low capacity has been driven directly by fiscal factors, on both the spending and revenue side. Low revenue extraction is another defining characteristic of the neo-patrimonial state, as any kind of revenue collection – duties, licences or taxes – is an opportunity to grant an exemption in exchange for a bribe (Ghura 1998). As van de Walle notes, it is not extractive capacity that is at issue here, rather it is 'the political logic of a system in which the authority of the state is diverted to enhance private power rather than the public domain' (2001 p 53).[91]

On the expenditure side, while spending on the civil service as a whole has been contained by dramatic falls in salaries, what van de Walle calls 'sovereignty' expenditure has not. The large size and expansion of cabinets meant a multiplication of ministerial and Permanent Secretary salaries, allowances to run ministerial offices and associated privileges such as foreign travel. van de Walle (2001 p 107) cites expenditure of $5 million by the Zambian government on foreign travel for senior civil servants in 1997 alone. Where civil service numbers have been reduced, the posts and allowances of senior civil servants have been protected. In a review of recent reforms in East Africa, Kjaer (2004 p 394) notes that:

> Reforms cutting off broader clienteles, such as retrenchments of staff at the lower end of the public hierarchy, seem to be relatively easily carried through. The type of reform which has been blocked in East Africa appears to be that hurting elite interests, such as the downgrading of senior staff, or the reduction in the number of ministers in government.

To an extent, World Bank civil service reform advice reinforced such distinctions, as this advice urged 'decompression' of salaries, meaning large rises at the top.

Equally, the size of legislatures has grown steadily, from an average of under 90 seats in the early 1960s to 149 in 1997 (van de Walle 2001 p 106). While legislators tended to receive smaller allowances and budgets than ministers, this also represents an additional drag on scarce budgetary resources.[92] A further form of largesse for elites is Presidential Commissions and advisory councils, with Cote d'Ivoire leading the way in the multiplication of offices over the 1980s and 1990s.

Finally, while the rules and offices of the formal state are needed to facilitate corruption, a *degree* of state weakness is also needed. In many countries, basic statistical and budgeting functions broke down in the 1980s and 1990s, undermining rational policy-making and accountability, but also preventing the easy identification of fraud and bribery. Most countries lack independent and well-resourced auditing institutions.

Beyond the breakdown of the 'service' state, the weak capacity produced by neo-patrimonial politics has also had important implications for economic development. The evidence in chapter 2 above showed low growth over the last 30 years, a failure to diversify production and exports away from raw commodities, and a decline in the productivity even of commodity production. These problems are rooted in a lack of investment, not only FDI but also domestic investment (we have already seen that there is a massive capital flight problem in Africa). After comparable levels of private investment in the 1970s, trends for Africa and East Asia diverged. In Sub-Saharan Africa total investment has declined from 26 per cent of GDP in 1980, to 22 per cent in 1990 and 20 per cent in 1998, with most of the fall coming from private investment. In East Asia, private investment rates since the 1970s have been on average 82 per cent higher than Africa's (Fosu et al 2001 p 2).

In the more extreme cases of spoils politics, this is not hard to understand. A lack of basic functions of the state, including providing security of property rights, courts reliable enough to fairly resolve commercial disputes, electricity, water supply and roads, are clearly going to put potential investors off. Political instability in these cases is also a deterrence (Gyimah-Brempong and Traynor 1999).

The only industries willing to invest in such countries are those that can be sure of high returns and create enclave investments where they themselves can control all aspects of operations, including infrastructure, security and supply lines. These are of course the extractive industries – oil, mining and forestry – that do operate in spoils politics states such as Angola, Liberia, Congo, Equatorial Guinea and DRC. To operate in these countries, large foreign investors (as no domestic investors have sufficient capital to enter) need to become closely intertwined with regimes to insure themselves effectively against political risk (see Global Witness 2004 for the cases of Equatorial Guinea, Angola and Congo-Brazzaville). Returns are sufficiently high for these companies for the costs of patrimonialism and Presidential enrichment in the form of oil and mineral rents to be worth paying.

However, even in the 'centralized bureaucratic' states, such as Ghana, Kenya and Tanzania, there are problems for investment that arise from relatively weak capacity. Beyond basic infrastructure and functioning utilities, investment in manufacturing or tourism needs a range of resources and services, including telecommunications, rapid and predictable customs clearance, an educated workforce, and financial and insurance services including banking, while investment in agriculture needs rural roads, a reasonable level of taxation on farming, marketing infrastructure, good research and extension services, credit, enforced contracts, veterinary services for livestock, and dispute resolution mechanisms between farmers and herders, (Fafchamps et al 2001 pp 15–17). In most cases, corruption and erosion of civil service capacity has undermined the capacity of the state to provide, and above all maintain good infrastructure and support services.

The logic of the neo-patrimonial state acts to increase unpredictability of macro-economic policy, along with uncertainty about the implementation of state functions, including customs, licences, courts and taxes. All of these factors work to increase risk, and there appears to be a broad consensus that it is risk that deters investors in Africa, rather than returns, which are often higher than in other developing regions (Fafchamps et al 2001 p 27, Collier and Gunning 1999, Mlambo and Oshikoya 2001, Gunning and Mengistae 2001).[93] There is also direct evidence that corruption has a negative impact on African industry (McArthur and Teal 2002). Collier and Gunning (1999a) argue that Africa suffers particularly from the risk problem because a reputation has arisen that deters foreign investors more than they should be on the basis of evidence. Countries that are trying to provide better infrastructure, more predictable environments and better support services may therefore not benefit as much as they should do in terms of FDI inflows (see also Commission for Africa. 2005 p 294).

All of the above applies to policies associated with the 'enabling' state and openness to FDI. However, if African countries wish to approximate the rapid growth in manufacturing production, productivity and exports of East and South-east Asian countries, they will have to go further, and build the capacity to design and implement 'good' interventions to address informational and coordination market failures. Soderbom (2001) argues that firm level problems of low efficiency, lack of training and capital shortage exist in Africa even where there is macro-economic policy stability and lower risk, and that these need to be overcome if African firms are to grow and become sufficiently efficient to export successfully. Some of these interventions are those that are classically *dirigiste*, including tariff and non-tariff trade barriers, state ownership of enterprise, favouring of domestic capital over foreign capital, and implicit or actual selective taxation of agriculture and industry. It is easy to get these interventions wrong, and in Africa in the past this has most commonly been the case (Lall 2000, 2002).

Above all, neo-patrimonial states have struggled and largely failed to build an effective national capitalism, one which can not only compete at home but also in world markets. Africa does face challenges in the international trade environment, especially with China's rise, but the most fundamental barriers to diversification and increased value added lie on the supply side, including the ability to enter rich world markets. Tackling these barriers, which include poor infrastructure, education and training, as well as a weak set of institutions in customs, banking, legal services, etc, certainly needs capital, but it also needs a state that has a clear objective of raising productivity and exports, and also has the ability to make those institutions work. The neo-patrimonial state delivers neither of these requirements, as its leadership is focused more on managing political survival and needs to distribute opportunities for rent-seeking to clients, that have the effect of undermining institutional effectiveness.

All of these policies depend upon elements of state control over the economy, and so they also all represent opportunities for rent-seeking, or 'government failures'. As discussed in chapter 3 above, this is precisely why the thrust of donor-prescribed economic reform programmes in Africa has been towards liberalization. However, the 'government failure' model is static and abstract. It does not explain why some governments do fail at this type of intervention and others do not. The neo-patrimonial account of the African state offers an explanation with some political and historical logic. It implies that the price of political survival has been, at best, limited economic growth and at worst, economic collapse. It also implies that the 'developmental' state, in Chalmers Johnson's particular meaning of a state that prioritizes growth, productivity, competitiveness and investment in human capital, and that guides the market via a core group of civil servants politically isolated from interest groups, will not operate effectively unless and until the clientelist elements of African politics are tightly controlled or eradicated.

Of course, some of the most successful developmental states – including Japan, South Korea and now China – have also been deeply corrupt. At first sight this may be confusing, since it implies that clientelist politics is at work in these states as well (eg Mkandawire 1998). However, as Mushtaq Khan (1996, 2002) has investigated at some length, there are key differences in how corruption operates in politically strong states able to resist capture by external interests such as large companies, and weak states with clientelist politics. In the former case, which he calls the 'patrimonial settlement', bureaucrats and politicians in a politically dominant state dispense rights and resources (licences, government contracts, subsidized credit, etc) and get a share of the benefit as bribes, or additional political support, but they can still enforce performance from the client company, and they are not politically dependent on that client. This form of corruption may add some cost to the taxpayer or the company, but it is does not disrupt the process of investment and accumulation. Khan argues that it is this variant of corruption that has been observed in countries such as Korea. By contrast, in the 'clientelist settlement' the state is less powerful and has more need for the client's political support, so clients can extract a more favourable deal: 'Compared to the patrimonial political settlement, the preferential allocation of rights to politically powerful clients amounts to a payoff which the clientelist coalition gets from the state' (Khan 1996 p 19).

In the African case, the weakness of the political bargain is not so much between the state and external agencies such as companies or trade unions, as these are even weaker; rather it is a political weakness of the political centre (essentially the President) in relation to the elites surrounding him, each representing different factional, regional or ethnic constituencies. While Presidents have done all they can to gather power to them, they still need to buy off these constituencies. Indeed, to keep the many different client groups happy, the central state also has to multiply the rights and

resources available (Khan 1996 p 19). This is perhaps the best way to understand the expansion of ministries and large number of cabinet posts in so
many African countries, each with their own opportunities for rent-seeking.
The economic result of corruption in the African clientelist settlement is
also different, since state resources and rights are used as much for consumption as for investment, and the political centre cannot (or will not) discipline
the client in the same way. Thus there are many instances of Presidents
retaining or reintroducing cabinet members who have been convicted of
corruption.

The impact of economic reforms

Above, I argued that both donors and NGOs have not engaged sufficiently
with the evidence that conditionality did not work as effectively as it was
supposed to (as both parties often claim), but rather worked only patchily
and over a long period of time. I also argued that it is possible to understand
this as the outcome of a process of implicit negotiation and compromise
between donors and governments. Clientelist politics and the neo-
patrimonial state provide a framework for this approach. As noted, reforms
were aimed primarily at relinquishing state controls over the economy – over
foreign exchange, trade, domestic markets, state ownership, and banking –
all of which would threaten to remove opportunities for rent-seeking that
could be allocated to elites and their clients. On the other hand, the depth
and permanence of the economic crisis mean that by the late 1980s it had
become clear that (except for the oil or mineral rich, where deals with multi-
national oil and mining companies were easier to cut), aid would be a key
state resource and some kind of deal had to be done with donors, if only to
maintain the clientelist system. According to van de Walle 2001 p 159:

> In this second phase, which can be very roughly linked in time to the
> second decade of the crisis, top state leaders have sought to accom-
> modate themselves to the permanent crisis in several ways. While the
> complete removal of state interference in the economy might have
> eliminated rent-seeking, leaders have understood that partial reform
> and the actual implementation process would provide them with new
> kinds of rents, as well as discretion over the evolution of rents within
> the economy. They understood that the uncertainty and chaos of the
> reform process might cut into the overall size of rents, but these condi-
> tions would certainly increase rent-seeking, and they determined they
> would seek to increase their control over the latter. In other words we
> have witnessed an *instrumentalization* of the reform process, in which
> donor pressures and the logic of reform are used by leaders to justify
> measures that are often not at all in the spirit of economic liberalization,
> but which serve to enhance political control.[94]

One way in which they did this was to seek further centralization of control, both over rent-seeking but also over the reform process, with an increase in the powers and budgets of the President's Office (van de Walle 2001 pp 160–61). Another was, rather than resisting donor reform programmes (and attached budgets), instead subverting them for clientelist aims. van de Walle (2001 pp 162–63) gives the examples of World Bank privatization programmes in Cote d'Ivoire in the 1980s and 90s that actually led to larger and more centralized parastatals, and Moi's restructuring of the tea and coffee sectors to reward key allies and actually make cooperatives into parastatals, while receiving donor support. In yet other cases, new political leaders seeking to weaken old patronage networks and establish their own used the rhetoric of liberalization – for example Diouf in Senegal or Chiluba in Zambia (van de Walle 2001 p 164, Boone 1994).

Privatization is an example of a reform wave that was initially resisted (Hutchful 1995) and subverted, and has since been adopted more widely. While some utilities have more recently been put under management contracts, they still typically remain in state ownership. However, many SOEs have been privatized. For example Tanzania had sold off some 40 per cent of SOEs by the late 1990s (Temu and Due 2000), and between 1987 and 1999 Ghana sold 324 SOEs, or 70 per cent of the total (Appiah-Kubi 2001). Why was initial resistance dropped? One likely reason was that elites saw the opportunity to acquire businesses or concessions cheaply – Kelsall (2002 p 610) gives the example of the scramble for gold mining rights in Tanzania in the 1990s. The other, which may be more important, was the rent-seeking opportunity in the divestment process itself. For example, in Ghana, local elites have bought into a majority of the privatized enterprises, but mainly in small and medium size enterprises. The Ghanaian share of all privatized enterprises is only 10 per cent of the total. However the lack of transparency and widespread allegation of corruption surrounding the selection process for choosing which enterprises to sell, and in the choice of bid winners are common features of African privatization programmes. In Ghana, one third of the total value of divestiture transactions going back to 1991 were still outstanding 10 years later; a fact, Appiah-Kubi concludes, that 'underlines the use of the divestiture programme as a political instrument' (2001 p 224).

Thus clientelist politics and the neo-patrimonial nature of the state are remarkably persistent, and have adapted to, rather than been disposed of, by liberalizing economic reforms. In fact, there will always be a limit to the project of eliminating rent-seeking through liberalizing reforms. This is because even the Washington Consensus, following Adam Smith, requires the state to have some role in the economy. Even the most minimal 'enabling' government must provide law and order, police, courts, public goods like education, and infrastructure, and must raise revenue to pay for it, which means some form of taxation. This provides plenty of grounds for rent-seeking and clientelist politics.

Again, reform processes may be able to reshape these phenomena, but they cannot eradicate them. A good example is taxation. Typically African countries taxed both exports and imports, the latter directly through levies and the former often implicitly through parastatals that paid low prices for export crops or paid late or even not at all. Many countries have indeed reformed these systems, with parastatals replaced by private marketing agents and tariffs reduced. Many countries have now liberalized to the point where revenue from tariffs is falling[95] (UNECA 2004 ch 6). At the same time, they are under pressure from the IMF to raise revenue-to-GDP ratios, and donors are keen to widen the tax base in most countries. The result is that as trade taxes have fallen, taxation has grown elsewhere in the economy. Many countries have introduced VAT systems, but there has also been a sharp increase in local taxes in countries that have decentralized (for example see Balihuta and Sen 2001 for the case of Uganda). As a result, many of the opportunities for both rent-seeking by bureaucrats and clientelist politics have been relocated to the local level. In Tanzania, district councils were levying up to 60 different types of taxes in the late 1990s (Fjeldstad 2001 p 3). This gave scope for extensive fiscal corruption amongst local authorities, with the connivance of senior officials, and also for councillors seeking polit-ical support to offer exemptions: 'Tax collectors interviewed stated that councillors obstructed tax collection and talked "cheap politics"' (Fjeldstad 2001 p 8). As a result, not only are there chronic gaps between projected and reported revenues, but also in a large majority of councils a fall in revenues in the 1995 election year.

Finally, clientelist politics and the nature or the neo-patrimonial state are important for understanding why anti-corruption and wider governance reforms have been so unsuccessful without the backing of 'political will'. As van de Walle (2001) argues, the donor community has played down the significance of clientelist politics as anything more than 'incidental', focusing instead of the symptoms of weak capacity and corruption. This leads to a technical approach, with capacity building programmes and anti-corruption reforms that promote greater administrative 'hygiene' and technical expertise. This ignores the real nature of the hybrid neo-patrimonial system:

> a striking reality is that most anticorruption strategies being devised in the policy community simply assume that there is a rational-legal logic at the apex of these states that will be available to carry out the strategy; in fact, all too often, leaders at the apex of the state choose to undermine these strategies, which threaten practices they find useful and profitable. (van de Walle 2001 p 127)

Overall then, clientelist politics and the nature of the neo-patrimonial state provide good explanations for many of the problems underlying Africa's record on trade and investment, conditionality and failed governance reforms. They also provide a way of understanding why states have col-lapsed, as spoils politics has spiralled out of control, often over who controls natural resource rents. Most of all, they provide an explanation of why Africa's problems have been so chronic, persisting over the last 25 years through changes in the policy regime. Indeed, Africa is now in a type of political and economic trap. Clientelist politics disables the state, which in turn has made economic adjustment and transformation impossible. The result is a lack of investment, and poverty, which further weaken the state and economy. This in turn makes it harder to establish political alternatives to clientelism.[96]

In many ways, this is a pessimistic take on Africa's situation. It is especially so as populations suffering from weak and corrupt states have also been hit hard by the AIDS epidemic. The prospect of treatment for the many rather than the few in Africa has been brought nearer after campaigners won a partial victory over enormously greedy pharmaceutical companies in the TRIPS and Health Agreement in the WTO. However, such treatment still has to be delivered through effective health systems. Again, this potentially provides clientelist politicians and neo-patrimonial state functionaries with opportunities for rent-seeking and selective and partial performance. This is of course not a reason for not trying to tackle the crisis and deliver ARTs, but it is another reminder of the deeply destructive nature of the political trap that Africa is in.

At the same time, my argument in this book is not primarily a moral one, but rather one about the logic of political and state institutions. Clientelist politics was a perfectly reasonable response to the dilemma presented to nationalist movements on the eve of Independence. It has meant, in turn, that African states have a particular character. Certainly, some of the excesses of predatory elites are morally reprehensible, and the anti-developmental nature of neo-patrimonial states is, I believe, a major factor in the persistence of deep poverty in Africa, with all the human suffering it entails. However, my aim here is not apportioning blame, but rather seeking understanding and solutions.

In these circumstances, three questions are highly important, and the last three chapters address them in turn. The first is: are some states in Africa actually showing signs of becoming 'developmental'? The second is: what will African developmental states look like? The third is: what can international NGOs and donors do?

8 Are developmental states now emerging in Africa?

A NUMBER OF COUNTRIES in Africa potentially raise questions for the neo-patrimonial approach. One is Botswana, the only country on the African mainland with an exceptional growth record. The others are group of countries that have shown signs of more effective states, rapid economic growth and development of manufacturing industry, either in the 1990s (Ghana and Uganda) or in the 2000s (Tanzania and Mozambique).

What are the implications of these cases? How can the case of Botswana be accounted for? Do the other cases mean that clientelist politics and a neo-patrimonial state are not incompatible with growth and export diversification? Or are some countries actually eradicating or moving out of clientelism altogether?

Botswana

Botswana's record on growth and human development exceeds even that of East Asia, and is quite exceptional in mainland Sub-Saharan Africa. According to the UNDP it is the country that has made most progress on human development indicators since 1960 (along with Malaysia). Real per capita income has grown from $80 in 1967 to $6,000 today, the result of an average annual growth rate of over 10 per cent during the 1980s. It has also achieved universal primary education, access to potable water for over 80 per cent of households, and until the AIDS epidemic took hold, infant mortality had been reduced three fold (Taylor 2002).

Botswana's rapid growth has mainly been based on diamonds, which by the early 1980s had replaced beef as Botswana's main export earner. However, unlike as in other African states with extractive resources windfalls, such as Nigeria or DRC, revenues have not been stolen or wasted, and macro-economic management has been good. Rodrik (1998 pp 27–28) argues that:

> a lot of Botswana's success has to do with its superior governance. The bureaucracy in Botswana is honest and competent, attaches great

value to economic expertise and has consistently produced sensible macro-economic policies. There have been no urban bias and no white elephants.

The government has intervened in the economy, and public expenditure has been high, but 'what distinguished economic interventions in Botswana is its quality, not quantity'.

What explains Botswana's high quality of governance and economic management? Rodrik argues that Botswana's trade was well managed because of its membership of a customs union with South Africa, SACU, which meant that until 1976 Botswana didn't have an independent trade policy or even its own currency until 1976. Government officials had no control over customs revenue, which was collected by South Africa. He sees this as an extreme case of an 'agency of restraint' (Rodrik 1998 p 28). But while this may be true, it begs the question of why the political and policy elite in Botswana decided to follow this route. It is also insufficient to explain the broader aspects of economic management in Botswana, which include a renegotiation of SACU on improved terms in 1969 and a landmark 50:50 share ownership deal with De Beers in the country's diamond mines. To account for this we must look at the nature of the state and politics.

In many respects, Botswana has many features of a classic developmental state. It had strong leadership in Seretse Khama in the period leading up to and following Independence, who like Chiang Kai-shek in Taiwan, sought political stability by offering collective and long-term development of the economy within a pre-existing (Botswana) nationalism, rather than particularistic pay-offs immediately. Indeed, he emphasized the need to 'work for development' and even make sacrifices (Taylor 2002 p 5). The capitalist nature of the developmental project was explicit. Charles Harvey argues that the interests of politicians and senior civil servants in cattle ownership and exports kept the government from adopting the anti-export bias seen elsewhere in Africa (cited in Rodrik 1998). As in East Asia, there was a close relationship between political leaders and civil servants, with the latter playing a major role in decision-making. Botswana's current President came from a life long career in the finance and planning ministry. As elsewhere in Africa, the ministry of finance has been dominant. However, the fiscal prudence function in the ministry has been balanced by a more developmental function as the outcome of a struggle over objectives in the 1960s, and since 1970 the two have been merged into a single ministry (Taylor 2002 p 16).

While there were distinct fractions within the elite, it was, by comparison with other African countries, relatively coherent. Although Botswana since Independence has been a multi-party democracy, the ruling Botswana Democratic Party (BDP) has always been in power, until recently in a completely dominant way. There was therefore little party political competition, and even relatively little competition within the party. The cabinet has been disciplined and relatively small by African standards, with currently only 14 ministers. The Tswana ethnic identity dominated the economy and politics. Unlike the other newly independent states where power needed to be centralized and bureaucratized across a larger and ethnically more diverse population (Tanzania, Zambia, Kenya, Senegal), Khama enjoyed high status and traditional authority as a former chief of a single ethnic group. He also benefited from a pre-colonial active institution of decision-making, the *kgotla* council, that emphasized consensus building through debate, and which survived colonial rule (Acemoglu et al 2004). Nevertheless, like other centralizing leaders, Khama removed the power of the traditional authorities and made them subordinate to central government in the Chieftancy Act of 1965, actually predating formal Independence. Thus, as Allen (1995 p 321) notes, Botswana already had a version of the 'centralized-bureaucratic' political system before Independence.

In certain ways, however, Botswana's developmental state lacks some of the key characteristics of those of Asia. Most of all, its developmental success has rested on the careful management and use of diamond revenues, rather than on the development of a high-value manufacturing industry. It remains relatively unindustrialized, with manufacturing contributing about 5 per cent to GDP over the last five years. Attempts to tackle informational and coordination failures in the economy through agencies such as the Botswana Development Corporation (established in 1970) and the Financial Assistance Programme aimed specifically at SMEs (1982) failed to produce manufacturing investment. One problem has been the strength of the currency against the South Africa rand (Taylor 2002 p 17).

Another feature of Botswana that sets it apart from the East and South-east Asian experience is that it is extremely unequal in terms of wealth and incomes. The concentration in ownership of the main asset – cattle – already marked at Independence, has become more acute as the elite gained most from infrastructure and institutions built up for livestock marketing and exports. However, the underlying reason for high inequality is the same as it is elsewhere in Africa – the lack of industrialization and employment. Botswana has been a low-wage labour reserve for the South African mining industry (with employment limited by its capital intensity), with diamonds, beef and some low-volume tourism as the only domestic activities, none of which use much labour. As a result, unemployment is unofficially estimated at 40 per cent (Taylor 2002 p 21), and mass education has not resulted in equalizing growth as it did in East Asia. While effective use of diamond revenues has cushioned Botswana from the impacts of the failure to industrialize, it has also meant that there has been a lack of urgency in trying to diversify. There are now even signs that the political unity and discipline around the developmental project is beginning to unwind (Taylor 2002 p 23), with political challenges to the BDP growing, and one of the highest prevalence rates of HIV in the world.

Overall, it is possible to understand the Botswana experience as a developmental state with diamond windfalls. With a strong nationalist ethos and charismatic leader who moved swiftly to centralize power, an elite from a single dominant ethnic group with independent wealth in the form of cattle, and minimal needs to feed a clientelist network in order to maintain political stability, this was one of the most successful regimes in Africa, combining the stability of the centralized bureaucracies with the revenue cushion from diamonds. But most of all, the weakness of elite competition in the 1960s meant that Botswana has avoided the features of the neo-patrimonial state, although there are signs that this may be changing in the last few years. At the same time, the combination of diamonds and a small population have meant that the ultimate economic test of a developmental state – constructing industry – has not been faced.

Entirely different from the Botswana story is the emergence of a group of African countries that have seen better-than-average economic performance over the late 1990s and early 2000s. None of them is a major oil exporter. Most of them are clearly examples of centralized-bureaucratic systems. Here I look particularly at Uganda, Ghana, Tanzania and Mozambique. These are countries that have been or currently are donor 'favourites'. They feature prominently in the success stories of the Commission for Africa report. All currently receive substantial aid from DfID (Table 8.1), part of it in the form of direct budget support.

Table 8.1   DfID bilateral allocations 2002–03

	£ million	£ per capita
Sierra Leone	33.0	6.88
Rwanda	35.3	4.25
Malawi	51.7	4.34
Zambia	37.7	3.52
Ghana	52.9	2.58
Zimbabwe	30.8	2.41
Uganda	53.2	2.13
Tanzania	75.5	2.08
Mozambique	30.6	1.65
Lesotho	2.7	1.50
Kenya	42.4	1.34
Sudan	19.1	0.58
Ethiopia	40.3	0.58
DRC	12.9	0.25
Nigeria	29.2	0.24

Sources: DfID (2004b), UNDP (2004).

Uganda

With the victory of the NRA in 1986, Museveni led the reconstruction of Uganda's society and economy from the chaos and violence of the Amin and Obote years. From running at several hundred percent in the mid-1980s, inflation was brought down to 5 per cent by 1994. Economic growth was in the range 5–10 per cent in first half of 1990s, and the headcount poverty rate was reduced from 56 per cent in 1992 to 35 per cent in 1999 (Moncrieffe 2004 p 37), although the surveys exclude areas affected by war. From total collapse in 1986, revenue collection rose to 11 per cent of GDP by 1996.

From 1987, Museveni introduced elements of a developmental state. He instituted a new political order, replacing traditional authorities with National Resistance Movement councils at local and regional levels in a classic centralized-bureaucratic move. For over a decade the 'no-party' system brought stability and was a political price donors were prepared to pay to their star performer. Following the war, Museveni ran a large cabinet to accommodate a national reconciliation agenda, but began to press for public sector reform in a serious way. From a situation where there were 72 junior and senior ministers across 32 ministries in 1990, he disbanded 11 ministries in 1992, and pushed through a civil service reform package that saw 150,000 retrenchments in the early 1990s and large scale pay reform. However, most of these were at the junior level and senior posts were largely protected (Kjaer 2004).

Donors helped create a powerful Ministry of Finance, Planning and Economic Development (a similar combination to Botswana's), which has focused on providing a stable macro-economic framework[97] (Moncrieffe 2004). A key technical policy group has been established inside the Ministry with considerable power and autonomy. However, this group is only partially insulated from political pressures, and indeed these sometimes come from Museveni himself. Museveni's inclination has been towards interventionism, but this has been restrained by the relationship with donors. In the 1990s he fought battles with the World Bank over roads and education, and also over tariff reform (Mosley 1995).

Uganda's economy is still doing well relative to many other African countries, but it has not sustained its initial burst following recovery from the crises of the 1980s.[98] Economic growth was as high as 8 per cent in 1998, but has since decelerated somewhat to 5 per cent a year since 2001. Growth remains tied to agricultural production and the weather, showing signs of limited structural transformation. Recently it has emerged that Uganda's long run in reducing poverty has ended, as the headcount rate increased to 38 per cent in 2003 (Moncrieffe 2004 p 38). Revenue as a percentage of GDP declined slightly from mid-1990s levels and is just back up to 12 per cent, which is fairly low.

Although the general business environment in Uganda is relatively good by African standards, manufacturing growth has slowed down more sharply than growth generally, and industry currently makes up only about 10 per cent of GDP. Industry is predominantly focused on light manufactures of consumer goods competing with imports for the domestic market, rather than exports. Investment is struggling to get clear of 20 per cent of GDP (Table 8.2). Private investment remains steady at about 16 per cent of GDP. The high cost of credit may be a problem; private sector credit growth is strong, but most of it is going to trading, rather than agriculture or industry. There have been some limited experiments in stimulating industry, including special zones with tax holidays, import duty exemptions on inputs and export duty exemptions, and 'investment incentives' given to selected investors.[99] However, exports are still mainly focused on a few commodities, and the balance of payments position is still dependent on commodity price movements.

As the 1990s progressed, two key problems emerged in Uganda. One was the war in the North, and the other was an increasing level of corruption, and both have had a negative impact on the economy. Some see a connection between the two. The Ugandan army seems unable to stop attacks by the Lords Resistance Army rebels, with locally organized civilian defence militias apparently able to do a better job.[100] At the same time, for as long as the war goes on, army officers continue to receive allowances (Moncrieffe 2004 p 34), seen by many as an incentive for the army to drag it out. The conflict has placed pressure on the budget, and strained relationships with donors, who still covered 55 per cent of the budget in 2002–03.[101] The defence budget increased significantly in 2002–03 (although expenditure on the Poverty Action Fund and on education was protected).

At the same time, there are signs of growing clientelist corruption. Uganda now has one of the worst ratings on Transparency International's Corruption Perceptions Index (Table 8.3). This is of course a limited indicator, subjective and partial, in that it gives the views of business investors. Nevertheless it gives some idea of the impact of corruption in the economy. The score ranges from 1 to 10, with the countries judged less corrupt having a higher score. Uganda's score is very low, if rising slightly since 2001.

Table 8.2   Gross capital formation as a proportion of GDP in selected countries (%)

	2000	2001	2002	2003	2004
Mozambique	36.6	41.5	44.7	45.5	43.2
Tanzania	17.6	17.0	19.3	20.1	20.8
Uganda	19.9	21.6	21.5	21.5	21.7
Ghana	24.0	26.6	19.7	19.9	19.7

Source: OECD (2004).
Figures for 2003 are estimates and those for 2004 are projections.

Table 8.3   Corruption Perceptions Index score

	2000	2001	2002	2003	2004
Mozambique	2.2	–	–	2.7	2.8
Tanzania	2.5	2.2	2.7	2.5	2.8
Uganda	2.3	1.9	2.1	2.2	2.6
Ghana	3.5	3.4	3.9	3.3	3.6

Source: Transparency International Corruption (2004).

Uganda also shows signs of a bloated cabinet. To give an idea of the range of cabinet sizes associated with different political settlements, Botswana has 14 ministries while Nigeria has 50.[102] Currently Uganda has an extraordinary 68 cabinet ministers, 73 presidential advisers and what one observer calls a 'stadium-sized Parliament'.[103] Public sector reform initiatives halted in the late 1990s, and by 2002 numbers of employees were climbing again. Attempts to tackle corruption in the Revenue Authority have also largely failed, reflected in the low and sluggish revenue rates cited above (Fjeldstad et al 2003). On the other hand, some ministries, including health and education, appear to be models of openness and accountability.

Kjaer notes that in recent years 'considerations of political loyalty seem in some cases to have overshadowed considerations of competence' (2004 p 399). In 2001, two ministers who had previously been censured by Parliament for corruption were appointed to the cabinet. There have been numerous allegations of corruption associated with those close to Museveni, such as his half-brother Salim Saleh, including over the notorious World Bank-backed Bujagali Dam. It is widely perceived that Museveni is favouring regional groupings from western Uganda in appointments to the army and the government, while easterners see themselves shut out. Much of the corruption is associated with the military, where Museveni appears to be politically managing the army through offering the possibility of illicit business opportunities in DRC (Kjaer 2004), as well as general budgetary largesse with impunity (Moncrieffe 2004), despite pressure from Parliament. Up to last year, not a single leader had been faced with prosecution or punishment for corrupt military behaviour (Tangri and Mwenda 2003). A former commissioner-general of the Revenue Authority has stated that 'the rich and politically powerful don't pay taxes'.[104]

Anti-corruption measures in Uganda seem to suffer from some of the usual difficulties in neo-patrimonial states. An 'Inspectorate of Government' was established as long ago as 1987. However, although it has highlighted various high-level cases of flagrant abuse, it has limited powers to act. More recently a Directorate of Ethics and Integrity was created in the Presidents Office, but this basically focuses on educating, not pursuing cases. Attempts to impose a Leadership Code of Conduct on government officials is being challenged in court on grounds of invasion of privacy and is expected to have a limited effect. The judiciary is relatively independent, but unwilling to challenge the government openly (Moncrieffe 2004). However, overall Museveni continues to convince the donors that he will tackle corruption, and recent steps included the removal of a Presidential adviser and efforts to remove the backlog in the courts.[105]

The growth of clientelist pressures also poses political problems. As Museveni has found reasons to amend the constitution a number of times to stay in power, and as the pressure for full multi-party elections has grown, the 'no-party' system is fraying at the edges. Within Parliament there are caucuses representing different factions, including regional factions. Currently Museveni is giving way to demands for multi-party reforms, but is also seeking a constitutional change to allow him a third term. There have already been signs of winner-take-all behaviour in Museveni's campaign for the 2001 Presidential elections, with intimidation, beatings, voter fraud and control of the media (Moncrieffe 2004 p 22). In addition, elections are also now very expensive, with candidates required to have independent means or business backers; campaign spending is being used to win favour with electorate (Moncrieffe 2004 p 23).

The Ugandan case shows how persistent clientelist politics can be, and how they have limited, and even threaten to derail, the Uganda success story. There has been a partial attempt to create a developmental state in the 1990s, with some basic success but no take off into industrial growth. The policy stance of the donors and the group they backed in the MFDEP also meant that opportunities to experiment with interventionist policies for manufacturing growth were limited. Nevertheless a degree of economic momentum was created, and Uganda is a lot better off now than it was in 1986. However, Museveni's leadership has not been sufficient to prevent the re-emergence of a clientelist politics in the regions and the army, and the consequences are currently evident in terms of politics and corruption. In terms of state capacity and the economy, the picture seems mixed, with the possibility of either further growth or stagnation. Donors have invested heavily in Uganda, both financially and in terms of reputation. However, the first increase in measured poverty rates for 15 years, the current shape of political competition and entrenched corruption in the army are ominous signs. Most of all, this shows that the project of building a developmental state cannot be built on political leadership alone, but needs to involve the permanent transformation of political systems.

Ghana

Similarly to Museveni, Rawlings inherited an economy 'mismanaged, abused and pillaged by civilian and particularly military politicians on an unprecedented scale.' (Booth et al 2004 p 9). Excessive taxation of cocoa, gold and timber exports, competition for rents through corruption, expansion of state employment, and 'pork barrel' allocation of state amenities and services gave the state a spoils politics character that saw political instability and coups culminating in the excesses of the Acheampong–Akuffo period. Also, as with Museveni, Rawlings seized power from within the military but then created a degree of developmentalism as a civilian leader, moving from coup maker in 1981 to elected President in the 1990s (Ibrahim 2003). Following an initial path of repression and human rights abuses in the 1980s, Rawlings began to seek legitimacy, ended military rule and opened up the political system. However, he did not stand for election until he had carefully deepened his power base and established the state's authority over traditional leaders in the rural areas through decentralization reforms (Ibrahim 2003 p 22). Finally, just as Museveni, Rawlings turned to the IFIs and pursued a path of partial liberalization. This produced economic growth in the 1990s, and for a while Ghana was the IFIs 'star pupil' (Hutchful 1995). However, as Hutchful explains, Ghana's reforms in the 1980s very much followed the 'partial reform' pattern described above, with Rawlings seeking to carry out those only those reforms that would work for him politically.

From collapse in the 1970s, Ghana's long recovery has continued into the 2000s, and it is often seen as one of Africa's more hopeful economies. However, there are signs of persistent limits to economic transformation. High economic growth in the 1990s has slowed to around 5.5 per cent in recent years.[106] The basic productive structure of the economy has remained the same as it was thirty years ago (Booth et al 2004 p 18), and growth remains driven by agriculture. Exports remain dominated by gold, cocoa and timber. The industrial sector is about 25 per cent of GDP, but manufacturing is a much smaller proportion and has not expanded significantly following the contraction of the early reform years in the 1980s. Manufacturing growth currently is only 4–5 per cent (Table 8.4), and some sectors are still contracting. From about 25 per cent of GDP in 2000/01, investment has fallen back to under 20 per cent (Table 8.2), mostly because of a decline in public investment. Revenue as a proportion of GDP, at around 17.5 per cent

Table 8.4   Recent manufacturing growth in selected countries (%)

	2000	2002
Mozambique	4.1	5.1
Tanzania	5.0	8.0
Uganda	6.3	6.6
Ghana	3.7[a]	4.8

Source: OECD (2004).
[a] Figure for 2001.

is higher than some other African countries,[107] but static (Table 8.5). There are also recurrent fiscal and inflation problems.

From being seen as a 'star pupil' in the 1990s, Ghana's relationship with donors has slipped somewhat. A cut in civil service numbers in the 1980s was reversed after the first elections in the 1990s. However, there are still staff shortages in key front line skills and outside Accra. Poor management and incentive structures remain and general performance has reached 'a very low ebb' (Booth et al 2004 p 26). Budgeting is poor, with large deviations between budget estimates and actuals, and very large leakages of funds between their allocation from the centre and their arrival at the point of service delivery (up to 50 per cent for education and 20 per cent for health of non-salary resources).[108] Overall, high-level political commitment to public sector reform is still lacking. Similarly the privatization programme has ground to a halt; of 12 companies to be 'fast tracked' in 2002, only one has been partially privatized.

Beyond a lacklustre service state, Ghana also appears to have a poor enabling state, let alone a successful interventionist developmental state. A pledge from the new government in 2000 to help business has failed to usher in an age of achievements. A lack of dynamism in the Ghanaian private sector means that what growth there has been has come from the multiplication of small enterprises rather than growth of large enterprises. High taxes coexist with widespread tax evasion. Investors continue to complain about short-ages of credit (crowded out by the public sector), uncertain power supplies, high transportation costs, excessive regulation and bureaucratic delays, problems with contract enforcement, corruption at many levels, and a lack of secure property rights.[109] The 2000 government's election claims that it would tackle corruption have been dented by its record. Ghana's Corruption Perceptions Index is actually somewhat better than many other African states, at around 3.5 (Table 8.3), but shows no strong signs of improving.

There are also signs that government's relationship with business is not one of support combined with discipline, but rather one of politicization, whereby each party favours its allied businesses and discriminates against those of its opponents when in office. Business–state relationships have

Table 8.5   Revenue as a proportion of GDP in selected countries (%)

	2000	2001	2002	2003	2004
Mozambique	12.1	11.8	12.5	12.9	12.6
Tanzania	10.6	10.6	11.1	12.3	12.8
Uganda	10.2	10.8	11.9	12.1	12.1
Ghana	16.3	17.2	17.5	17.5	17.2

Source: OECD (2004).
Figures for 2003 are estimates and those for 2004 are projections.

become about access to state favours on a discriminatory basis, so that businesses and business associations press for favours rather than an improvement in general conditions. As noted in chapter 7 above, the privatization process has been marked by corruption. Booth et al conclude that: 'neither party [state or business] applies rigorous performance standards to the other, except perhaps in a crisis' (2004 pp 10–11).

It is thus clear that Ghana still has a neo-patrimonial state. In the post-colonial period, unlike as in Tanzania or Uganda, the chieftaincy structures of Indirect Rule and nascent civil society organizations, including trades unions, professional associations, and farmers groups were not destroyed or co-opted by the state. Neither was there a single party system. Instead, over a number of elections in the 1950s and 1960s, two party political 'traditions' built up and sustained party bases through patronage systems; one more allied to chiefs and private business, and the other to state led development and trade unions (Booth et al 2004). In Allen's terms (Allen 1995), the lack of a centralizing bureaucratic system provides a good explanation of why Ghana suffered so much instability and spoils politics up to 1980. Rawlings ushered in precisely such a system, and political traditions were attenuated, although not so much that they did not re-emerge in the 1990s. The political reforms of the 1990s have returned some features of Ghana's earlier political landscape – a relatively independent judiciary and election authority, an increasingly active Parliament and a vibrant media and civil society, for example. These are major developments. However, weaknesses in accountability and rule of law remain, along with Rawlings' legacy of powers heavily concentrated in the Presidency, enabling extensive patronage. These include the power to appoint any number of ministers to cabinet. Ghana had a relatively large cabinet comprising 33 ministries in 2001 and now has 30.[110] Given the need still for parties to receive political support from local figures, party competition at national level also gets enmeshed with local disputes. Political liberalization thus opened up traditional political competition, and clientelist forces began to reassert themselves. In a manner both parallel to and as a possible warning to Uganda, a democratic Ghana was so corrupt by the end of the 1990s that the new President, John Kufuor, won power from the Rawlings' ruling NDP party on an anti-corruption ticket.

Booth et al (2004) argue that, given Ghana's particularly strong history of civil society groups, the net effect of political competition will be to attenuate neo-patrimonialism over time. Interest groups, including urban youth, cocoa farmers, Native Authority elites, professional and business elites, and unionized workers are all relatively well organized, and although patronage still exist, these groups provide a potential identity and solidarity that can cut across patron-client relationships. This means that political parties have to compete for their support, and have to offer the prospect of collective, rather than particularistic benefits. Most of all, Booth et al argue, the fact that the incumbent party lost the 2000 elections means that the power of patronage is not invincible when it comes to political competition.

Meanwhile, the scrutiny of an increasingly active media and civil society means that the political costs associated with corruption are rising. Over time, they consider that the likely gains of democratization outweigh the risks and costs, moving Ghana, over time, along the journey made in Latin America from patronage-based politics towards issue-based politics.

This judgement is offered tentatively by Booth et al (2004). Clearly, one change of government does not necessarily mean the end of clientelist politics, as the case of Zambia alone shows. They are also clear that Ghana is rather unusual in Sub-Saharan Africa in the strength of its civil society, implying that this path may be much more difficult for other countries. It is also true that a democratic, interest-group based politics has rarely produced a developmental state leading nations to rapid economic transformation and poverty reduction. This theme is taken up again in the next chapter.

Tanzania

Much change in Tanzania has been relatively recent, following Benjamin Mkapa's election to the Presidency in 1996. Unlike his predecessor, Ali Hassan Mwinyi, Mkapa has been apparently committed to both economic and political liberalization. He has increased the pace of public sector reform, and the civil service is both smaller and better paid than previously (Kjaer 2004 pp 399–400). He also cut the number of ministries in the large cabinet he inherited from 33 to it current size of 26,[111] although even Mkapa has had to distribute some patronage through the creation of independent portfolios (Kjaer p 401).

The 1990s also saw the advent of multi-party reforms, although the process has been heavily controlled by the ruling Chama Cha Mapinduzi (CCM) party,[112] which has never been out of power since Independence (Baregu 2000). On the one hand, many parties are widely branded as *ruzuku* (subsidy) parties, their leaders merely chasing the financial provision for and opportunities in forming political parties, for personal gain. In 2000, for example, MPs were allotted an official allowance for 'hospitality' during elections (Kelsall 2002). On the other hand, uncertainty over rules and procedures, restrictions, a heavy emphasis on law and order, the harassment of leaders and dirty tricks at election time have all prevented strong challenges from emerging. In 1999 CCM established youth vigilante groups in every region, with echoes of Mugabe's use of youth militias in Zimbabwe. Funding for political parties is based on seats in parliament rather than popular vote, a system that favours CCM (Baregu 2000 p 67). Baregu (2000 p 71) describes CCM as a state party rather than a political party: 'It is a ruling machine designed to maintain a grip on power rather than an engine for socio-economic development.' Presidential powers, already centralized by Nyerere in the 1960s, were bolstered still further in 2000 with a right to appoint 10 MPs to Parliament. At the lower political levels, from district down to the 'ten-cell leader' local party representative, a fusing together of party and government remains (Kelsall and Mmuya 2004). It is therefore clear that nominal political liberalization in Tanzania, unlike as in Ghana, has not yet produced the emergence of political traditions that can form parties and win elections.

Economic liberalization has had rather different effects. At the macro-level, Tanzania's economy is currently performing well by African standards.[113] Following collapse up to the late 1980s, and hesitant recovery since, growth has not been spectacular, but it has been consistent; 4.6 per cent in 1996–2001, 6.2 per cent in 2002, and around 5 per cent since then, in real terms. Agriculture still dominates growth, but industry is expanding. Manufacturing industry has grown at between 5–8 per cent in recent years (Table 8.4), but the real boom has come in mining, especially gold, where annual production growth is in double figures. This sector is also attracting investment, both in the form of FDI and from local sources, with some going into export-oriented production including in textiles, and processed agricultural products. Investment has grown from 17.6 per cent of GDP in 2000 to 20.8 per cent in 2004 (Table 8.2). Despite persistent problems of corruption in the Revenue Authority (see below), revenue has also been rising, from 10.6 per cent of GDP in 2000 to a predicted 12.8 per cent in 2004 (Table 8.5), with the most recent claims being that exemptions have been cracked down on. This may reflect the growth of large-scale gold mining, which is more easily taxed.

There are also signs of some structural transformations, especially in exports. The share of traditional products in exports, such as coffee, sisal and cotton, has declined and that of non-traditional items, including gold, manufactures, and fish products have rising sharply in the last five years. The privatization programme continues, with 266 enterprises privatized to March 2003, a large majority being sold to Tanzanians or joint ventures (see also Temu and Due 2000). The government has been relatively active in stimulating the private sector, beginning a scheme to promote investments by domestic entrepreneurs in 2002, and establishing an export credit guarantee scheme. There has also been support to agriculture in the form of tax exemptions on export crops, support to input purchases, and micro-credit. Nevertheless, Tanzania remains extremely poor. Up to 2000, progress on reducing poverty has been 'painstakingly slow' (Sen 2002 p 1), with hardly any fall in the percentage of those living below the poverty line since 1990.[114] Inequality has risen sharply, implying that a few have done well out of recent economic changes, while the majority have not. Equally, despite growth and economic dynamism, the country is still highly aid dependent, with aid covering 45 per cent of government expenditure in 2002–03.

On the face of it, Tanzania is showing elements of a developmental state. The centralized-bureaucratic party system put in place by Nyerere (see above ch 6) has survived political liberalization so far. Indeed, Kjaer attributes Mkapa's ability to bring about reform to Tanzania's high degree of 'political institutionalization', meaning that an institutional mechanism for succession, and an ethnically united and dominant party means Mkapa has not had to worry about securing a power base: 'Institutionalisation reduces the dominance of clientelism, increases stability and thereby enables real reform.' (Kjaer 2004 p 402). Additionally, the country has a leader apparently committed to economic growth through capitalist accumulation. It may indeed be the case that of all of the four cases reviewed here, Tanzania is the one that has most resembled a developmental state. However, there are two problems with this view. The first is that there is sufficient evidence to cast doubt on the developmental nature of the relationship between state and business. The second is that there are signs that the very political reforms introduced in the 1990s and 2000s, backed by the donors, may be undermining the stability that Tanzania has enjoyed for so long. Indeed, there appears to be a resurgence of classic post-Independence locally based clientelism in Tanzanian politics. Kelsall (2002) concludes that Tanzania is seeing the paradoxical pattern of donor-led reforms and growth of civil society advancing side by side with patrimonial politics.

According to Kelsall and Mmuya (2004), political elites in Tanzania have responded to recent liberalizations, and the declining importance of parastatal employment and rents based on government control of the economy, by locating themselves increasingly in one of three worlds. Some have allied themselves with donor agendas and resources, including the development of a new class of (urban) NGOs through the PRSP process. Others have moved into various legal and illegal business, including import–export trade, land grabbing, urban real estate, and exploitation of tax loopholes. Many opportunities arose from privatization: 'Divestiture of parastatals also introduced a spoils character into Tanzanian politics, as politicians positioned themselves to receive kickbacks or to become part owners of the newly privatized companies' (Kelsall 2002 p 610, see also OED 2004 p 94). The classic expression of this straddling has been in the grabbing of concessions in the new boom activity of gold mining (Chachage 1995). There are thus questions about whether those who have acquired newly privatized businesses in Tanzania are interested in accumulation via investment, or in the use of business for personal enrichment and political influence. Critically, it is still unclear whether the state will be able to discipline politically powerful capitalists as well as support them. While the data on investment and industrial growth are encouraging, the political reading urges more caution.

A third, entirely new, phenomenon is that of localization. Retired politicians, especially those associated with the older, parastatal patronage era, have gone back to their home areas, getting involved in local institutions including churches and cooperatives societies, as well as setting up their own local NGOs and trust funds, such as District Development Trusts (Kelsall 2002, Kelsall and Mmuya 2004). These trust funds, often defined on an ethnic or locality basis, provide money for local elites to educate their children, to build local prestige, and sometimes to embezzle. Meanwhile national politicians donate to the trusts because 'in a context of political liberalization, local support is important to securing national power, and local elections are becoming more competitive.' (Kelsall 2002 p 611). Additionally, local contacts are increasingly important to national level politicians and businessmen because of new opportunities for enrichment via natural resource extraction outside of the cities. Kelsall concludes that clientelism has re-emerged more strongly in Tanzania, with a new system replacing the centrally controlled bureaucratic structures, even though it is still working mainly within the dominant party. The new system consists of:

> local elites, operating out of ethnic trust funds, NGOs and district councils, cultivating strong personal ties and exchanging favours with national elites, including national politicians. National politicians, for their part, increasingly group themselves into regional blocs, with the aim of securing the attention of government. (Kelsall 2002 p 612)

There are two consequences of this new politics. One is that despite Mkapa's obvious intentions and notwithstanding considerable efforts at public sector reform, clientelist corruption has not been tackled in Tanzania. Corruption emerged in Tanzania in the 1980s, and came to full expression under Mwinyi (see eg Cooksey 2003). When Mkapa came to power he established the 1996 Warioba Commission on corruption and launched a big anti-corruption drive. But this could not be maintained politically, and it became clear that the 'big fish' would not be netted (Kelsall 2002 p 605). Instead, Mkapa came to an accommodation with those who had amassed fortunes under Mwinyi but still had considerable political bases. Some of these figures came back into the cabinet. As a result (Kelsall 2002 p 606): 'While the President's own integrity is rarely called into question, the stance of several members of the government with respect to reform is now ambiguous.'

With donor-backed anti-corruption programmes, there is a public, national discourse opposed to corruption, but at the local level, according to Kelsall and Mmuya 2004, voters often expect to be bribed. As Cooksey (2003 p 17) notes, moving from the one-party system to competitive politics has, despite CCM's heavy management, 'undermined security of tenure for incumbent regimes, making elections more costly and outcomes less predictable. The scale for politically motivated corruption has consequently escalated.' As described in chapter 7 above, fiscal decentralization has led to new forms of rent seeking and politically motivated corruption in local taxation (Fjeldstad 2001). World Bank-backed projects designed to strengthen and clean up the Tanzania Revenue Authority 'largely failed to target the root causes of widespread corruption in the TRA.' (OED 2004 p 92, see also Fjeldstad et al 2003), and the Bank's evaluation department concludes that taxpayers are still vulnerable to 'arbitrary assessment and harassment' from officials (OED 2004 p 94). This study also recognizes that increasing civil service salaries may have had little effect on corrupt activities, since the chances of being caught have not increased. Overall, although Tanzania is now judged to be less corrupt than Kenya or Uganda on Transparency International's Corruption Perceptions Index, and its rating has improved somewhat, it is still one of the most corrupt countries on the index (Table 8.3).

A second effect of political liberalization, and especially the new localism, is political destabilization. The centralized, bureaucratic, one-party system in Tanzania, as elsewhere in Africa in the 1960s, meant that clientelism was controlled and relatively non-destabilizing while not eradicated (Allen 1995, Kelsall 2002 p 598). Links between national and local elites were weak, giving the centre a degree of autonomy. Key positions were dispensed at the centre, via ministries or the party national executive. MPs and regional party chiefs were screened centrally, so for national elites central approval, not local support, was essential. Regional, ethnic and religious demands and tensions were muted and managed as the parastatal sector was a 'sufficient reservoir of patronage with which to satiate the educated elite of Tanzania's various regions.' (Kelsall 2002 p 609. See also van Donge and Liviga 1986 pp 628–29). This system is now changing. Localization has increased political competition at local level, and this is often expressed in ethnic or religious idioms. These are now also more closely linked to the national level (as in Ghana) and are sometimes played out in Parliament. Regional, ethnic and religious identities and demands are all stronger politically than they were previously (Mmuya 1999). Kelsall (2002) points to a rising incidence of violence, both at elections and in regions where there are clashes over resources.

Tanzania thus poses a key dilemma for the emergence of developmental states in Africa. Like Botswana and the East Asian developmental states, its state had a degree of central autonomy, and it currently has a leader interested in economic growth. It may even develop sufficient bargaining power with donors to experiment with interventionist policies. However, there are signs that the power of the centre may not hold, and that Tanzania's stability (which underlies its economic performance) may be in jeopardy from political liberalization and decentralization – a contrast to the prognosis for Ghana of Booth et al (2004).[115]

Mozambique

Mozambique's long and devastating war ended in the early 1990s. Reconciliation between Frelimo and Renamo and elections in 1994 opened the door to period of recovery. From the very low base of the post-war situation, economic growth was in the region of 10 per cent in the 1990s (Ostheimer 2001). High growth has continued into the 2000s (Gastrow and Mosse 2002). The end of the war also saw a shift from the one-party system to nominal multi-partyism, although as Ostheimer points out, Frelimo have carefully controlled this process so as to minimize the risk to their hold of power. 1998 elections saw a Renamo boycott and widespread abstentions. Renamo is a significant political force, with strong regional bases, and heads a coalition with almost half the seats in Parliament (World Bank 2003 p 11). Nevertheless, the Mozambican state bureaucracy is still deeply entangled with the Frelimo party apparatus.

From being a controlled war economy in the 1980s, heavily protected from imports, Mozambique has liberalized substantially, especially in external trade, with licences abolished and customs simplified. The regime has also undertaken a large privatization programme. The economic indicators give the impression that Mozambique's recent economic performance is exceptional not only by African standards but by global standards. Economic growth has been running at over 10 per cent per year up to 2001 (except for the flood year of 2000), and since then at around 8 per cent.[116] Investment rates are extraordinary; rising from over 35 per cent of GDP in 2000 and peaking at 45.5 per cent in 2003 (Table 8.2).

However, these figures are a reflection of a new development in the Mozambican economy – the so-called 'mega-projects' – a small number of which dominate an otherwise tiny and rather slow moving economy. Two very large projects especially dominate the data from the late 1990s through to the early 2000s: the Mozal aluminium smelter and the Sasol gas pipeline, which also account for a boom in construction. Manufacturing growth more generally is somewhat lower, at around 5 per cent per annum (Table 8.4). There are also big project investments in agriculture (60 per cent of land under sugar is in large scale farms), which makes up around 20 per cent of GDP. While some sectors are expanding (cotton and sugar amongst them) others, notably cashews, are not, as prices collapsed in 2000.

From the very high levels of poverty at the end of the war, peace, recovery and a lot of aid[117] have brought some reduction in headcount rates. Progress on reducing poverty has been quite slow, hampered in the early 1990s by spending caps introduced by the IMF that meant cuts in health and education expenditure. The caps were only removed after donors protested that they were obstructing the spending of reconstruction funds (Hanlon 2004). In late 1990s incomes were rising in Maputo, but not elsewhere, and regional inequalities were increasing. The latest government survey, carried out with IFPRI, registered a fall from 69 per cent living under the poverty line in 1997 to 54 per cent in 2002–03. However, this average masks a lot of regional variation, with Maputo and the other infrastructure and communications 'corridors' doing well while other regions (especially in the south) seeing the persistence of poverty.

These trends have led to the emergence of what the World Bank calls 'two economies' in Mozambique (World Bank 2003 p 6). One economy is based on mega-projects, controlled by South African capital, and reliant mainly on natural resource extraction, especially in the 'minerals and energy complex' (MEC). Investment, 75 per cent of which is FDI, is heavily concentrated in MEC large projects. Almost half of all FDI is from South Africa (Castel-Branco 2004). Between 1990 and 2003, South African corporations have been the driving force in 18 per cent of investment projects, but these have absorbed 85 per cent of FDI, 75 per cent of private investment and c. 45 per cent of total gross investment. Thus a few very large projects in a few industries controlled by a few large foreign corporations dominate. The industries include natural gas and sands in minerals, and aluminium, energy, sugar, beer, soft drinks and cereal milling in manufacturing. The classic example is the Mozal aluminium smelter plant near Maputo. This is an investment totalling $2.2 billion in two phases that is estimated to add 7 per cent to Mozambique's GDP and double exports. Mozal uses twice the amount of energy than the rest of the Mozambican economy combined.[118]

On the one hand, such massive investments might appear to be a sign of a developmental state. However, on closer inspection, the benefits are less clear and the process not part of a strategic approach. As Castel-Branco (2004 p 13–22) makes clear, the Mozambican government has not followed the approach of developmental states in East Asia by taking advantage of competition between capitalists (in this case between BHP Billiton, the backers of Mozal, and Kaiser) to extract the best possible deal. It has only a tiny fraction of the share ownership, and has taken on considerable debt to fund that. The scheme is exempt from paying import duties and VAT on inputs, and pays corporate tax of only 1 per cent of sales. On the employment front, Mozal's capital-intensity means job gains are small. The initial capital cost per job in Mozal is over 25 times that elsewhere in manufacturing. As the World Bank itself notes (2003), projects such as Mozal will not produce the 3.7 million jobs needed to lift 20 per cent of the population out of poverty. On present trends, $10 billion of such investment would only create 20,000 jobs. Finally, Mozal is not such a clear winner in terms of exports either. Despite now providing an estimated 60 per cent of Mozambique's exports, Mozal sucks in a lot of imports, including around 500,000 tonnes of bauxite, and electricity from South Africa's Eskom. Exports net of imports (ie trade gains) are estimated at $400 million (Castel-Branco 2004 p 15), but net of profit repatriation, payment of investment services, and transfers of wages of foreign workers, this goes down to $100 million. Of this, the Mozambican economy is estimated to make direct benefits of only $45m in the form of wages, and product and financial linkages. While these recent net earnings from Mozal are still substantial for Mozambique, they do not help Mozambique escape vulnerability to price instability, and also bring problems of 'Dutch disease.'[119] Mozal makes Mozambican exports highly dependent on aluminium prices, which can be volatile (they fell by 15 per cent in 2000–03). A 10 per cent change in the aluminium price will change Mozambican export earnings by $80m, which is more than the rest of other manufacturing export earnings together (Castel-Branco 2004 p 22).

The Mozal economy contrasts with the small-scale sector (Castel-Branco

2004 p 9): 'Outside the dynamics of mega and large projects, especially of Mozal, industrial outputs and exports are stagnant, manufacturing output actually declined in 2003, and the MVA share of GDP, without Mozal, has fallen to the levels of 1971.' The World Bank also notes the shortage of investment in this sector, low productivity and weak employment growth (World Bank 2003 pp 5–6):

Most firms lag regional competitors in skills, management and manufacturing techniques; and labor-intensive manufacturing . . . has not been able to compete. Moreover, linkages to large-scale projects remain limited. Despite Government incentives, the sector still faces many challenges. In general, Mozambique remains a risky and difficult market: it is poor and small; and it has high operating costs (due to poor infrastructure); low labor productivity (low wages are offset by poor skills and health) and high transactions costs (due to an inefficient bureaucracy).

Much development in Mozambique is therefore of an 'enclave' nature, and contrasts with industrialization processes in developmental states where there has been great focus on technology transfers from FDI, domestic linkages and joint ventures.

A final impact of the 'two economies' path is regional inequality. With the exception of tourism, all the large-scale industry projects are concentrated in or near Maputo. The capital city and its region contribute 70 per cent of trade, transport and telecommunications and 75 per cent of financial services and construction. It absorbed 75 per cent of FDI and 88 per cent of private manufacturing investment in the period 1990–2003 (Castel-Branco 2004 p 12). This explains the much of the disparity in poverty reduction noted above.

Overall Castel-Branco (2004 p 18) concludes that: 'no matter how much FDI flows into the Mozambican economy, there is no substitute for strategies and policies that effectively create domestic business and productive capabilities, including entrepreneurial capacities and a qualified and motivated workforce.' This has clearly not yet happened. Instead, there are signs that the dominant state faction, far from being developmental in character, has elements of spoils politics.

Unlike most African independence movements, Frelimo fought a successful bush war against their colonizers. This meant a high degree of discipline and central control during the struggle. Early post-Independence leaders such as Samora Machel had personal integrity and were committed to rooting out corruption (Gastrow and Mosse 2002 p 46, Hanlon 2004). However, following his death in 1986, Frelimo began to change, and under Chissano corruption and crime have emerged high up in the party (Gastrow and Mosse 2002 p 47, Hanlon 2002). Hanlon (2004 p 4) notes that the privatization process was corrupt, with small firms passed on to 'friends and family of the leadership', in what became known as 'silent privatizations' (Ostheimer 2001).

The civil service is understaffed and heavily bureaucratic even by African standards (World Bank 2003, Ostheimer 2001), and there are morale problems due to low pay. Salaries of civil servants were actually cut in the early 1990s, worth one third in 1996 of what they had been in 1991. Demands for bribes for services are common. A survey in 2001 found that 45 per cent of respondents said they had to give a bribe in last 6 months. Most common demands were from officials in health, education and the police (Hanlon 2004 pp 2–3). Revenue as a percentage of GDP has been level at below 13 per cent for the last few years (Table 8.5). Until late 2002, Mozambique had no central revenue authority. A 2001 Country Financial Accountability Assessment found that risk of waste and misuse of budget funds remains, along with payments made off budget, outdated accounting and recording systems, and weak auditing and Parliamentary oversight (World Bank 2003 p 13). The police and judicial services are also corrupt (Hanlon 2004 p 4).

Beyond corruption in the 'service' state, there are also signs of political corruption in relation to the private sector, without a balancing discipline. Hanlon (2004 p 5) cites cases of loans going to favoured businesses that are never repaid, for example. There have been two major bank scandals in recent years, with more than $400m stolen, in which senior Frelimo figures are implicated (see Hanlon 2002 for details). Two journalists probing the case were assassinated, with subsequent investigations into their murders blocked at high level. Foreign investors are frequently asked for commissions or shares by political leaders. On Transparency International's Corruption Perceptions Index, Mozambique's rating – below 3 in 2003/04 – is about the same as Tanzania's but below Ghana's (Table 8.3).

There also appears to be high-level regime involvement in organized crime, including drug-trading, large-scale smuggling and money laundering (Gastrow and Mosse 2002). A report by the Attorney General in 2002 stated that the criminal justice network has been discredited by the impunity with which gangs work. Gastrow and Mosse (2002 p 62) state that a widely held view within the country is that Mozambique has a 'gangster state'.

Hanlon (2004) argues that in the past donors have taken a sanguine view of corruption in privatization, and in the use of loans. Certainly, Mozambique received HIPC debt relief when there must have been serious questions about misuse of funds (Ostheimer 2001). However, recent IFI analyses are fairly candid about corruption issues (eg World Bank 2003 p 12). Economic governance is judged to be 'weak', and corruption 'a growing concern'. Similar problems are recognized by DfID.

However, as is by now familiar, the donor approach remains fairly technical, and it cannot grapple with the deeper political issues:

> Donors continue to align themselves with a predatory elite faction that sees state capture as the only way toward rapid development of a

national bourgeoisie. At the same time, donors reject the appeals of a more critical, 'developmental' faction of the elite, who promote a longer-term entrepreneurial perspective requiring a more interventionist, functioning and honest state (Hanlon 2004 p 5).

An open verdict

This review of four African countries was not intended to be exhaustive. I have focused on the question of whether countries showing some stability and growth, especially in manufacturing, may be emerging as African developmental states. The findings are not particularly optimistic. In Uganda, an initial political drive has become bogged down in the re-emergence of clientelist politics. In Mozambique, what looks like outstanding economic performance is the result of a criminalized elite who have opened the country to the strategies of South African corporations, but have no strategy of their own for gaining the most from FDI for the country. The more hopeful countries are Ghana and Tanzania. In Ghana, democracy in a context of unusually strong civil society may be changing the nature of politics, which may then lead to a better functioning state. However, one change of ruling party does not make a developmental state, as the case of Zambia shows, and Ghana shows few signs of economic transformation as yet. Tanzania shows most signs of a developmental project, with a history of stable politics, and strong growth across agriculture and manufacturing. However, even here there are signs that political liberalization may be bringing a stronger voice to regional, ethnic and religious groups that demand a more explicit and powerful clientelist politics to accommodate them.

In all cases, clientelist corruption (as opposed to 'patrimonial' corruption, on Khan's typology) is persistent and has defied donor attempts to tackle it through governance reforms. In all cases, donors have persistently tried to shape reform programmes that lead away from state intervention, towards liberalization. The actual outcomes have been more complex, but this relationship has made it difficult for the more competent looking governments to experiment with active trade and industrial policies. With manufacturing in most countries now a little stronger than in the 1980s but still focused on domestic markets rather than on exports, this is a pressing problem. This is a key shift that developmental states need to lead industry through.

A final comment is about scale. The four countries I have focused on here are in many ways some of the most hopeful in Africa in terms of their economies and political stability. However, their combined populations amount to around 100 million people, less than one-sixth of Africa's total. The three large African countries – Nigeria, DRC and Ethiopia – are not even on the qualifying list for developmental states, especially the first two. It is clear that for the continent as a whole the prospect of active successful states leading rapid growth and poverty reduction is still a long way off.

9 What will a developmental state in Africa look like?

THE STORY OF BOTSWANA – economically the most successful country in Africa – and the assessment of four candidates for more recent developmental states on the last chapter, brought out some sobering conclusions. The unusual circumstances of Botswana's history confirmed the significance of political factors in effective state performance and economic development in Africa. Of the four other countries, only Tanzania might be said to have some enduring characteristics of a developmental state, and even these are vulnerable to political change.

However, these case studies also throw up some broader issues about what developmental states in Africa are likely to look like when they do emerge. In this book I have been making comparisons directly between the most successful East Asian states and African states, as do UNECA (2004) and others. But some are of the view that it is unrealistic to expect African economies to look like their East Asian counterparts, arguing that they may end up looking more like the 'in-between' cases of Latin America or Southeast Asia. Others apply similar reasoning to political structure, seeing the characteristics of Korea and Taiwan as being too historically specific to be relevant for Sub-Saharan Africa. Thus rather than assuming that African developmental states should and will end up looking like this or that other example, it may be appropriate to ask the more open question of what political characteristics they might have.

Political form

Wade's discussion of East Asian developmental states is nevertheless helpful. He introduces two dimensions of political organization to help explain the success of Taiwan. The first is the traditional political contrast between authoritarian states (where leaders were not brought to power by popular consent) and democratic states (where they are). The second dimension is about the relationship between the state and interest groups, with a contrast between a corporatist arrangement (where states exercise a considerable degree of control over how interest groups expressed their demands), and a pluralist arrangement (where states are much more open to lobby groups, and therefore also to 'capture') (Wade 1990 p 27). He characterizes Taiwan and Korea as essentially authoritarian and corporatist. By contrast, 'developed' countries like the US and European countries are democratic and pluralist.

These are useful concepts. However, the corporatist–pluralist dimension needs to be understood in a slightly different way in most African contexts. Demands on the central state and leaders in Africa have been expressed in a particularistic way – as demands for resources by individuals, often regional or ethnic leaders who claim to be able to deliver the political support of groups defined on identity. Some of these resources are used in conspicuous consumption, while some may be passed on in turn to more minor clients, again in a particularistic way. This contrasts with the more conventional understanding of interest group politics, as demands for collective benefits accruing to functional or class groups, such as a particular industry, or trade unions. Therefore the pluralist/corporatist distinction in Africa has a rather different meaning, whereby it reflects the degree to which clientelism is controlled, coinciding with Allen's distinct between centralized-bureaucratic states and spoils politics states (see above ch 6). On this view there would be a continuum from Botswana at one end (maybe with Tanzania nearby) as more corporatist, and collapsed states on the other, where competition between warlords might be seen as the extreme end of pluralism.

What are the likely characteristics of African developmental states? I focus first on the authoritarian–democratic dimension.

After the fall of the Berlin Wall, many saw the shift towards multi-party democracy as holding out new hope for Africa, as they associated the authoritarian regimes of the past – whether one-party states or military governments – with the failure of development. It is often pointed out that the two successful Sub-Saharan countries – Botswana and Mauritius – had democratic states. In the mid-1990s, Gordon White called for democratic developmental states on the basis that democracy is a 'massive developmental good in its own right' (White 1995 p 30). And although in favour of authoritarian rule in the case of developmental Taiwan, Wade (1990 p 350) argued that, where regimes were predatory, 'enhancing the power and autonomy of the state could be disastrous.'

Booth et al (2004), in relation to Ghana also argue for the limited relevance of the authoritarian East Asian states, and for the potential of democratic politics (and specifically of political competition), on balance, to erode clientelism. Thus, despite the problems that have persisted in multi-party systems, the obvious appeal of democracy still leads many to see the future for Africa as lying in this direction: 'the constitution of "democratic developmental states" may be the single most important task on the policy agenda in Africa' (Mkandawire and Soludo 2004).

However, the case for democracy is far from straightforward. Statistically the general relationship between democracy and poverty reduction is weak (eg Moore et al 2000 pp 8–9). In Africa, the advent of multi-party systems did not make a decisive difference to overall economic performance in the early 1990s (van de Walle 2001 pp 247–54). It is also true that regimes that did *not* introduce a centralized one-party system soon after Independence in Africa tended to become more unstable, often leading to military coups and sometimes state collapse (Allen 1995). In some cases (but certainly not all), political stability has been created out of chaos by authoritarian rule, Rawlings and Museveni being two examples. More recently, while political competition has led to changes of government in elections in countries other than Ghana – including Zambia and Kenya – it hasn't necessarily led to the decline of clientelist politics and a newly effective state (see van de Walle 2001 pp 265–66 for Zambia after Chiluba replaced Kaunda).

However, in practice it is hard to see the widespread political reforms of the early 1990s being reversed. International political pressures for at least formal democracy in almost all African countries[120] are fairly widespread (even Museveni is giving way on this). Clearly then, what matters is not just the presence of absence of a multi-party electoral system, but rather, the quality of democratic processes. As Gordon White notes, to deliver developmental performance, democracy needs to be deep enough, and the state strong enough:

> Democratization without a serious effort to reform and/or strengthen the state may mean that a diversification of political elites through multi-party competition will just mean more snouts in the trough and successful private sector development will just mean fattening more frogs for snakes. (White 1995 p 31)

One key factor here is the strength and structure of civil society. Booth et al (2004) explicitly reject the authoritarian models of East Asia as irrelevant for Ghana, and argue that, on balance, democratic, party-political competition will work to weaken clientelist corruption, and promote a more effective state. However, they do so on the basis that Ghana has a civil society that is unusually strong by African standards. This, they argue, means that the 'horizontal' identities that people acquire through membership of specific groups (such as cocoa farmers organizations, professional associations, unions, business associations, etc) have the potential to cut across patronage relationships, and may lead to interest groups expressing issue-based politics and demands for collective resources, rather than individuals pursuing particularistic pay-offs.

This strengthening of civil society is associated with a move from 'subject' to 'citizen', which Mamdani (1996) identifies as key to progress in Africa (see ch 6 above). It may indeed be the case that in some countries with strong civil society, this shift is happening. Alongside Ghana, the 2003 elections in Kenya, which saw a deep rejection of the corruption of the Moi regime, may be signs of an emerging sense of citizenship that can underpin a deeper and more accountable democratic state. However, the fragility of gains in Kenya is already visible. And in many African countries a weak concept of citizenship, especially in rural areas, means that rule by a combination of patronage, disempowerment and repression is still effective (for Uganda see Moncrieffe 2004 p 30). Political identity and claims are still shaped by region and ethnicity (see, for example, Abah and Okwori 2002 on notions of citizenship in Nigeria). In many countries it is still difficult to establish rights as a citizen. And in the absence of a strong sense of citizenship, civil society itself will be organized along lines of patronage, as appears to be the case for many of the new local NGOs in Tanzania (see above ch 8).

A sense of where countries are in this process may be sought in the relationship between the state and civil society (including Parliament), where the latter is strongest (urban areas) and on the issue that touches most of the mechanisms of clientelism (the budget process). If analysis and demands for accountability in this area are weak, as in Malawi (Rakner et al 2004), then the building of a citizenship concept in rural areas is likely to be a long way off. Where they are stronger, as in Ghana (Booth et al 2004), this may indeed be the sign of the emergence of civil society.

The major problem with the position of Booth et al (2004) is the relatively uniqueness of Ghana, which they themselves point to. In most countries, lacking such a strong civil society, the increased political competition that comes with democratization may accentuate a clientelistic politics, such as in Tanzania. In these circumstances, although formal multi-party elections are virtually inevitable, the countries most likely to control clientelism enough to embark on a developmental project are likely to be those that have de facto one-party states, such as Botswana and Tanzania.[121]

Access to the state

Beyond the question of the quality of democracy, there is the separate question of whether even deep democracy in Africa can actually deliver developmentalism of the type seen in East Asia. Democracy tends to produce open competition for resources between interests where they exist as organized groups. Wade's view is that developmentalism is tied up with corporatism, where competition for state support is controlled by the state, and where the state can extract performance in return for support, allowing a degree of long term planning and insulation from short-term political pressures. It is not at all clear in the African context that a pluralist democracy, even if a non-clientelistic one) would produce investment in increasing productivity and exports.

A key relationship here is that with the private sector. Africa countries desperately need effective national private sectors, ones that can, with state support, begin to compete in global markets. The state must have sufficient power to award support to chosen firms, but also to discipline them, a relationship that might allow 'patrimonial' corruption in the terms of Khan (1996), but prevents state capture by specific interests.

One of the most interesting issues in Africa currently is whether the (largely corrupt) privatization process might nevertheless create a new commercial class from parts of the political elite. In the past, African elites have often had a punitive approach to the private sector – not so much disciplining companies as tormenting them. But in the post-privatization phase this may change. In the words of Brian Cooksey (commenting on Tanzania):

> If the former apparatchiks can eventually transform into real capitalists (initially and inevitably, through political corruption and cronyism!), then there might be some limited hope of some African economies eventually 'taking off'. (Cooksey 2003 pp 18–19)

If such a class does emerge, the question is what its relationship will be with the state. The case of Ghana discussed in the previous chapter implied that the state there has not yet moved to imposing rigorous performance demands on client businesses, and that the state-private sector relationship is still largely particularistic. In Tanzania, where part of the political elite has straddled across into business, it is not yet clear what will happen. Most particularly, it is unclear whether this new group can politically be pushed into investment and accumulation, or whether they will rather seek to milk their acquired businesses for resources to spend in political careers.[122]

Leadership

To Wade's two dimensions determining the performance of states, I would add a third: the nature of political leadership. This is partly because African politics is likely to continue to be characterized by Presidential rather than collective rule. Writing in 1986, before multi-party democracy in Africa seemed a viable option, and assuming that only neo-patrimonial states can survive politically, Richard Sandbrook argued that the best outcome would be a 'revolution from above' – modernizing leadership that could mobilize political support for the gradual displacement of clientelism and the building of an effective state (Sandbrook 1985 pp 155–56). He saw this as working through:

> Decent, responsive and largely-even handed personal rule. Although neopatrimonialism is virtually the only workable mode of governance in tropical Africa, Houphouet-Boigny's neopatrimonialism is infinitely preferable to that of an Idi Amin. The point is that there is personal rule and personal rule. (Sandbrook 1985 p 157)

Beyond decency, however, the question is whether a particular leader is interested in a developmental project. Wade's whole analysis of developmental states assumes:

> benign political leaders, whose concerns go beyond using state power to support the affluence of a small group. Some rulers . . . are predatory, in the sense that their efforts to maximize the resource flow under their control erode the ability of the resource base to deliver future flows. In these circumstances enhancing the power and autonomy of the state could be disastrous. (Wade 1990 p 350)

This points to the fact that successful developmentalist leaders in Africa have to be sufficiently committed to establishing an effective state that they are willing to tackle the extremely difficult task of transforming a clientelist politics. Many leaders at certain points have seemed interested in controlling and minimizing clientelism, including the first generation of national leaders who established centralized-bureaucratic systems, as described in chapter 6. Nyerere was genuinely concerned about corruption, for example. More recently, Museveni and Rawlings were clearly initially determined centralize control so as to force through their version of a developmentalist project.

However, even benign, developmentally minded African leaders have found it hard to maintain such a stance. This is because of the pervasiveness of clientelist politics, deeply established not just amongst political elites, but also amongst the widespread networks of clients a in the wider population. Chabal and Daloz (1999) argue that while some leaders, like Nyerere or Museveni, may well have a relatively modest personal need for the status of Big Man and may genuinely aim to transcend the short-term view in favour of longer-term developmental goals:

> [the] fact remains . . . that the ability of such exceptional leaders to move the political system beyond its present rationality is limited, not primarily because of a lack of ambition but much more fundamentally because of the nature of existing forms of political legitimacy. In the end, there is an interlocking neo-patrimonial logic between the deep ambitions of the political elites and the well-grounded expectations of their clients. (Chabal and Daloz 1999 p 162)

Leaders such as Museveni, Rawlings, Nyerere and Kaunda did attempt to strip out clientelism from traditional rural structures, and to some extent within their own political movements. However, all failed to prevent its resurgence. Even Museveni appears to have become dependent on a clientelistic relationship with the army in Uganda. In these circumstances, future leaders with these ambitions will need all the support they can get.

Overall, given that multi-party systems in Africa are here to stay, it may be that the most likely political form of the African developmental state will be like that of Botswana – formally democratic, (but with electoral politics dominated by a single party) and corporatist in relation to clientelist politics. Tanzania comes closest to this model, and from the review in chapter 8 above, seems the most likely candidate for a developmental project, if its politics do not unravel. In this case, political leaders will not only have to be committed to a developmental project, they will also need to cement a power base sufficiently powerful and resistant to clientelist politics to eradicate the latter.

However, if civil society and concepts of citizenship radically strengthen in the next few years, Africa may see the emergence of more cases like Ghana. These will not be developmental states along the lines of East Asia, and are unlikely to mirror the exceptional growth, industrialization and poverty reduction of the latter. Their developmental path is likely to be slower and more meandering as the state is pulled in different direction by different interest groups. The state may indeed become 'captured' by dominant groups that do not have a developmental agenda (in Ghana perhaps the extractive resources industry, for example). A common analysis of some central and Latin American states is that they were likewise captured by landed interests little interested in industrialization, poverty reduction and structural transformation.[123] However, regardless of which interest groups come to predominate, the argument is that politics will have been transformed from its current clientelist basis, and within democratic politics, it will actually be possible for different interest groups with coherent sets of policies to fight for control of a functioning state.

10 Towards developmental states in Africa – what agenda for international action?

THE MESSAGE OF THIS book is that politics and the state matter for development. I have argued that the nature of politics and the state in Africa are a central part of the explanation for persistent low growth and poverty arising from a failure of accumulation through investment, and marginalization from the global economy. They are also part of the story of the failure to tackle the AIDS epidemic. Africa's predicament is the outcome of a particular political history, combined with the difficult economic niche it inherited from the colonial powers. That history has bequeathed a structural political feature – clientelism – that pervades a neo-patrimonial state, and has proved remarkably entrenched in the face of economic crisis and subsequent partial economic and political liberalization. Some states have been virtually destroyed by it; others have managed to contain it for long periods, but none whose political existence relied on it have managed to escape its consequences for any length of time. While it is driven by its own logic, clientelism is highly damaging for economic development and for prosperity – not only has it prevented the emergence of developmental states, it has actually led to the evolution of *anti-developmental* states.

This final chapter looks at the question of what external agents – international NGOs, and donor governments and institutions – should do in response to this situation. From Independence up until the end of the Cold War, clientelist regimes in Africa were heavily supported by the West and the Soviet bloc. Even after 1990, donors have not fully engaged with the nature of African politics and its developmental implications. It is likely that the argument in this book is a difficult one for donors, for understandable reasons. Official donors largely give government-to-government aid; publicly at least they see recipient states as 'development partners' rather than neo-patrimonial and anti-developmental. The World Bank, by its charter, cannot make political judgements in the allocation of loans. The tendency to fall back into 'governance' mode is strong. Nevertheless, engaging with the political nature of Africa's development problems can, I believe, lead to a coherent policy agenda. Getting donors to adopt that agenda is an entirely different matter, since the primacy of politics applies to donor governments as much as to African ones. In this respect, campaigning NGOs have a crucial role to play, but also a crucial responsibility.

Current donor objectives are nominally dominated by poverty reduction, in the form of the Millennium Development Goals. The most rapid declines in poverty, and the most rapid increase in human development in recent history have come from East and South-east Asia. I have argued in this book that the rapid and broad-based economic growth underlying this experience, based on high levels of productive investment and successful industrialization, has been led by highly interventionist 'developmental' states. I have also argued that the most significant contrast between this experience and Africa's stagnation has been in the nature of states in the two regions. Finally, I have argued that the key factor in African countries' pervasive state failures has been clientelist politics, a form of politics that constantly works to undermine the effectiveness and capacity of those states. It is easy to see that this approach leads to the conclusion that rapid development and poverty eradication will only be possible in Africa if clientelist politics can be transformed. In the words of Gordon White, what is needed is not just 'good governance' but also 'good politics' (White 1995 p 31).

It is also fairly easy to see that this transformation is only going to come from within Africa – in the final analysis, only Africans can change their own politics. As Herbst and Soludo (2001 p 675) note, locating the failure of adjustment lending in Nigeria in the political nature of public spending:

> the Nigerian program did not fail because of a lack of [policy] ideas . . . What is needed is to develop new ideas about how Nigerian politics should operate, something that the World Bank, the IMF and the bilateral donors cannot provide. Only the Nigerians can do that.

The international community can play only a minor, supporting role in this drama, despite the fact that it is used to seeing itself as the *prima donna*. This is the first and hardest lesson for donors to accept.

However, while only a small role, it is one worth playing. The overall goal of the international community with respect to Africa, towards which all policies should be aligned, should therefore be *to support political transformations that change a clientelist political system with a logic of consumption, to a developmental political system and state with a logic of productive investment*. Robert Wade (1990 p 350) uses the striking image of the 'vampire state' vs the 'ruminant state': 'The vampire extracts so much as to debilitate, the ruminant grazes the resource base while fertilizing it at the other end'. The objective is thus to support transformation from vampire to ruminant.

The key question for donors and international NGOs, therefore, is about what kinds of existing or potential processes of political change they should support, which they should avoid supporting, and what this means for development policies. I look in turn at aid policy, debt relief, trade policies, and banking and corporate responsibility policies.

An agenda for aid

Aid for Africa is currently a hot topic, since one of the few possible 'deliverables' from the G8 for 2005 might be a sharp increase in aid to Africa, possibly linked to the need to tackle HIV/AIDS. It is also the most complex of the policy issues discussed here.

Both the Chancellor and UK NGOs in the 'Make Poverty History' campaign are calling for a sharp increase in aid and debt relief generally, and to Africa in particular. Oxfam has argued that Africa needs an additional $25–35 billion a year to meet the Millennium Development Goals (Oxfam 2003). The Treasury is proposing the International Financing Facility to accelerate the delivery of extra aid resources. Others have called for aid of the order of 20–30 per cent of Africa's GDP (around $60–90 billion) every year until 2015 (Sachs et al 2004 p 26), or a doubling of aid by 2008 (Commission for Africa 2005).

The Chancellor has referred specially to a Marshall Plan for Africa, with the image of rebuilding a country with shattered infrastructure after war. In fact, the Marshall Plan aid arrived only after the major reconstruction effort, and was too small an amount to stimulate a growth effect (Bradford de Long and Eichengreen 1991). Nevertheless, the basic idea is a profound one – that Africa's infrastructure and human capital needs are so great that a very large amount of capital is needed to kick start the development process. Sachs et al (2004) underpin this idea with a plausible theoretical analysis proposing that returns to investment are increasing, not decreasing, in very poor economies.

However, the record shows us that increasing flows of development finance to Africa has in the past not succeeded, in itself, in getting growth and poverty reduction going. In 1980 the OAU called for a doubling of aid to Africa in the Lagos Plan of Action, a proposal that the World Bank seconded in the 1981 report *Accelerated Development in Sub-Saharan Africa* (van de Walle 2001 p 217). Aid did subsequently increase by over 130 per cent between 1980 and 1990. Yet this period became known as the 'lost decade', as per capita incomes fell and poverty increased.

It is tempting to conclude that aid will be of no value without changes in governance.[124] However, there is considerable macro-economic evidence (summarized in ch 4 above) suggesting that aid is useful even in Africa, leading to higher growth regardless of policies, with the greatest effect in the poorest countries. In this sense, aid works, and there is a case for increasing it. At the same time, the story of the 1980s shows that, while more aid may not be useless, aid itself is not the key to sustained high growth rates, and we must look at how aid interacts with other factors if we want to see a step change in progress.

I have argued that to achieve rapid and sustained growth, the nature of politics and the state will have to be transformed, by leaders who have the combination of commitment and political power to overcome clientelism, in order to undertake a developmental project. If this is true, then there is another way of looking at the role of aid. This is that aid flows have maintained regimes in power in Africa that do not have such commitment and political power.

At an aggregate level, I would argue that this is the case for most of Africa, since almost all African countries have variants of neo-patrimonial rather than developmental states, while at the same time Africa as a region attracted an increasing share of aid up until the 1990s, still has the highest aid-to-GDP ratios and is now again receiving increased aid allocations. Within Africa, it is generally thought that, post-Cold War, the allocation of aid has a more developmentally-based rationale. However, while aid allocations are now theoretically supposed to reflect 'good' performance, and going off track on conditionality is supposed to mean an interruption of aid, in practice most countries in Africa have continued to receive aid funding. van de Walle (2001 p 225) argues that despite claims by the World Bank to the contrary, aid allocations do not reflect economic performance or adherence to donor policy packages. More broadly, Alesina and Weder (1999) argue that more corrupt governments receive no less aid than less corrupt ones. Tables 2.7 and 8.1 above also show that allocations of total aid, and of aid-per-head from DfID show that 'poor' performers can come quite high up the aid rankings. While the conventional criteria of good or poor performance are not quite the same as the strength of clientelism, the general point that aid allocations do not follow a clear pattern holds.

There are a number of reasons for this (Alesina and Dollar 1998, Stiglitz 1998). Some are internal to aid institutions, with strong pressures relating to career development, as well as inter-donor pressures (eg Kanbur 2000). All of these mean that there is reluctance to actually interrupt programme aid even if countries go off track. In recent years there has also been external political pressure from campaigning NGOs, especially in the UK, to increase debt relief and aid flows to African countries quite broadly, without much distinction in terms of state effectiveness (eg for Cameroon see van de Walle 2001 p 188, for Mozambique see Hanlon 2004). Not engaging with 'poor performers' (now called 'difficult environments' by DfID and Low Income Countries Under Stress' by the World Bank) is not seen as an option, and donors have sought ways to develop new aid delivery mechanisms for these countries.

Another reason is that, in Africa, donors have become caught in a kind of aid-dependency trap. The build-up over the years of very high levels of aid in relation to both GDP and government expenditure, has now made many economies in Africa vulnerable to the cutting of aid, not just in terms of macro-economic stability, but also in terms of the broad functioning of government. In some countries aid makes up more than half of government spending. This again makes it difficult to suddenly cease programme aid or budget support. Moreover, as van de Walle (2001 ch 5) describes, donor institutions and personnel have taken over not only much of the developmental functions of governments, but also the details of planning and decision-making. Donors have become deeply involved in attempts at micro-management.[125] Given that they are also very poor at coordinating time-tables and procedures both with each other and with recipient governments, this adds huge burdens and inefficiencies (Commission for Africa 2005 ch 9). This dynamic is one of the major ways in which the developmental capacity of states has been eroded by the aid regime over the years. There has, of course, been some recognition of this by both donors and NGOs, and attempts at pulling back from micro-management and at capacity building have been popular in recent years. However, as we saw from chapter 5 above, these very attempts at state building (ie governance reforms) have themselves again become micro-managed by donors. Technical assistance in Africa, for example, remains mainly supply, rather than demand driven. Once the institutions have developed, old habits die hard.

The basic dilemma for donors is therefore that, while there are powerful humanitarian and economic arguments for giving aid, it has also become part of a system that is supporting neo-patrimonial states across Africa.[126] In its current form, aid may be working to prevent political transformations that could lead to much faster levels of growth driven by committed leaders driving through institutional change.

The key policy question then becomes: *is there a way of giving aid that meets short-term needs but doesn't undermine the longer-term goal of trying to foster developmental states by acting as a resource for clientelist politics?*

I believe that there are ways of doing this. They would have to be based on two basic principles:

- For both humanitarian and basic aid efficiency reasons, there is a case for some kind of 'floor' of assistance to all countries in Africa, allocated in a way that is biased towards poorer countries.
- There is a strong case for using (some) aid to create a clear and consistent incentive system – based on carrots rather than sticks – for leaders to overcome clientelist politics and forge a developmental path.

However, such innovations would require transforming the aid delivery system, involving considerable change to donor institutions in-country, and would largely abandon conditionality.

The first element is a basic floor of aid to all countries in Africa. Given the relative ineffectiveness of donor-led governance reform efforts in the absence of political commitment (see ch 5 above), there is little case for packaging this type of aid to encourage policy or institutional change (unlike the current LICUS scheme). There is a case for targeting it at the provision of very basic public goods, especially infrastructure, and at health, most especially at tackling the AIDS epidemic and providing ARTs.

It would be justified on humanitarian grounds, and on the evidence that aid, broadly, leads to growth via investment at a certain level even in countries with poor institutions (see ch 4 above). There is also an argument for holding the functions of the central state together, so that if there are political challenges to a corrupt order, there is something to take over, reducing the risk of a descent into regional or ethnic warlordism (see chapter 6 above). On the same argument, there may be a case both for direct military intervention by donor countries to prevent conflicts spreading, and building AU capacity to do so (but see also comments on the AU below). Given the greater effectiveness of aid in poorer countries (Gonamee et al 2003), there is also an argument for allocating aid on the basis of a fixed dollar amount per head, so that the 'floor' would become less important as countries grow. It would have to be pitched at a level where moral hazard incentives for governments attempting to keep per capita income low were not too strong.[127]

Given the relative inefficiency of conditionality in using aid to lever policy change, such 'floor' aid would probably benefit from keeping any conditionality to a minimum (probably mainly aimed at preventing excessive macroeconomic instability), and all steps should be taken to ensure that the design and implementation of this conditionality learns from past mistakes (Mosley et al 2003). Donor institutions might, however, be quite involved in delivery, since it would be assumed that state capacity would be very low. Inter-donor coordination would therefore be a priority.

However, at this point the by-now familiar dilemma of aid in a clientelist environment poses itself very acutely here; how do donors avoid getting into a situation where they are simply maintaining a Charles Taylor, Abacha or Mobutu in power (ie playing a similar role to that of oil and mineral resources)? This why an aid system for Africa needs to incorporate a strong incentive element aimed at supporting political transformation.

A second element would therefore need to be designed purely to create incentives rewarding the emergence of developmental regimes, and providing the resources that are needed for infrastructure and to crowd in investment in such regimes (Commission for Africa 2005 pp 294–95). This would have to be rather different from existing aid mechanisms, involving a simple allocation rule instead of conditionality, and rapid and progressive withdrawal of donor institutions from micro-management.

Key to such a system would be an allocation rule for amounts of aid large enough to create an attractive incentive.[128] To avoid the familiar problems of donor micro-management, resources additional to the 'floor' would have to be allocated to countries on the basis of a very few final outcome indicators of developmental performance. To avoid penalizing poorer countries, these would have to be proportional or rate-of-change indicators. If poverty reduction is the overriding objective of donors, then the primary indicator should be reduction in the poverty headcount. Other indicators could include signs of developmental state outcomes, including economic growth, investment in manufacturing or services as a proportion of GDP, progress in diversification of exports, for example. All donors would have to agree to the same small, simple set of criteria. The desire to add to this set will be very strong, since donors almost always want to pursue multiple objectives with aid (often encouraged by NGOs). However, this system will only work by keeping the focus on the emergence of developmental regimes.

This is a radical notion, and it is immediately tempting to slip back towards micro-management through a wider set of output indicators. What about school completion rates? Or how about governance criteria, such as prosecutions where there is clear evidence of corruption? Surely governance criteria, in particular, would be needed to root out the neo-patrimonial aspects of the state? Minimal fiduciary conditionality?

Here, however, the central argument is that the single most important dynamic of development is learning (Rodrik 2002 p 4). Thus it is important to reward and support developmental outcomes, however reached, so as to allow governments the space to learn and experiment. This is essential for building the capacity to make and implement policy and undertake planning. Donor micro-management and conditionality have severely dampened the learning dynamic in Africa over the last 30 years.

For donors, one of the most difficult issues will be about state intervention in the economy. As we have seen, the whole drive of donor conditionality has been towards liberalizing African economies. However, while this approach is based on an Anglo-American theoretical orthodoxy, and on the observation of government failures and rent-seeking in Africa (which UK-based NGOs have played down), it cannot engage with the history of successful intervention in East and South-east Asia, or heterodox models elsewhere. The danger is, therefore, that this approach will produce a 'poor but stable and efficient' Africa (Mkandawire and Soludo 2004). The African challenge is not how to neutralize the neo-patrimonial state, but rather how to transform an anti-developmental state to an actively developmental one.[129] For economic policy, the record shows that what works in one setting will not necessarily work in another (Rodrik 2002 p 3), so, given that the basic political commitment is there, the essential task is not to prescribe a set policy agenda, but rather to support the development of learning capacity through experimentation.

The same applies to governance and political change. Again, it is tempting to argue, that, using studies such as the excellent DfID 'Drivers of Change' series[130] as a basis, this extra aid should be tied to political or governance change criteria. However, the review of potential candidates for developmental states in chapter 8 above, and the general lessons emerging in chapter 9, show that it is hard to second guess the political form of developmental states in Africa. African political leaders committed to a project of overcoming clientelism are more likely to know how best to tackle the task than are donors. It is also true that the least effective type of conditionality is political conditionality (Crawford, cited in Killick 2004).

However, this does not mean that donors should not encourage governments to receive advice about how to manage economy and state. Many of the army of advisers in Africa could indeed remain there if contracted by governments, although countries should perhaps be encouraged to seek advice from those who have managed successful entry into world markets more recently, such as retired Korean and Taiwanese administrators. Instead of 'Do as we say, not as we did', the message from donors should be 'Try doing as they did, and if that doesn't work, try something else'. The crucial difference is that this would be advice that governments had sought themselves, rather than being an imposed part of the aid package.

Rather than worrying about the details of exactly how African countries should be achieving developmental outcomes, donors would instead have to put their effort into ensuring that they do actually disburse aid in line with their allocation rules. This would, as noted, require a change in current donor practice, a political point that I will return to below. Since the 'floor' provides a way of meeting humanitarian concerns, donors should actually cease to give additional incentivizing aid if countries do go off track on the outcome criteria. The fact that donors are not trying to run countries themselves should help here.

It is important to remember that this additional aid would not be given to all countries (indeed it may be only a very few to begin with), but rather only to those that are demonstrably showing an interest in pursuing and achieving developmental outcomes. This of course raises the issues of monitoring and exogenous influences on outcomes.

Such a system would work best with accurate up-to-date information, so that the relationship between government management, outcomes and aid rewards is as close as possible. This is the only area that donors would have to micro-manage, in the sense that they would have to ensure that such data was available, rather than leaving it to government choice, However, to avoid suspicions of data-massaging by donors, data collection would have to be managed by a third party.

There is a well-known objection to outcome-based aid systems, ie that exogenous factors beyond the control of the government, such as a drought or a fall on commodity prices, may lead to lower growth through no fault of the government. Beyond a certain point, developmental states will seek to minimize their vulnerability to both natural and economic shocks, but in the early stages for African countries, it will be necessary to develop a visibly fair system for adjudicating cases. This again would have to involve a third party, but obviously one acceptable to donors.

Equally, aid programmes that have frequent interruptions of aid built into them are problematic, as they deter investors and growth. This means that an effective incentive system will have to have a fixed, known period of time between when it is judged that a country has gone off-track and when aid is ceased and the country reverts to the 'floor'. This could be quite long, say, two to three years, so that if the government can get back on track again it would be possible to manage the situation without an interruption. For investors, in any case, the credibility of political commitment is probably the key thing, which they will also have to make judgements on.

Finally, there is a trade-off involved here. On the one hand, there is a case for giving aid quite broadly across all African countries on humanitarian and aid effectiveness grounds, but skewed towards poorer ones. On the other hand, there is also a case for using aid as an incentive for political change. A key question is how to divide a total aid pot for Africa, say $50 billion a year, between the two, and therefore where the balance lies.

Any sensible development assistance programme for Africa can clearly not afford to ignore the debt problem. Debt relief should also be part of the system.

There are two broad reasons for giving debt relief. One is basically humanitarian, in that debt service in Africa is competing for government expenditure. If commercial creditworthiness is not a practical concern, then it doesn't make any sense for aid flows to a country to be returned in the form of debt service. The other rationale for debt relief is economic; that an excessive debt 'overhang' can put off potential investors in a country (Elbadawi et al 1997). However, Africa's chronic debt problems are closely related to its primary commodity dependence, and unless countries diversify their exports somewhat, a sustainable exit from debt will be elusive (see ch 3 above).

For countries which are showing no signs of a developmental state, there is thus a humanitarian case for freezing or at least cutting debt *service*, similarly to the way in which a debt service freeze has been arranged for disaster hit countries (for example for Central American countries after Hurricane Mitch in 1998, and Sri Lanka and Indonesia after the recent tsunami disaster).

Where there are signs that leaders can seriously overcome clientelism and put together a developmental project that includes diversification and attracting investment, then it becomes important to ensure a generous write-off of debt *stock*, so that investment and growth is not held back.

Ideally, although these measures of debt service freeze and debt stock write-off should be attached to a basic 'floor' aid package and an incentiv-ized aid mechanism respectively, the resources for such debt relief measures would be additional to aid budgets. However, whether this actually happens is down to political will and pressure from campaigners in creditor countries.

The politics of the aid agenda

There might appear to be some similarities between this idea and the US government's Millennium Challenge Account.[131] However, the underlying analysis and the type of criteria for allocation are very different. First, the MCA uses a much greater range of indicators, linked to multiple objectives, some of which (such as democracy) are only very weakly correlated with

economic development and poverty reduction at early stages of development processes. Second, the MCA indicators often use levels instead of rates
of change, which unfairly penalizes the poorest countries. Finally, there are
signs that the US administration is already bending its own rules (Lucas and
Radelet 2004).

The MCA, which includes all sorts of indicators of democracy and
human rights, is explicitly a political aid instrument. The incentive mechanism I am proposing is also political, in the sense that it is aimed at supporting
processes of change in African politics and states. However, while I believe
that sustained developmental success is only possible with such change, the
mechanism I am proposing specifies only developmental outcomes.

It may be thought controversial to propose a political role for aid, and a
liability to have a similar approach to the MCA. But it becomes less so if the
simple fact that aid will always have a political impact is recognized. Donors
are already politically involved, willingly or not. Indeed, my approach is
based on the observation that aid has been helping to support clientelist
regimes in Africa over a long period. Obviously the degree of political impact
will vary from place to place, depending on the form and amount of aid
given, as well as the political system. But even small amounts of aid can have
considerable political consequences.[132]

In the 1970s and 1980s, the recognition of the political aspect of aid
was widespread. Both superpowers fairly explicitly deployed aid to Africa as
part of Cold War politics. The left in the West supported explicitly political
solidarity movements. The end of the Cold War has in one sense been a good
thing, as it allowed development and poverty eradication to emerge as the
avowed ultimate goal of aid policy. However, the de-politicization of aid, the
decline of solidarity movements and the rise of NGOs have left all players
with a major blind spot.

No mention has been made so far of NEPAD and the Africa Union. At
the moment there is considerable hope being invested in NEPAD's Africa
Peer Review Mechanism (Commission for Africa 2005 ch 4). However, it
seems that this has been confined to a review of economic governance,[133]
rather than of political performance, which will fall under the AU, as it
did under the OAU (Olivier 2003 p 818). In the past, OAU leaders were
notoriously reluctant to condemn clientelist practices, repressive rule, spoils
politics and state failures amongst themselves. While the name and some of
the principal protagonists have changed, will the AU be any different?

The signs so far are that the domestic preoccupations and interests of
political leaders will continue to dominate over an attempt to produce a
systematic political transformation across the region. In 2004 and 2005, the
AU has acted decisively on Cote d'Ivoire and Togo, but not on Zimbabwe or
Darfur. This pattern suggests that leaders from other countries are not
troubled so much by repression or political violence as long as the ruling
regime in the country concerned is in control. Situations of more evenly
matched civil war (or its prospect in the case of Zimbabwe) are more

worrying to neighbours. The case of Togo also suggests that openly flouting the rules of the democratic game is now less acceptable, partly because it is now understood, post 1990s, that this particular form of politics is especially important to the international community.

Thus where the AU seems most useful, as was the OAU, is in intervening and mediating in conflicts that have arisen in the extremes of spoils politics regimes on the verge of collapse. Mbeki's forays into Cote d'Ivoire are a recent example. This is an important role, and is based on the fact that, while almost all African countries have a clientelist element to their politics, there is some variety in how they have managed it. Leaders from more centralized and bureaucratic states will be in a position to offer guidance to those where clientelist pressures have run out of control. Donors should think about supporting more intra-Africa technical or political assistance in this area. If all else fails, this process can, and has, facilitated an early exit for some of the worst offenders (eg Charles Taylor).[134]

I have proposed principles for an aid system for Africa that would need a number of changes from the current system. What it looks like in detail is less important that the principle underlying it: that if donors want to see a step change in development in Africa, then they have to become serious about creating incentives for regimes to embrace developmentalism. My argument is that although the current system is not as ineffective as some critics make out, its impact is so modest and incremental that it is drowned out by the deeper political dynamics. Only by making a concerted effort to tackle the latter will there be the prospect of rapid transformations in Sub-Saharan Africa.

However, using aid as an incentive system to support the emergence of developmental regimes may not very effective (although it will be more sensible than the current use of aid in Africa). This is because, since most African countries are now and will remain formal multi-party democracies, it is the people who can make regimes change (ie African populations, both as voters and as clients in patronage networks), but the message and the incentives of the aid mechanism are distant to most people in Africa. For such a system to really work politically, donors would have to signal both their analysis and their strategy very strongly to African voters and civil society. Currently donors do not really do this at all.

As noted in chapter 9 above, the appeal to adopt a developmental path needs to be made credible not only to leaders, but also to ordinary Africans, who have adapted to clientelist realities over the years. They have to be convinced that a new way of organizing politics will really bring benefits that will be greater than those they might hope to get under the present system. As Chabal (2002 p 461) argues, in the related context of explaining why the wave of democratization of the early 1990s did not trigger political transformation:

It is not just that authoritarian (or 'evil') elites have sought to block

reform demanded by 'enlightened' populations. It is, more significantly, that the essence of neo-patrimonialism is derived from the
socio-cultural milieu which both elites and populations share. The fact
that this system of government is . . . profoundly unfavourable to the
prospect of development and that, as a result, the economic situation
of most African countries continues to worsen is as yet insufficiently
compelling to challenge the very prevalence of the clientelistic 'logic'.
The present failings of most African states are not always interpreted
as by the populations – as so many outside observers automatically
assume – as evidence of the bankruptcy of patrimonialism and of the
desirability of 'democracy'.

In other words, you can't eat democracy (Chabal 2002 p 449), and
although you may not eat much under the present system, at least you can
expect something.

Changing this situation will be a huge job. Current approaches, which
do not really engage with the nature of clientelist networks, need to be re-
thought. It has now become part of the aid orthodoxy that transparency
and accountability of governments to the public (and perhaps especially the
poor) needs to be strengthened in Africa, and this is a task many NGOs,
with donor support, have now embarked on. But on Chabal's argument,
under clientelism greater accountability can mean greater demands on
patrons, greater competition for resources and increasing political instability
as patronage networks break down (Chabal 2002 p 454).

Therefore if it is to be done, it needs to be done properly. Work on
'accountability' especially has to be about changing its meaning, as well as
increasing it. Past reforms based on the technical 'governance' framework,
have often had an apolitical approach to understanding this issue, and have
run aground. The Commission for Africa report appears to revisit this same
terrain. Fiscal decentralization provides a good example. Moving both
expenditure and revenue collection decisions to the local level was supposed
to increase accountability because, it was argued, people would be nearer to
decision makers. However, it is clear that this has only rarely worked. Gloppen and Rakner (2002) report that tax reforms in East Africa have not
increased accountability, while Fjeldstad's review of decentralization and
corruption (2004 pp 11–12) finds problems across procurement, revenue
collection, financial management, human resource management, and land
allocation and control, concluding that: 'There are many cases of obvious
failure, but few cases of obvious success.' As argued above, the limits of
changing the form of government without addressing the underlying political culture – still based on the patronage and authoritarianism of the local
'big men', rather than on a fully embedded citizenship identity – shows how
hard it will be to build accountability through participation in Africa, most
especially rural Africa (see Golooba-Mutebi 2004 for the case of Uganda).

There is thus a huge job of basic civic education to be done. Progress can be made; for example, Nyamu-Musembi and Musyoki (2004) report on the way in which NGOs in Kenya are beginning to establish a more substantive discourse of rights in rural areas, and connecting accountability to the political context. However, much of this work is at present funded only in a patchy and short-term way. Most donor funding to civil society organizations goes to urban-based groups (Hearn and Robinson 2000), rather than to rural areas, where the political legacy has left the most acute need (see ch 6 above). Similar considerations apply to civil society (including Parliamentary) involvement in monitoring of budgets, expenditure tracking and PRSPs at the national level. Beyond the widely recognized problems of capacity (Lucas et al 2004, Hearn and Robinson 2000), there is the danger that the project of increasing accountability becomes undermined by patronage and political cooption. For example, Gould and Ojanen (2003 p 14) write of the dominance of the PRSP process in Tanzania by a small group of civil society organizations, privileged by donors 'who have made a survival strategy of adapting themselves to the rollercoaster ride of donor whims.' Rakner et al 2004 p 20 note the enthusiasm of MPs to pass budgets without much scrutiny in Malawi because they want to get funds to their home areas.

Overall, then, aligning accountability and transparency work in Africa to the goal outlined above would require not only a large increase in funding for this work, but also making the primary goal of the work a change in the meaning of accountability.

An agenda for trade

I have argued that the goal of policies amongst the international community towards Africa should be to support a move away from clientelist politics and neo-patrimonial states towards a developmental project. I have also argued that this change will principally come from within Africa, where it is political commitment that will be decisive in building supply side capacity on trade, increasing productivity and diversifying exports away from primary commodities. However, there are some supporting steps that the rest of the world could take, not only in the USA and EU, but also amongst the larger middle-income countries, India and China.

Some of these steps are already part of the established policy debate and NGOs are running campaigns on them. OECD countries can and should eliminate agricultural subsidies their own economies. This elimination should be complete rather than partial, for Africa to benefit (Achterbosch et al 2004). However, I have argued above in chapter 3 that the net benefits to African countries are likely, at best, to be quite small. Of course, the fact that OECD subsidy elimination will only produce a relatively small impact for Africa is not a reason for not undertaking it. However, given the need for African countries to retain policy space, this should not come at the cost of locking countries into a radical opening of their own markets, especially under the Agreement on Non-Agricultural Market Access.

WTO members should therefore agree to binding and generous special and differential treatment (S&DT) on these and other agreements in the Doha Development Round for LDCs (covering a majority of African countries). Equally, the proposed EU–ACP Economic Partnership Agreements under Cotonou should be strictly non-reciprocal (which will require a WTO waiver or an amendment to Article XXIV of the GATT), offering African non-LDCs duty free access to EU markets without requiring reciprocal arrangements. Of course, clientelist regimes with neo-patrimonial states will not make good use of such flexibility, but where political transformation does occur, developmental states will, especially if they are no longer constrained by liberalizing conditionality from aid donors, and if they gain an accurate picture of freedom of manoeuvre in the WTO.

Likewise, turning to preferential access schemes, it is important to distinguish the reasons why countries do not fully or even partly use these schemes. As discussed in chapter 3 above, this is partly because of supply side weakness largely linked to neo-patrimonial states, and here trade-related capacity building schemes by donors will not really work until there is political interest in them (see ch 5 above). However, there are other reasons why some schemes do not deliver as many benefits as they should. In the case of the EU's Everything But Arms scheme, part of the problem are restrictive rules of origin (Brenton 2003) and the use of SPS regulations as non-tariff barriers (Stevens and Kennan 2003 pp 4–5). In the case of the US's Africa Growth and Opportunity Act (AGOA), it is that not all countries have been given preferences in the most useful area of garments (Brenton and Ikezuki 2004). Indeed the USA should extend the range of products covered in the AGOA. This is fairly familiar territory, and action could and should be taken in these areas. There may be some trade diversion as a result, but as Stevens and Kennan (2004) argue in relation to rules of origin, it is better to err on the side of over-liberality.

On garments, however, it may now be too late, as the MFA has now ended, and exporters in Africa will have to compete for OCED markets, without quotas, against India and China. This raises the other point made in chapter 3 – that the rise of these countries, especially China, is now the greatest external problem that African exporters face. This is an early example of preference erosion, and while Africa may be able to negotiate compensation for loss of future preferences, it will receive none on textiles and garments. The loss of these preferences is a particular problem because, while EU–ACP preferences were largely on agricultural commodities, AGOA garment preferences were on one of the few areas in manufacturing where real preferences could be granted. African manufacturing is so small, and the value of stimulating it is so high that it would be worth considering positive discrimination for African manufacturing exports into EU, US and Japanese markets, possibly in the form of 'negative tariffs' (ie subsidies to African imports)[135] or, more radically, in the form of reverse VERs, ie 'voluntary import quotas' that would have to be administratively distributed. To avoid creating preference-dependence there would have to be a clear signal that these would phase out over time, but some sort of device such as this would be of great help to exporters in fledgling African developmental states.

Finally, emerging developing country 'superpowers', including China, Brazil and India should also consider giving Sub-Saharan African exports duty free access, offsetting their threat as competitors by the opportunities presented in their growing markets. Within Africa, the regional giant of South Africa should also consider non-reciprocal preferential access for its neighbours across the continent.

An agenda for coherence

Finally, there are a number of other ways in which the policies of the international community need to be aligned to the goal of supporting the transformation of African politics away from clientelism. This agenda is fundamentally about constraining the ability of spoils politicians to operate internationally, thus raising the costs of such politics in Africa (and indeed anywhere else). Again, leading OECD countries have taken this agenda on in recent years, but there is still a significant gap between rhetoric and implementation. Most of these issues require a wide international consensus, and so the G8 could help create change. However, to be effective, these measures need to be applied consistently. US client dictators (eg Karimov in Uzbekistan) should not be exempted, as this will undermine the enforceability of these measures with respect to Africa.

Over the years, elite figures from spoils politics regimes have been able to operate easily at the international level, moving state resources to personal offshore accounts through the international banking system, buying property in Europe and the US, forming cosy relationships with transnational corporations, especially in oil and mining, and obtaining arms for purposes of internal repression. Chabal and Daloz (1999 p 135) talk of informalization and the 'instrumentalization of disorder' at the international level, with regimes becoming involved in international criminal activities.[136] We are all familiar with Mobutu's villas in France, Moi's vast personal fortune largely held abroad and the Abacha family's exporting of billions of dollars of Nigeria's oil revenue to accounts in London and Switzerland. Recent estimates are that African assets equivalent to half the continent's external debt are held in foreign bank accounts (Commission for Africa 2005 p 151).

The ability to operate freely in this matter helps elites, making their economic (and therefore political) positions more stable, as they can diversify their portfolios and protect their resources against currency risk. Bribes from transnational corporations are a direct source of resources for clientelism. And of course, shopping and holidaying across the world is a key element of the conspicuous consumption that leaders and elites are partially motivated by. All of these mean that there is no incentive for elites to make their own states and economies function better.

Action on money laundering and banking secrecy has been spurred on by the 'War on Terror', and a standard for records and disclosure by the banking industry (including offshore centres) has now been devised by the Financial Action Task Force. This includes due diligence on 'politically exposed persons' (basically people who hold public office). A shrinking list of countries is judged to be 'non-compliant'. This is, on paper at least, an improvement on the situation in the late 1990s when the Abacha family laundered an estimated $4 billion through banks abroad, including $219 million in the City of London, at a time when EU sanctions were in place. However, it is worth noting that disclosure was supposed to have been made at that time as well, but was not, and no clear sanctions have been brought against the offending banks. Global Witness also points to the case of accounts held by President Obiang of Equatorial Guinea in a Washington DC bank as recently as 2003 (Global Witness 2004 pp 55–57). The G8 needs to show leadership on this issue by ensuring that the FATF standard is adhered to and that sanctions are actually applied. Some countries, including the UK,[137] have also been slow to bring into force action on asset recovery and repatriation, whereby new governments can recover wealth stolen by former regimes.

Spoils politics and conflict in Africa is especially associated with oil and mineral exporting countries. This makes efforts to increase transparency and accountability in these industries particularly important. However, movement is very slow. The main tool for tackling corruption by transnational corporations is the 1999 OECD Convention Against Bribery, but its conversion into legislation and enforcement is patchy. The All Party Parliamentary Group on trade and industry has recently criticized the DTI for failing to allocate sufficient resources to investigate allegations by the UN that British companies breached OECD guidelines on prolonging conflict.[138]

Meanwhile the voluntary Extractive Industries Transparency Initiative, announced at Evian in 2003 has recently gained support from the USA but has been criticized as under-resourced, erratic and slow-moving (Global Witness 2004 pp 80–81). The Kimberley Process, a more advanced voluntary scheme for diamonds, aimed mainly at preventing the trade fuelling civil wars, has also had credibility problems, due to an absence of independent monitoring. Critics are now calling for schemes that have a mandatory element, such as Publish What You Pay. Given the temptation of governments and companies to simply do what looks good, rather than really tackling the problems, and also the lack of incentives to comply, mandatory schemes make sense.

Slow progress is a familiar story in another area – control of small arms. And again, while an international agreement on action was reached in 2001, and laws are now on the statute books, control regimes in some countries remain weak or non-existent, and there is no joined up control across agencies.[139]

In many cases, it is not only difficult for potential developmental leaders to build a political movement, it is positively dangerous to do so. They may well need to do so initially from a position of exile (as indeed Museveni did in the 1970s and early 1980s in Tanzania and Mozambique). In these circumstances it is highly counter-productive for Western countries – especially European countries – to operate restrictive asylum policies based on out-of-date political analysis and a lack of information.

A final issue is that of sanctions. The EU and other OECD countries have developed 'smart' sanctions against named individuals in an elite, meaning that they cannot travel to and operate in many developed countries. These are a great improvement over broad trade sanctions, and also directly hit the enjoyment of conspicuous consumption by those leaders targeted (typically those in countries where repression has emerged most strongly alongside patronage). However, as recent shopping trips by Grace Mugabe to Malaysia show,[140] there are now attractive global destinations outside the OECD. Equally, Zimbabwe is Africa's biggest market for Mercedes cars after South Africa.[141] Here G8 leaders need to show that they have sufficient diplomatic skills to persuade other countries to extend a global reach to smart sanctions.

I have outlined a basic policy agenda that arises from the goal of supporting a process of political transformation in Africa, in turn derived from an analysis that emphasizes the centrality of politics and the state. Of course, some points will have been missed, and some ideas here may be unworkable. My aim is really to stimulate debate about policies that address what I see as a central concern, but one that has remained very much obscured.

At the same time, this is in some ways a radical and idealistic agenda, in the sense that it is difficult to see the international community signing up to it quickly and enthusiastically. All sorts of institutional and political barriers to it exist.

It is therefore important to consider briefly the first steps along the road towards such a policy vision, and in particular, key steps the UK government and UK NGOs would have to take to develop such an agenda

An agenda for the UK government

It is clear that the UK government has some considerable influence when it comes to policy on Africa. The UK is a significant voice in the EU, in the multilateral institutions[142] and within the G8. Of course, 2005 is also the year that it holds the Presidencies of the G8 and the EU, so there are opportunities for raising the issue of Africa (although it is less clear that there is a lot of room for agenda setting, especially in relation to the EU Presidency). The UK has also led on the creation of the Commission for Africa. However, what the UK government does with its 2005 opportunities depends on what kind of analysis it has, and where it stands in relation to the policy agendas.

In parts of the UK government there are signs that elements of the analysis presented above are accepted. For example, thinking with DfID has developed to the point that the 'Drivers of Change' studies were commissioned, although it is not clear how they will be used. Equally, the Commission for Africa, with policy and research being directed from the Treasury has governance issues high up on its agenda.

However, it is not clear that the implications of a more political analysis for policy have been thought through. Most of the emphasis is being put on the Africa Peer Review Mechanisms. At the same time, the big aid and trade ideas still appear to be increasing aid and debt relief through the IFF, and cutting OECD agricultural subsidies in the Doha Development Round.

The government is still a long way off the agenda outlined here. Probably the most difficult ideas to accept will be on aid. The UK is one of the leading thinkers amongst donors on problems with conditionality and the inefficiencies and ineffectiveness of aid micro-management. It has untied aid, sought new thinking on technical assistance, and committed to the Rome Agenda on harmonization, for example. But the UK position on conditionality remains ambiguous: despite a position paper that acknowledges its lack of effectiveness, elements of conditionality still will guide aid disbursements and allocation. A more radical move away from conditionality and a stricter adherence to simple allocation rules still seems to be a step too far.

On the trade agenda, the government has now stated that it will not take a universally liberalizing approach, and is re-prioritizing non-reciprocity in the EU–ACP Economic Partnership Agreements negotiations. Whether it would go further, to the point of embracing 'negative tariffs' for African imports into the EU, is unclear. Here, there is the familiar issue of how the UK can be a more effective voice on trade policy within the EU. With the arrival of Peter Mandelson as trade commissioner, there is a special relationship. However, early signs are that Mandelson will prove to be, if anything, even more of an aggressive liberalizer in relation to developing countries than Lamy was.

On asylum policy, there is plenty of anecdotal evidence that asylum decisions made by the UK government suffer from the defects of out-of-date information mentioned above, and as a result, potential opponents of spoils politics regimes are being deported to face torture or murder. The political intelligence aspect of the asylum system needs an urgent overhaul, and is an area where, in the UK, DfID, FCO and the Home Office should be working together.

On the other areas discussed, including money laundering and TNC corruption, UK government thinking is largely in the right direction; it is more the lack of action that is the problem. For example, on asset recovery, legislation that would require action now exists in the form of the 2002

Proceeds of Crime Act, but the Home Office has been slow to bring into force the international part of the Act. On overseas bribery and corruption, the UK is again particularly vulnerable, and if it wishes to lead progress on overseas bribery it needs to make enforcement more convincing.[143]

This last point can be made more widely. Almost all the changes proposed here rely on concerted international action: all donors acting together on an aid incentive structure; WTO members agreeing to appropriate deals for LDCs; the EU member states agreeing to negative tariffs for African imports; action on banking secrecy, sanctions and the arms trade. One of the biggest problems about Africa is that the international community has rarely been able to agree on a single approach, especially on aid. This is reflected in the debates about how hard it is to get donor coordination and harmonization.

A major factor is that in most donor governments, aid ministries and agencies are weak relative to other foreign policy, commercial or broader geo-political interests and ideologies within governments, even in relation to Africa. If donor agencies had to agree only with each other, coordination might be possible. But the policies of each donor agency are being driven by larger political forces. Within Africa this a particularly important problem, since the two largest bilaterals are the US and France (Table 10.1), each of which have their own strong ideas about what to do that do not always coincide with those of others, including the UK. For example, the rise of a neo-conservative agenda in the US is now strongly reflected in a belief in the use of aid to promote a particular model of democracy and economic rules, rather than development.

At the same time, unless all major donors line up behind some form of incentive mechanism for the support of developmental politics, it simply will not happen. As noted, the UK does have influence, and some power, on the international stage. However, it will need all the analysis and credibility it can muster to move others, especially the USA. It therefore urgently needs to set its own house in order.

Table 10.1   Major donors to Sub-Saharan Africa in 2003 ($ million)

All donors	23,749
Multilateral	6,439
US	4,642
France	2,974
Germany	1,894
UK	1,446
Japan	529

Source: OECD [online] www.oecd.org/dac/stats/idsonline

An agenda for campaigning NGOs

Much of the pressure to do so will only come from NGOs. Across Europe and the USA, NGOs represent the progressive end of the development debate. As long as progressive NGOs fail to develop a good analysis of politics and the state in Africa, the agenda will be set by right-wing analysts, who have largely made the topic their own. Indeed, the danger is that simply raising issues of African politics, governance and states in the UK NGO context comes to be seen as reactionary.

Most UK development NGOs[144] would share elements of the analysis in this book. For example, the importance of policy space has become a major theme. Equally, while none appear to follow the particular political analysis developed here, it is widely argued that African governments are often unaccountable, in the conventional sense, to the poor, and that this issue needs to be addressed, somehow, in order to make aid more effective. However, in practice much of the campaigning effort under Make Poverty History is going into cutting agricultural subsidies in the rich world and doubling aid. The push for 'better' aid is really about a removal of economic policy conditionality.

While these are OK as far as they go, what NGOs essentially lack is a framework for putting all of these elements together which would also give them some of them missing pieces. The current (largely implicit) model that most NGOs seem to use concentrates on the policy constraints put on developing country governments by international institutions such as the WTO, World Bank and the IMF, in a globalized world with highly unequal players (Western transnational corporations vs workers and small farmers). But the impact of globalization is different in different countries, dependent on domestic institutions. For countries where states are basically pursuing a capitalist developmental path, seeking accumulation through productive investment, broad-based growth through education plus employment through labour-intensive manufacturing and services, and an investment in welfare, these constraints are very real and serious. For a number of developing countries with a socialized capitalism, including large parts of East and South-east Asia, and to some extent India and Brazil too, this focus is appropriate. However, African states are not developmental, and their economies do not have an established capitalist dynamic.

To put it another way, a just world order is a desirable thing in itself, and worth campaigning for. However, it will help people in Africa a lot less than those in other parts of the developing world, because of the natures of the states they are ruled by. Equally, a fairer global order will not, in itself, help change the politics that are a major factor in African poverty. Political change will come from within Africa, but the rich world could support that process. However, this support will have to be of a specific type. A different frame of understanding is needed, such as the one I have presented here, one that produces a different kind of policy and campaigning focus.

Obviously, NGOs in the UK can only campaign on what can be changed from the Northern end, and they may feel fairly far removed from African politics. Indeed, I have argued that the key political changes will be made from within, and only a supporting role can be played by outsiders. However, this role is still worth playing. At the same time, if NGOs don't adopt an analysis that engages with politics in Africa, they run the risk of campaigning for change that will not help, or even make things worse. For example, campaigning for a doubling of aid or debt relief without a clear strategy for how to deliver that aid with incentives for political change might bring some small economic benefits, but it will also prolong a highly damaging political trap.

Campaigning for more aid and debt relief will continue to be necessary, since some donor and creditor governments remain reluctant to countenance this. However, as noted, there is little point in more aid without a suitable system in which to deliver it, and a simple call for an end to economic conditionality is not enough. The call must be for some kind of system that supports political change along the lines outlined above, and this call must be given prominence.

Campaigning for cutting OECD agricultural subsidies is not a priority for Africa, whereas campaigns on the Economic Partnership Agreements, rules of origin in the Everything But Arms agreement and negative tariffs for African manufactured exports to the EU would be. (It is also the case that a campaign in the UK on subsidies of questionable value since the UK government already wants to eliminate them. This is a campaign for France and Italy. This point has wider relevance. Certainly on aid, any effective system will require concerted action by the major donors to Africa, which are mostly in other countries than the UK.)[145]

Campaigning for policy space for African governments is still worthwhile, for example in the form of a generous and binding Special and Differential Treatment under WTO agreements, or in opposition to economic policy conditionality from the IFIs. However, it will always be more difficult to campaign on this issue credibly and effectively without the kind of framework adopted here.

UK NGOs should also put a lot more campaigning effort into the issues of corporate corruption and money laundering. More resources should be put into the Publish What You Pay campaign and campaigning against the trade in small arms.

As long as the Northern, campaigning parts of UK NGOs work with an incomplete framework of analysis, there will be tensions with partners and offices in Africa. For example, under the Jubilee campaign, Northern NGOs pushed for debt relief to be delivered as quickly as possible. However, in 2001 Mozambican civil society organizations lobbied sympathetic donors to delay HIPC debt relief because of concerns about corruption (Hanlon 2004 p 10). In fact, for most organizations, much good political knowledge and analysis is to be found within their Southern offices and partner organizations, and within the programme parts of their organizations. What is needed is for Northern organizations to recognize the significance of such knowledge, and integrate the analysis properly into their campaigning messages. Some have tried to do this to some extent, and much more should be done.

Inasmuch as the African parts of international organizations are involved in attempts to increase accountability within Africa through advocacy and other means, there is scope for some fruitful dialogue and reflection on what this means in an African context, how these efforts might be supported by international campaigning, and indeed how concepts of accountability in Africa can be transformed, as discussed above. Northern offices should try to replace the tension that is often present with a genuine, evidence-based solidarity.

This will also be useful when communicating with supporters and the general public in the UK. This public may have an exaggerated and distorted view of corruption in Africa, and may not understand the causes, but their concerns are sufficiently rooted in a reality to create problems for campaigning NGOs who do not have credible answers, for example to the question of how aid money can be guaranteed to reach the poor. This was a perennial issue in media debates during the Jubilee debt campaign, and will definitely be re-appearing in 2005 as NGOs push for a doubling of aid. NGOs, like donors, have become hostages to sovereignty, in the sense that their campaigns have become too reliant on the notion of solidarity with governments, rather solidarity with people or political movements.[146] Although a brief allusion to building accountability is now almost always included in campaign documents, these are often not totally convincing to the supporting public. A proper analysis, and tying campaigning messages to that analysis, are the only ways to build a different type of solidarity that goes beyond sovereignty. I am not saying this lightly, since I know from personal experience how hard it is to bring supporters and the public along a path of understanding complex issues. However, unlike understanding the IMF or the WTO, this issue is not that technical, just a lot more political.

In a recent speech in Edinburgh, the Chancellor of the Exchequer Gordon Brown spoke of the 'enormous power of human compassion to build anew'.[147] He is right. But real compassion needs understanding as well as emotion, and is built on solidarity as well as charity. We need to give the people of African the support they actually need, not what we think they need, or what makes us feel good.

Endnotes

1 See World Development Movement (2004a) pp 11–15. After the emergence of crisis in the 1970s, early assessments and action plans included the influential 1981 'Berg report' from the World Bank proposing agricultural liberalization, and the 1980 Lagos Plan of Action from the pre-cursor of the African Union (AU), the OAU. The 1980s saw the establishment of the multi-donor Special Programme for Africa (SPA), and by the end of the decade the Bank published another big-picture report, entitled (sadly ironically with hindsight) *Sub-Saharan Africa: From Crisis to Sustainable Growth*. In the same year the UN Economic Commission for Africa responded by launching the African Alternative Framework to Structural Adjustment Programmes (AAF-SAP). By the mid-1990s the World Bank and IMF launched the HIPC debt relief initiative, which was mainly focused on African countries, while in 2000 the US government created the African Growth and Opportunity Act (AGOA) with the avowed aim of increasing African exports. In 1996 the UN system launched a Special Initiative for Africa. Reports from the World Bank, UNCTAD and UNECA continue to appear, including *Can Africa Claim the 21st Century*. In 2002, the leaders of Senegal, South Africa and Uganda proposed a New Economic Partnership for Development (NEPAD), which has quickly gained a permanent secretariat in the AU. The G8 responded in 2003 with an 'Africa Action Plan'.

2 See for example Amaoko (2004).

3 Although I do take education into account as an important potential factor in raising productivity.

4 In the 1970s and 1980s there was a large literature on whether capitalism had become established in Africa, and if so, what form it took. All I am asserting here is that capitalist accumulation (as distinct from marketing activity) in Africa is extremely weak, especially in agriculture and manufacturing. The only sectors where it is evident on any scale are oil and mining, where it is dominated not by domestic companies but by MNCs. South Africa is a special case, where capitalist accumulation has developed much further, but the socialization of part of the surplus accrued almost entirely to the small, white proportion of the population up until the mid-1990s.

5 The two small countries of Botswana and Mauritius are the only exceptions.

6 This is true more generally of mineral and non-mineral exporting LDCs – see UNCTAD (2002a p 124).

7 The Gini coefficient is a measure of inequality, ranging in theory between 0 and 100. The higher the figure, the more acute is inequality. Most OECD countries have a Gini coefficient in the range 25–35.

8 Sachs and Warner showed a negative relationship between abundance of natural resources in a country and the rate of economic growth. There is now a considerable literature on the issue, with the quality of institutions being an important factor.

9 ie Trade in goods. Merchandise trade does not include trade in 'invisibles', such as services, where tourism is a particularly important foreign exchange earner for Africa.

10 For non-LDC oil exporters such as Nigeria and Gabon oil and related products make up more than 90 per cent of exports.

11 Notably cotton prices for Burkina Faso and coffee prices for Ethiopia. See IMF HIPC completion documents for details and [online] www.jubileeresearch.org [accessed 15 April 2005] for analysis of these cases.

12 [online]   http://www.oecd.org/document/11/0,2340,en_2649_34447_ 2002187_1_1_1_1,00.html [accessed 15 April 2005].

13 OECD International Development Statistics On-line http://www.oecd. org/dataoecd/50/17/5037721.htm [accessed 15 April 2005].

14 Richard Dowden *The Observer*, 9 January 2005.

15 [online]   http://www.oecd.org/document/11/0,2340,en_2649_34447_ 2002187_1_1_1_1,00.html [accessed 15 April 2005].

16 Even in South Asia, again initially much poorer than Africa, per capita incomes now exceed those in Africa.

17 See also sources at [online] http://www.odi.org.uk/hpg/aidsresources. html#food [accessed 15 April 2005].

18 See the resources at [online] http://www.odi.org.uk/hpg/aidsresources. html#variant [accessed 15 April 2005].

19 World Development Indicators (2003), gross national income at purchasing power parity. Comparison of GNI using exchange rates makes Sub-Saharan Africa's economy smaller than Holland's.

20 [online] http://www.lfc.co.uk/business_briefings/bb_999.pdf [accessed 7 October 2004].

21 Here I use the phrase 'agricultural subsidies' to mean support in the broadest sense, incorporating both direct support and export subsidies.

22 eg Actionaid (2002), Oxfam (2002a ch 4, 2002b) Christian Aid and CAFOD (2000 p 47), CAFOD (2004).

23 eg HM Treasury and DTI (2004 pp 49, 53), DfID (2000 p 70), DTI (2004 pp 87–91).

24 [online] http://www.kenyalink.org/sucam/ [accessed 15 April 2005].

25 'Forget Maxwell House, would you like a cup of Kenco Sustainable?', *The Guardian*, 22 November 2004. The fair trade guaranteed price in

2004 was $1.21 per pound of green beans, a premium of 65 cents per pound, or a little under double the price. Cooperative supermarkets are selling own brand products with full fair trade certification from the Fair Trade Foundation.

26 Robin Murray, Twin Trading, personal communication.

27 It is possible that apparent recent US interest in reviving the coffee agreement is to make coffee growing more competitive with coca growing in Colombia.

28 Again, the experience of the fair–trade chocolate brand *Divine* is instructive. Launched in 1998, and giving cocoa producers a share in the retailing company, it is now beginning to carve out a small market in the UK, with sales expected to rise to £5.7 million in 2004. However, this has been a long hard struggle. Niche marketing has been key, as *Divine* is one of the few fairly traded chocolates on the market. In the early years there were losses, which were underwritten by sympathetic NGOs (including Christian Aid) and foundations. There have also been difficulties in getting credit at reasonable rates (personal communication, Robin Murray, Twin Trading).

29 Even the USA has been a major producer and export of commodities, and has pursued a growth strategy in part based in increasing productivity in this area. However, as with other successful countries, this was only ever *part* of its strategy, which included manufacturing and services.

30 To be fair to Oxfam, they do also recommend export diversification.

31 See also similar arguments by the FAO at [online] http://www.fao.org/docrep/005/y4852e/y4852e02.htm [accessed 15 April 2005].

32 The MFN system of tariffs and quotas is the most basic system of trade protection a country applies to imports. It offers equal treatment to all countries covered at the rate offered to the 'most favoured nation'. Thus if the US offers duty free access on a product within the MFN system to say, Australia, and Chile is MFN-eligible, then the US will also have to offer Chile duty free access on that product. The GSP was a system introduced in the 1970s that offers developing countries lower tariffs to developed country markets than were available within the latter group.

33 At the beginning of 2005, China voluntarily put a tax on its own exports of garments, so as to head off a protectionist response from the USA. It is unclear whether this will be enough to allow African exporters to maintain some competitive edge.

34 Most famously in Japan's MITI (Johnson 1982).

35 As discussed below, this does not mean that corruption was absent from these countries, but it did mean that the corruption did not distort policies and create inefficiencies that disrupted the growth strategy significantly (Khan 1996, 2002).

36 In some cases governments turned a blind eye to patent laws, a pattern echoed more recently in India's successful development of its pharmaceutical industry.

37 A good example would be the Pohang steel mill in Korea, a SOE established by the government using Japanese aid in 1973, designed to provide cheap steel to stimulate the formation of downstream industries. It quickly emerged as a global producer (Kim 1995 p 92).

38 OECD International Development Statistics On-line http://www.oecd.org/dataoecd/50/17/5037721.htm

39 [online] http://countrystudies.us/south-korea/56.htm [accessed 15 April 2005].

40 See Wade (1996) and Amsden (1994) on the World Bank's attempts to re-frame the East Asian story as a success for free market policies.

41 Malawi and Cote d'Ivoire have been claimed as states supporting rather than taxing agriculture.

42 ie Government corporations.

43 See also Lall (2002).

44 See Datta-Chaudhuri (1990) for a review of both concepts.

45 Melamed (2002 p 5–6) is one of the few NGO analysts to explore this explicitly. However, the subsequent policy recommendations solely relate to the importance of maintaining policy space.

46 Common arguments about Africa are that is has more malaria, lower population densities, inherited poorer infrastructure and human capital at independence, etc.

47 Here I take a broad definition of aid, to include both grants and the grant element of concessional loans, and to include both bilateral and multilateral donors.

48 Data from the US Government Energy Information Administration [online] http://www.eia.doe.gov/emeu/cabs/orevcoun.html [accessed 15 April 2005].

49 There has been a subsequent debate about whether there is a non-linearity in the aid-growth relationship, suggesting that there is a threshold above which aid has no effect, or a negative one. However, Gonamee et al (2003) argue that this is due to poor specification.

50 These findings also suggest that aid plays an important part particularly in African economies with small populations. Because official aid is government-to-government, its allocation has developed a 'sovereignty' bias (van de Walle 2001 p 199) which still applies. It can be seen from Table 2.7 that of the top ten aid recipients ranked by proportion of aid-to-GDP, only three had populations over 10 million people and only one (Ethiopia) over 20 million.

51 This is seen more generally in the significance of the Africa 'dummy' variable in growth equations (Collier and Gunning 1999a).

52 [online] http://www.makepovertyhistory.org/aim3.html [accessed 15 April 2005].

53 See White (1996) for a useful review. The challenge of the counter-factual has remained the biggest barrier to systematic assessments.

54 This was a major focus for the NGO-WB Working Group, for example.

55 It features heavily in the DfID 1997 White Paper, for example.

56 See Wood and Lockwood (1999) and Wood (2004) for rare exceptions.

57 Van de Walle (2001 p 71–72) gives examples from Gabon, Niger, Congo, Guinea-Bissau and Nigeria.

58 In more technical terms, constraining government failures through liberalization may bring short-term benefits for parts of the economy, moving the economy towards static allocative efficiency on the 'production possibility frontier', but it will not allow the intervention to address market failures and produce dynamic effects that underlie a higher investment and growth path, actually shifting the frontier back.

59 Mosley et al (2003) present evidence that, along with political stability, other factors also affect compliance with conditionality, including economic performance during the adjustment period, initial macroeconomic conditions and the level of adjustment funding. Although their sample size is small, their model predicts well. Some of their underlying explanatory variables, including implementation capacity and a favourable economic environment during the adjustment period could well be the outcome of political factors underlying state capacity and economic management. Nevertheless, this study suggests that there are things that donors could do in terms of the design and application of conditionality that would improve compliance. However, the basic point about the need to recognize recipient country governments as political actors remains.

60 See Wood and Lockwood (1999) for a review of these.

61 This issue in respect of the World Bank was the subject of the Wapenhans Report of 1992.

62 This is one reason why donors have recently become more interested in 'soft' conditionality in the form of 'technical assistance'.

63 When I worked with the Zimbabwean Council of Churches on spending priorities in the budget in 1997, one of the most striking issues was the way in which initial budget plans were completely changed by a supplementary budget submitted by the President that circumvented the normal budgetary procedures, and took precedence.

64 I witnessed this at a workshop on aid in Kenya in 2002, for example.

65 In one of those curious historical resonances, the current positions have echoes of the debates of the 1970s between dependency theorists such as Gunder Frank and Dos Santos, and neo-Marxists such as Robert Brenner. In the view of the neo-Marxists, dependency theory made an error in viewing capitalism as a system of 'world exchange', since this overemphasized the relationships between the industrialized economies of North America and Europe ('centre') and the countries of the South ('periphery') at the expense of analysis of the relationship between classes *within* the periphery, and trade at the expense of production. Although the language and framework is very different, I am arguing that many NGO positions today have elements of dependency theory

in them. NGO campaigning discourse, established in the late 1980s and early 1990s, was perhaps developed by people who had studied dependency theory.

66 Cited in Lieven (2004 p 84).

67 Cited in [online] http://www.commissionforafrica.org/economy/ trends_and_evidence.pdf [accessed 11 November 2004].

68 Zimbabwe in the late 1990s or Kenya in Moi's last years are good examples of where an independent press reported widely and frequently on high-level corruption cases on which no action was taken.

69 It might be argued that the democratization wave of the early 1990s is a major exception. However, van de Walle (2001 pp 239–41) shows that this wave was driven more by the collapse of the Soviet one-party model, and by internal crises of economics and legitimacy and ensuing protest than by donor pressure. Democratization happened fastest in countries like Benin and CAR where patronage politics had gone deepest and where the crisis was most acute.

70 Killick and White were writing a publication for the World Bank, Wood is currently DfID's chief economist, Collier was Head of Research at the World Bank until late 2003. See also UNCTAD (2002a) for a similar argument made for LDCs. Sachs et al (2004) unusually make the argument that governance is not really a problem for many African countries, on the grounds that they are no worse on governance scores than low income countries in general. However, since African countries predominate amongst low income countries, this comes close to saying that governance in African countries is no worse than the African average! Countries that they consider as having 'good' governance include Malawi and Ghana, countries with severe problems in budget processes and with corruption (eg Rakner et al 2004, Booth et al 2004), while CAR and Mozambique are described as 'average', even though the former had a coup in 2003 and has a scarcely functioning state and the latter is seen by close observers as having a 'gangster state' (see below). This is generally not a convincing argument.

71 Especially transport links, as African countries are large, often landlocked, with small and poorly integrated colonial transport networks largely unchanged since independence, meaning that transport costs for Africa are much higher than elsewhere in the developing world (Wood 2002 pp 28–29, Sachs 2004).

72 The UK government is also supporting spending on trade related infrastructure, to the tune of about £600 million a year: [online] http:// www.dfid.gov.uk/pubs/files/trcbhandout.pdf [accessed 15 April 2005].

73 A broad observation about TRCB programmes is that in a general sense, they seem to have a weak impact on overall trade performance in Africa. For example, Kenya has had 10 TRCB/TRTA programmes running over the past few years supported by a whole range of donors (Blouin and Njoroge 2004 pp 9–12), but its trade performance has been

poor over that period. Malawi has had an astonishing 97 TRCB initiatives in the period 2001–03 without clear effect (Weston and Tsoka 2004 p 9). A much wider set of flanking factors – including the state of infrastructure and the education and health of workers – are therefore obviously still decisive in determining supply side capacity. These factors of course require competent governance.

74 Personal communication, Laura Kelly, Africa Policy Department, DfID.

75 Daniel Kaufmann, quoted in 'Tunnel vision on corruption' Moses Naim, *Washington Post* 21 February 2005.

76 See Ranger (1996) for the classic statement on the invention of tribe in Africa.

77 In the case of Portuguese colonies, a tiny number of 'assimilated' Africans were effectively allowed to enter civil rule.

78 See van de Walle (2001 p 51) for a list of sources on clientelism in Africa.

79 See van de Walle (2001 p 50).

80 These were common in the immediate post-Independence period. A stark contemporary example that I witnessed was the use of state funds by Mugabe in Zimbabwe (including almost certainly an IMF stand-by loan in 1999), to pay gangs of youths to intimidate and murder opposition politicians. Mugabe has also used funds from diamonds obtained through incursions in the DRC, and more latterly has sought to extract tax from international NGOs for the same purposes. Moi in Kenya followed similar if less extreme strategies in the early 1990s before elections.

81 The UK has 17 departments represented in the cabinet, even though its national economy is larger than that of all African countries combined.

82 For example, in the first five years of Independence civil service employment expanded by 50 per cent in Nigeria, and 250 per cent in Senegal.

83 It would also be true to say that Rawlings in Ghana and Museveni in Uganda instituted similar reforms after coming to power in the 1980s.

84 Allen (1995) also argues that Mobutu in Zaire made similar moves to centralize power and limit clientelism, but after 4 years abandoned this approach, making an abrupt turn to spoils politics.

85 'DTI failing to act on Africa's "dirtiest war" ', *Observer*, 6 February 2005.

86 By 'particularistic' I mean a relationship with an individual based on some connection of family, kin, ethnic group, possibly regional group, in contrast to a relationship with a group based on functional or class interests.

87 Much of this account is based on Coulson 1982.

88 Personal communication, Mary Myers.

89 In Ghana on the eve of regime change at the end of the 1970s, chaos and extreme rent-seeking had emptied the coffers of the central state.

The risk of collapse of the central state and the emergence of anarchy was very real. Following the 1981 coup, the Rawlings administration made addressing this situation a priority, making revenue collection their number one aim both in terms of the aims of macro-economic policy reforms, and in energetic tax raids (Hutchful 1995 pp 308–09). Museveni took similar steps to re-establish revenue functions after winning the war against Obote in 1986.

90 See below chapter 8 for the case of Ghana. A 2001 Actionaid education project in Kenya found significant 'leakage' of education funds at the regional level. In Uganda, World Bank studies in the mid-1990s of leakage in education funds led to quite successful attempts by the Museveni government to improve the situation.

91 The Commission for Africa (2005 p 297) argues that tax revenue is higher in Africa than in many other developing regions. Because of fiscal federalism in India and China, their figures for Asia are biased downwards. But more importantly, the average African figure of 19.4 per cent tax/GDP for 1994–98 masks large variation, typically between high ratio countries that have natural resource exports such as Botswana and Angola (35–40 per cent tax/GDP ratios) and much poorer countries, usually without extractive resources exports (10–14 per cent). Countries such as CAR, Chad and Sierra Leone had revenue ratios of below 8 per cent in the mid-1990s (van de Walle 2001 p 74).

92 Nigerian legislators notoriously demanded a US $3,500 furniture allowance in 1999, contrasting with an average civil service salary at that time of around $200.

93 See also Rodrik (1991) for a general analysis of policy uncertainty and investment.

94 Hutchful (1995) provides a good account of the instrumentalization of reform up to the mid-1990s Ghana.

95 Ie they are on the upwardly sloping part of the Laffer curve.

96 However, as seen in chapter 2, it does not follow that it is impossible for very poor countries to have effective states. Korea and Taiwan in the late 1940s were very poor countries. Vietnam is a more contemporary example.

97 However, Siggel and Ssemogerere (2001) argue that Ugandan industries have been discouraged from exporting by appreciation of the Ugandan shilling, driven by resource inflows from aid and capital flight reversal.

98 Recent information on the economy from OECD African Economic Outlook 2003/04 Uganda country study [online] http://www.oecd.org/dataoecd/45/40/32411656.pdf [accessed 15 April 2005].

99 However, this latter measure is now being phased out to harmonize with investment policy in the new East African Community.

100 'In come the vigilantes', *Africa Confidential* 44, 19 (26 September 2003).

101 'Model reformer stumbles', *Africa Confidential* 44, 19 (26 September 2003).

102 All cabinet information from [online] http://www.cia.gov/cia/ publications/chiefs [accessed 15 April 2005].

103 'Foreign aid sabotages reform', Andrew Mwenda, *International Herald Tribune* 8 March 2005.

104 Tangri and Mwenda (2003).

105 'Model reformer stumbles', *Africa Confidential* 44, 19 (26 September 2003).

106 Economic data from [online] http://www.oecd.org/dataoecd/24/28/ 32429910.pdf [accessed 15 April 2005].

107 This may reflect the ease of taxing Ghana's sizable gold industry.

108 [online] http://www.newsinghana.com/economy/stunning-revelation. htm [accessed 15 April 2005].

109 Booth et al (2004)

110 [online] http://www.cia.gov/cia/publications/chiefs/chiefs69.html [accessed 19 November 2004].

111 [online] http://www.cia.gov/cia/publications/chiefs/chiefs175.html [accessed 21 November 2004].

112 CCM was formed out of TANU following Tanganyika's union with Zanzibar.

113 Economic data from [online] http://www.oecd.org/dataoecd/45/38/ 32411720.pdf [accessed 15 April 2005].

114 See also the World Bank/IMF 2003 assessment of the PRSP [online] http://www.imf.org/external/pubs/ft/scr/2003/cr03306.pdf [accessed 15 April 2005].

115 There may be parallels with other reforming leaders who lack sufficient political control to eradicate clientelism, such as Kibaki in Kenya and Obasanjo in Nigeria. It is also true that combinations of economic and political liberalization (perestroika and glasnost in the Soviet context) have of course been experienced elsewhere. The contrasting cases of the former Soviet Union on the one hand, and countries such as China and Vietnam on the other would imply that economic liberalization before political liberalization produces a much more ordered and successful transition experience. On the other hand, China and also Mexico show that economic liberalization can cut off the corporatist branch on which the project relies. Tanzania's current situation combines elements of all of these. Its politics more resemble Russia's than China's. On the other hand, the President is trying to lead a process of economic liberalization while resisting political liberalization, but may not succeed. The outcome is thus uncertain.

116 Economic data from the Mozambican case study in OECD African Economic Outlook 2002/03 [online] http://www.oecd.org/dataoecd/24/ 23/32430193.pdf [accessed 15 April 2005].

117 Mozambique receives about $350 million a year in external grant assistance (World Bank 2003 p 3).

118 [online] http://www.mozal.com/ [accessed 15 April 2005]. Mozal

receives subsidized power from South African energy company Eskom, not from Mozambique. This is a big factor in its profitability as energy is the major input cost.

119 Dutch disease refers to the effect whereby exports of a natural resource radically improve the trade position of a country, and lead to appreciation of the national currency, which then creates competitiveness problems for other exports. It is named after problems experienced by Holland following the discovery of North Sea oil. It can be minimized by careful management of foreign exchange earnings.

120 Possibly with the exception of some of the West Africa oil states where the USA wishes to maintain friendly regimes.

121 As noted in chapter 8, the ruling party's grip is beginning to loosen in Botswana.

122 Similar questions have arisen in the Russian case.

123 Van de Walle (2001) pp 280–81, however, argues that many Latin American countries have neo-patrimonial states as well.

124 Eg Richard Dowden, 'A Marshall plan will just be more money wasted' *The Observer*, 9 January 2005.

125 Crucially, however, the only area that even donors cannot sustain over any length of time or major policy area, is implementation.

126 In extreme cases, the way in which these two aspects cut across one another is very clear – for example, in 2002 food aid distributed in Zimbabwe was captured by ZANU-PF cadres at local level and effectively used to strengthen the political control of the party over the population. However, it is also the case in a much broader sense.

127 This element would lead to changes in the allocation of aid, towards the larger countries.

128 Beyond an incentive for leaders to adopt such a path, such a mechanism could assist leaders undertaking political reforms, by making clear what would be lost by not embarking on such a path (Collier et al 1997). However, I would argue that this type of mechanism would be more effective than donor conditionality, since it would mean leaders deciding on reforms themselves, and thus genuinely 'owning' them.

129 An example of this problem is the donor approach to finance ministries, in distinction to trade and industry ministries. Donors have focused substantial attention and capacity strengthening on ministries of finance over long periods, mainly because they have a claim to control macro-economic policy and budgets. In many countries they have become the only other source of power than the President's office and have taken on control of many developmental functions, including poverty reduction (for example in Uganda). Under donor influence they have taken on a strong ethos and aim of fiscal prudence, which in the African context is a counter-balance to neo-patrimonial tendencies to spending and lack of revenue control. However, successful developmental states in East Asia had powerful trade and industry ministries,

and rather weak finance ministries (eg Wade 1990 p 209). Key policy-making institutions were headed by civil servants trained as engineers, (who are trained to think dynamically), rather than as economists (who are trained to think in terms of static equilibria) (Wade 1990 pp 220–22).

130 See [online] http://www.grc-exchange.org/docs/doc59.pdf [accessed 15 April 2005]. For case studies see http://www.grc-exchange.org/g_themes/politicalsystems_drivers.html. A number of African countries have been covered in the project, including Kenya, Uganda, Zambia, Nigeria, Tanzania and Ghana.

131 How the MCA will work in practice cannot be assessed yet. As of March 2005 the MCA had not disbursed any money. It had signed only one agreement for a $110 million grant over four years with Madagascar.

132 Again, Zimbabwe provides an extreme and therefore clear example. In August of 1999 the IMF, after some years of tense relations with the government and no lending, agreed to a new programme with the Mugabe regime, and the first tranches were released. Within weeks, the government had gone off-track, as was widely predicted by domestic observers. However, even this comparatively modest sum gave the government valuable resources at a time when the economy was beginning to contract, and it allowed the financing of a campaign of intimidation of and violence against the newly-formed opposition in a referendum on a new Constitution in early 2000. This was a valuable dry-run for the regime for later elections, and is part of a pattern of the use of state resources to ensure ZANU-PF supremacy.

133 Some have suggested a collective accountability mechanism for aid through the AU (or NEPAD), where one African country would set conditionality for another, or all would collectively set conditionality for each. This, indeed, is similar to the structure used in the Marshall Plan aid, where European recipient countries had to submit a plan to the Paris-based Economic Cooperation Association. This body was mainly made up of representatives from European countries, and it also set conditionality (Henry Northover, personal communication, Bradford de Long and Eichengreen 2001). A collective accountability mechanism would imply that aid for all would be cut if any member went off track. This is not necessarily an efficient way to give aid, as the poor performance of, say, Zambia, would penalize a good performer, say Senegal, meaning that an opportunity to use aid effectively would have to be passed up. Such a scheme might work if the collective can put sufficient pressure on each member to comply. However, as with the donor-recipient relationship, there is little reason to believe that domestic political considerations will not predominate, implying that leaders will in the last analysis do what they need to at home rather than obey their peers. It is therefore better to base an aid incentive mechanism on the former rather than the latter.

134 See, for example, Michaela Wrong's arguments, *New Statesman*, 10 May 2004.

135 I am grateful to Duncan Green for suggesting this idea.

136 An estimated $18 billion was laundered in eastern and southern Africa alone in 1999 (Commission for Africa 2005 p 152).

137 For example, up to the present the UK government has not cooperated with attempts by the Nigerian government to recover millions of pounds worth of oil revenues taken by Abacha's family and deposited in UK banks.

138 'DTI failing to act on Africa's "dirtiest war"', *Observer*, 6 February 2005.

139 [online] http://www.iansa.org [accessed 3 December 2004].

140 [online] http://pgoh.free.fr/mugabe_customer.html [accessed 15 April 2005].

141 'How Zimbabwe defies economic collapse', *Financial Times*, 10 March 2004.

142 As well as the UK having a sizeable shareholding in the IFIs, the Chancellor is also chair of the IMF's governing Monetary Committee, and the Secretary of State for International Development is on the World Bank's Development Committee.

143 Legislation giving British courts jurisdiction over corruption offences overseas was enacted in the UK in 2001. However, up until now no cases have been brought, despite allegations from overseas missions, authorities and the ECGD. The main problem is that responsibility for implementation lies with local police authorities (mainly the City of London police and the Metropolitan Police), and the Home Office is not providing incentives or resources to pursue cases (Hawley 2004). A dedicated unit is needed, and DTI and DfID should contribute resources to make it work. Another wrong signal sent out recently by the UK is the ECGD caving in to industry pressure to weaken new rules on corruption (*Financial Times*, 6 September 2004), leading to a judicial review of the process. In March 2005 the OECD published a highly critical report on the UK's lack of implementation of the Anti-Bribery Convention.

144 As will become clear, I am referring specifically to the UK offices of these organizations, rather than their African offices and partners.

145 As the only really successful mass campaigning organizations in the OECD, UK NGOs do realize that they have to start expanding their reach and work with counterparts in other EU countries and the US, but they have not so far put serious resources and thought into knowing how to do this. Even Oxfam, which does has an international advocacy presence, cannot yet get large numbers of mass actions in the rest of the EU and the US.

146 For me, this was summed up in Jubilee 2000's choice of figurehead with which to launch its campaign in 1998 – the deeply corrupt and

sporadically repressive Kenneth Kaunda, who presided over Zambia's disastrous decline through the 1970s and 1980s.

147 'International Development in 2005: the challenge and the opportunity', Speech by the Chancellor of the Exchequer at the National Gallery of Scotland 6 January 2005 [online] http://www.hm-treasury.gov.uk/ newsroom_and_speeches/press/2005/press_03_05.cfm [accessed 15 April 2005].

Bibliography

Abah, O. and J. Okwori (2002) 'Agendas in encountering citizens in the Nigerian context', *IDS Bulletin* 33, 2 pp 24–30.

Acemoglu, D., S. Johnson and J. Robinson (2004) 'An African success story: Botswana' in D. Rodrik (ed.) *In Search of Prosperity: Analytic Narratives on Economic Growth*, Princeton University Press.

Achterbosch, T. J., H. Ben Hammouda, P. Osakwe and F. van Tongeren (2004) 'Trade liberalisation under the Doha Development Agenda: Options and consequences for Africa', Report 6.04.09, Agricultural Economics Research Institute, The Hague.

Actionaid (2002) *Farmgate: the developmental impact of agricultural subsidies*, London.

Actionaid (2003) *Unlimited companies: the developmental impacts of an investment agreement at the WTO*, London.

Actionaid (2004a) *Trade traps: why EPAs are a threat to poverty reduction and development*, London.

Actionaid (2004b) *Money talks: how aid conditions continue to drive utility privatisation in developing countries* [online] http://websrv.actionaid. org/wps/content/documents/money_talks.pdf [accessed 15 April 2005].

Actionaid, CAFOD, Christian Aid, Fairtrade Foundation, ITDG, Oxfam, Save the Children UK, World Development and World Vision (2002) *A genuine development agenda for the Doha Round of WTO negotiations* [online] http://www.oxfam.org.uk/what_we_do/issues/trade/downloads/ wto_doha.pdf [accessed 15 April 2005].

Actionaid, CAFOD, Christian Aid, Oxfam, Save the Children and World Development Movement (2003) *Unwanted, unproductive and unbalanced: six arguments against an investment agreement at the WTO* [online] http://www.oxfam.org.uk/what_we_do/issues/trade/downloads/invest- ment_wto.pdf [accessed 15 April 2005].

Actionaid, CAFOD and Oxfam, 2004 *Fools Gold: the case for 100 per cent multilateral debt cancellation for the poorest countries* [online] http://www.oxfam.org.uk/what_we_do/issues/debt_aid/downloads/ wbimf_fools_gold.pdf [accessed 15 April 2005].

Actionaid USA (2004) *Inclusive circles lost in exclusive cycles: An Actionaid contribution to the first Global Poverty Reduction Strategies Com- prehensive Review* [online] http://www.actionaidusa.org/pdf/ Inclusive%20circles.pdf [accessed 14 April 2005].

Actionaid USA/Actionaid Uganda (2004) *Rethinking participation: questions for civil society on the limits of participation in PRSPs* [online] http://www.actionaidusa.org/images/rethinking_participation_april04.pdf [accessed 3 November 2004].

Adams, R. (2004) 'Hard to credit – review of IOU: the debt threat and why we must defuse it' by N. Hertz', *The Guardian*, 30 October 2004, London.

Addison, T., G. Mavrotas and M. McGillivray (2004) 'Aid, alternative sources of finance and the Millennium Development Goals', Paper presented to the Development Studies Association Annual Conference, November 2004, London.

African Development Bank (1999) 'Infrastructure Development in Africa' in *African Development Report 1999* Oxford University Press.

Ahuja, V., B. Bidani, F. Ferreira and M. Walton (1997) *Everyone's Miracle? Revisiting Poverty and Inequality in East Asia*, World Bank, Washington DC.

Ake, C. (1996) *Democracy and Development in Africa*, Brookings Institutions, Washington DC.

Alesina, A., and D. Dollar (1998) *Who gives foreign aid and why?*, Working Paper w6612, NBER.

Alesina, A., and B. Weder (1999) *Do corrupt governments receive less foreign aid?*, Working Paper w 7108, NBER.

Allen, C. (1995) 'Understanding African politics', *Review of African Political Economy* 65, pp 301–20.

Amaoko, K.Y. (2004) 'The capable state', *New Economy* 11, 3, pp 132–137.

Amjadi, A., U. Reincke and A. Yeats (1996) *Did external barriers cause the marginalization of Sub-Saharan Africa in world trade?*, World Bank Discussion Paper 348, Washington, DC.

Amsden, A. (1985) 'The state and Taiwan's economic development' in P. Evans, D. Rueschemeyer and T. Skocpol (eds.) *Bringing the State Back in*, Cambridge University Press.

Amsden, A. (1989) *Asia's Next Giant: South Korea and Late Industrialization*, Oxford University Press.

Amsden, A. (1994) 'Why isn't the whole world experimenting with the East Asian model to develop? Review of *The East Asian Miracle*', *World Development* 22, 4 pp 627–633.

Amsden, A. (2000) 'Industrialization under new WTO law', Paper prepared for a high-level round table on trade and development directions for the twenty-first century, UNCTAD X, Bangkok.

Andersen, O. (2000) 'Sector programme assistance' in F. Tarp (ed.) *Foreign Aid and Development: Lessons Learned and Directions for the Future*, Routledge.

Aoki, M., H.-K. Kim and M. Okuno-Fujiwara (eds.) (1996) *The Role of Government in East Asian Economic Development: Comparative Institutional Analysis*, Clarendon Press.

Appiah-Kubi, K. (2001) 'State owned enterprises and privatization in Ghana', *Journal of Modern African Studies* 39, 2, pp 197–229.

Arrighi, G. (2002) 'The African crisis; world systemic and regional aspects' *New Left Review*, 15, pp 5–36.

Aryeety, E. and M. Nissanke (1998) 'Asia and Africa in the global economy: economic policies and external performance in South-East Asia and Sub-Saharan Africa', Paper prepared for presentation at the UNU-AERC Conference *Asia and Africa in the Global Economy*, 3–4 August 1998, Tokyo.

Aventin, L. and P. Huard (2000) 'The cost of AIDS to three manufacturing firms in Cote d'Ivoire', *Journal of African Economies* 9, 2 pp 161–188.

Baffes, J. (2004) *Cotton: market setting, trade policies and issues*, World Bank Policy Research Working Paper 3218, World Bank, Washington, DC.

Balihuta, A. and K. Sen (2001) 'Macro-economic policies and rural livelihood diversification: a Ugandan case-study', LADDER Working Paper 3, School of Development Studies, University of East Anglia.

Baregu, M. (2000) 'The state of political parties in Tanzania, 1999', Paper presented at International IDEA-SADC Conference: 'Towards Sustainable Democratic Institutions in Southern Africa' [online] http://www.idea.int/ideas_work/22_s_africa/parties/3_baregu.pdf [accessed 24 November 2004].

Barnett, T. and A. Whiteside (2002) *AIDS in the 21st Century: Disease and Globalisation*, Macmillan.

Bates, R. (1981) *Markets and States in Tropical Africa*, University of California Press.

Bates, R. and A. Kreuger eds. (1993) *Political and Economic Interactions in Economic Policy Reform*, Blackwell.

Bayart, J. F. (1993) *The State in Africa: The Politics of the Belly*, Longmans.

Bayart, J. F., S. Ellis and B. Hibou (1999) *The Criminalization of the State in Africa*, James Currey.

Bennell, P. (1997) 'Privatization in Sub-Saharan Africa: Progress and prospects during the 1990s' *World Development* 25, pp 1785–1803.

Berg, E. (2000) 'Aid and failed reforms: the case of public sector management' in F. Tarp (ed.) *Foreign Aid and Development: Lessons Learned and Directions for the Future*, Routledge.

Bernstein, H. (1981) 'Notes on state and peasantry: the Tanzanian case', *Review of African Political Economy* 8, 21, pp 44–62.

Bigsten, A., D. Mutalemwa, Y. Tsikata, and S. Wangwe (1999) 'Aid and reform in Tanzania' World Bank, Washington DC [online] http://www.worldbank.org/research/aid/africa/tanzania2.pdf [accessed 15 April 2005].

Blouin, C. and I. Njoroge (2004) 'Evaluation of DfID Support to Trade Related Capacity Building: Case study of Kenya', North-South Institute, Ottawa.

Bollinger, L. and J. Stover (1999) 'The economic impact of AIDS', Futures Group [online] http://www.iaen.org/papers/index.php?search=1&view= search&open= per cent22economic+impact per cent22+Africa&submit= go&conjunction=all [accessed 15 April 2005].

Boone, C. (1994) 'Trade, taxes and tribute: market liberalizations and the new importers in West Africa' *World Development* 22, 3, pp 453–467.

Booth, D., R. Crook, E. Gyimah-Boadi, T. Killick and R. Luckham, with N. Boateng (2004) 'Drivers of change in Ghana: overview report' Centre for Democratic Development/ODI.

Borrell, B. (1999) 'Sugar: the taste test of liberalisation', Centre for International Economics, Canberra [online] http://www.intecon.com.au/pdf/ Sugar_taste_test_of_trade_lib_presentation.pdf [accessed 15 April 2005].

Boyce, J. and L. Ndikumana (2000) *Is Africa a net creditor? New estimates of capital flight from severely indebted African countries, 1970– 1996*, Working Paper 2000–01, Department of Economics, University of Massachusetts at Amherst.

Bradford de Long, J. and B. Eichengreen (1991) 'The Marshall Plan: history's most successful structural adjustment plan' [online] http://www. jbradford-delong.net/pdf_files/Marshall_Large.pdf [accessed 15 April 2005].

Bratton, M. (1989) 'Beyond the state: civil society and associational life in Africa, *World Politics* 41, pp 407–430.

Brautigan, D. (1995) 'The state as agent: industrial development in Taiwan, 1952–1972' in H. Stein (ed.) *Asian Industrialisation and Africa* Macmillan.

Brenton, P (2003) *Integrating the least developed countries into the world trading system: the current impact of EU preferences under Everything But Arms'* World Bank Policy Research Working Paper 3018, Washington, DC.

Brenton, P. and T. Ikezuki (2004) *The initial and potential impact of preferential access to the US market under the African growth and Opportunity act* World Bank Policy Research Working Paper 3262, Washington DC.

Brown, G. (2004) 'The challenges of 2005', *New Economy* 11, 3, pp 127–131.

Burnside, C. and D. Dollar (2000) 'Aid, policies and growth', *American Economic Review* 90, 4 pp 847–68.

CAFOD (2004) 'Briefing note on the EU cotton regime' [online] http:// www.cafod.org.uk/var/storage/original/application/phpzDnEyI.pdf [accessed 15 April 2005].

CAFOD, Actionaid and Oxfam (2004) 'Submission to the DEFRA consultation on sugar reform'.

Castel-Branco, C. (2004) 'What is the impact and experience of South African trade and investment on the growth and development of host countries? A view from Mozambique', Paper presented at a conference on Stability, Poverty Reduction and South African Trade and Investment in Southern Africa, Pretoria, 29–30 June 2004.

Castro-Leal, F., J. Dayton, L. Demery, and K. Mehra (1999) 'Public spend-
    ing in Africa: do the poor benefit?', *World Bank Research Observer* 14, 1,
    pp 49–72.
Chabal, P. (2002) 'The quest for good government and develoment in Africa:
    is NEPAD the answer?', *International Affairs* 78, 3 pp 447–62.
Chabal, P. and J.-P. Daloz (1999) *Africa Works: Disorder as Political Instru-
    ment*, Zed Press.
Chachage, C. (1995) 'The meek shall inherit the earth, but not the mining
    rights: the mining industry and accumulation in Tanzania,' in P. Gibbon
    (ed.) *Liberalised Development in Tanzania: Studies on Accumulation
    Processes and Local Institutions*.
Chang, H-J. (1993) 'The political economy of industrial policy in Korea',
    Cambridge Journal of Economics 17, 2, pp. 131–157.
Chang, H-J. (2002) *Kicking Away the Ladder: Development Strategy in His-
    torical Perspective*, Anthem Press.
Chang. H-J. and D. Green (2003) *The Northern WTO Agenda on Invest-
    ment: do as we say, not as we did*, South Centre/CAFOD.
Chen, S. and M. Ravallion (2001) 'How have the world's poor fared since the
    early 1980s?' [online] http://www.worldbank.org/research/povmonitor/
    MartinPapers/How_have_the_poorest_fared_since_the_early_1980s.pdf
    accessed 15 April 2005].
Christian Aid (2002) *Quality participation in poverty reduction strategies:
    experiences from Malawi, Bolivia and Rwanda* http://www.christian-
    aid.org.uk/indepth/0208qual/quality.htm.
Christian Aid (2003) *Too hot to handle? The absence of trade policy from
    PRSPs* [online] http://www.christian-aid.org.uk/indepth/0304toohot/
    toohot.pdf [accessed 15 April 2005].
Christian Aid (2004a) *Taking liberties: poor people, free trade and
    trade justice* [online] http://www.christian-aid.org/indepth/409trade/
    tradereport_final.pdf [accessed 15 April 2005].
Christian Aid (2004b) *A rethink of trade and governance: Christian Aid's
    position on the Africa* [online] http://www.christian-aid. org.uk/indepth/
    504africa/africacomsub.pdf [accessed 15 April 2005].
Christian Aid and CAFOD (2000) *A human development approach to
    globalisation* Submission to the White Paper on Globalisation.
Collier, P. (1997) 'The failure of conditionality' in C. Gwin and J. Nelson
    (eds.) *Perspectives on Aid and Development*, Johns Hopkins University
    Press.
Collier, P. (1999) 'Learning from failure: the international financial institu-
    tions as agencies of restraint in Africa' in A. Schedler, L. Diamond and
    M. Plattner (eds.) *The Self-Restraining State: Power and Accountabilities
    in New Democracies*, Lynne Rienner.
Collier, P. and Dollar, D. (1999) 'Aid allocation and poverty reduction'
    World Bank, Washington DC [online] http://www.worldbank.org/
    research/abcde/washington_11/pdfs/collier.pdf [accessed 15 April 2005].

Collier, P., P. Guillaumont, S, Guillaumont and J. Gunning (1997) 'Redesigning conditionality', *World Development* 25, 9, pp 1399–1407.

Collier, P. and J. Gunning (1999a) 'Explaining Africa's economic performance', *Journal of Economic Literature* 37, 1, pp 64–111.

Collier, P. and J. Gunning (1999b) 'Restraint, co-operation and conditionality in African trade policy' in D. Greenaway, A. Oyejide and B. Ndulu (eds.) *Regional Integration and Trade Liberalization in Sub-Saharan Africa* Macmillan.

Collier, P., A. Hoeffler and C. Patillo (1999) *Flight capital as a portfolio choice* World Bank Working Paper 2066, Washington, DC.

Commission for Africa (2005) *Our Common Interest* [online] http://www.commissionforafrica.org/english/report/introduction.html [accessed 15 April 2005].

Cooksey, B. (2003) 'Aid and corruption: a worm's-eye view of donor policies and practices', Paper presented at 11th International Anti-Corruption Conference, Seoul, South Korea, 26–29 May 2003.

Cornia, G., R. Jolly and F. Stewart (1988) *Adjustment with a Human Face* Oxford University Press.

Coulson, A. (1982) *Tanzania: A Political Economy*, Oxford University Press.

Datta-Chaudhuri, M. (1990) 'Market failure and government failure', *Journal of Economic Perspectives* 4, 3, pp 25–39.

De Waal, A. and J. Tumushabe (2003) 'HIV/AIDS and Food Security in Africa', DfID, 2003.

Deaton, A. (1999) 'Commodity prices and growth in Africa', *Journal of Economic Perspectives* 13, 3, pp 23–40.

Devarajan, S. (2001) 'Overview' in S. Devarajan, D., Dollar and T. Holmgren (eds.) *Aid and Reform in Africa* World Bank, Washington DC.

DfID (2000) *Eliminating World Poverty: Making Globalisation Work for the Poor*, White Paper on International Development, London.

DfID (2004a) 'Rethinking tropical agricultural commodities', mimeo.

DfID (2004b) 'Departmental Report' TSO, London.

DfID, FCO and HM Treasury (2004) 'Partnerships for poverty reduction: changing aid "conditionality"', Draft Policy paper [online] http://www.dfid.gov.uk/pubs/files/conditionalitychange.pdf [accessed 15 April 2005].

Dollar, D. and A. Kraay (2001) *Trade, growth and poverty*, World Bank Policy Research Working Paper 2199, World Bank, Washington, DC.

DTI (2004) *Making Globalisation a Force for Good* White Paper on trade and Industry, London.

Easterly, W. and A. Kraay (2000) 'Small states, small problems? Income, growth and volatility in small states', *World Development* 28, 11, pp 2013–2027.

Edwards, C. (1995) 'East Asia and industrial policy in Malaysia: lessons for Africa' in H. Stein (ed.) *Asian Industrialisation and Africa*, Macmillan.

Elbadawi, I., B. Ndulu and N. Ndung'u (1997) 'Debt overhang and economic growth in Sub-Saharan Africa' in Z. Iqbal and R. Kanbur (eds.) *External Finance for Low Income Countries* IMF.

Englebert, P. (2003) *Why Congo persists: sovereignty, globalization and the violent reproduction of a weak state*, Working Paper Series 95, Queen Elizabeth House, University of Oxford.

Fafchamps, M., F. Teal and J. Toye (2001) *Towards a growth strategy for Africa* mimeo, Centre for the Study of African Economies, Oxford University.

Fjeldstad, O-H. (2001) *Fiscal decentralisation in Tanzania? For better or worse?* CMI Report 2001:10, Chr. Michelson Institute, Bergen [online] http://www.cmi.no/publications/2001/wp/wp2001-10.pdf [accessed 15 April 2005].

Fjeldstad, O-H., I. Koldstad and S. Lange (2003) *Autonomy, incentives and patronage: a study of corruption in the Tanzania and Uganda Revenue Authorities* CMI Report 2003: 9, Chr. Michelson Institute, Bergen [online] http://www.cmi.no/publications/2003/rep/r2003-9.pdf [accessed 15 April 2005].

Foster, M., A. Norton, A. Brown and F. Naschold (1999) 'The status of sector wide approaches: a framework paper for the meeting of the Like-minded Donor Working group on SWAPs in Dublin', ODI/Irish Aid.

Fosu, A, K. Mlambo and T. Oshikoya (2001) 'Business environment and investment in Africa: an overview', *Journal of African Economies* 10, Supp. 2, pp 1–11.

Gastrow, P., and M. Mosse (2002) 'Mozambique' in *Penetrating State and Business: Organised Crime in Southern Africa*, Institute for Security Studies, South Africa [online] http://www.iss.co.za/pubs/Monographs/No86/Chap3.pdf [accessed 15 April 2005].

Ghura, D. (1998) *Tax revenue in Sub-Saharan Africa: effects of economic policies and corruption*, IMF Working Paper WP/98/135, Washington DC.

Gilbert, C. (1996) 'International commodity agreements: an obituary notice', *World Development* 24, pp 1–19.

Gilbert, C. and J. ter Wengel (2000) 'Commodity production and marketing in a competitive world', Paper produced for CFC-UNCTAD panel in Bangkok, 13 February 2000 [online] http://www-econo.economia.unitn.it/cgilbert/UNCTAD_paper.PDF [accessed 15 April 2005].

Gillson, I. (2004) *Developed country cotton subsidies and developing countries: unravelling the impacts on Africa*, ODI Briefing Paper [online] http://www.odi.org.uk/iedg/Projects/cotton_brief.pdf [accessed 15 April 2005].

Global Witness (2004) *Time for Transparency: coming clean on oil, mining and gas revenues*, Washington, DC.

Gloppen, S. and L. Rakner (2002) 'Accountability through tax reform? Reflections from Sub-Saharan Africa', *IDS Bulletin* 33, 3, pp 30–40.

Goetz, A. M. (2005) 'Managing successful governance reforms: lessons of design and implementation', mimeo, Institute of Development Studies, Brighton.

Golooba-Mutebi, F. (2004) 'Reassessing popular participation in Uganda', *Public Administration and Development* 24, 4, pp 289–304.

Gonamee, K., S. Girma and O. Morrisey (2002) *Aid and growth in Sub-Saharan Africa: accounting for transmission mechanisms*, CREDIT Research paper 02/05, University of Nottingham.

Gonamee, K., S. Girma and O. Morrisey (2003) *Searching for aid threshold effects: aid, growth and the welfare of the poor*, CREDIT Research Paper 03/15, University of Nottingham.

Gould, J. and J. Ojanen (2003) *Merging in the circle: the politics of Tanzania's poverty reduction strategy*, Policy Paper 2/2003 Institute of Development Studies, University of Helsinki [online] http://www.eurodad.org/upload store/cms/docs/mergingthecircleIDSTanzPRSP.pdf [accessed 15 April 2005].

Green, D. and S. Priyadarshi (2001) 'Proposals for a "Development Box" in the WTO Agreement on Agriculture' [online] http://www.cafod.org.uk/ var/storage/original/application/phpjYUKOy.pdf [accessed 15 April 2005].

Gunning, J. and T. Mengistae (2001) 'Determinants of African manufacturing investment: the micro-economic evidence', *Journal of African Economies* 10, Supp. 2, pp 48–80.

Gyimah-Brempong, K. and T. Traynor (1999) 'Political instability, investment and economic growth in Sub-Saharan Africa', *Journal of African Economies* 8, 1, pp 52–86.

Hanlon, J. (2002) 'Bank Corruption Becomes Site of Struggle in Mozambique', *Review of African Political Economy* 91, pp 53–72.

Hanlon, J. (2004) *How Northern donors promote corruption: Tales from the new Mozambique*, Briefing No. 33, The Cornerhouse.

Hansen, H. and F. Tarp (2000) 'Aid effectiveness disputed', *Journal of International Development* 64, 2, pp 547–70.

Hardstaff, P. and T. Rice (2003) *More market access for less policy space – a bad deal for development*, Actionaid and WDM [online] http:// www.actionaid.org.uk/index.asp?page_id=790 [accessed 15 April 2005].

Harrold, P., M. Jayawickrama and D. Bhattasali (1996) *Practical lessons for Africa from East Asia in industrial and trade policies*, Africa Department Technical DP 310 World Bank.

Hawley, S. (2004) *Enforcing the Law on Overseas Corruption Offences: Towards a Model for Excellence*, The Cornerhouse.

Hearn, J. and M. Robinson (2000) 'Civil Society and Democracy Assistance in Africa' in P. Burnell ed. *Democracy Assistance: International Cooperation for Development*, Frank Cass.

Herbst, J. and G. Mills (2003) *The Future of Africa: A New Order in Sight?* Adelphi Paper 361, International Institute of Strategic Studies.

Herbst, J. and C. Soludo (2001) 'Nigeria' in S. Devarajan, D., Dollar and

T. Holmgren (eds.) *Aid and Reform in Africa*, World Bank, Washington, DC.

Hilary, J. (2003) *GATS and water: the threat of service negotiations at the WTO*, Save the Children UK.

Hill, A. (1992) 'Trends in childhood mortality in sub-Saharan mainland Africa' in E. van de Walle, G. Pison and M. Sala-Diakanda (eds.) *Mortality and Society in Sub-Saharan Africa*, Clarendon Press.

HM Treasury and DTI (2004) *Trade and the global economy: the role of international trade in productivity, economic reform and growth*, London.

Hutchful, E. (1995) 'Why regimes adjust: the World Bank ponders its "star pupil" ', *Canadian Journal of African Studies* 29, 2, pp 303–317.

Hyden, G., Olowa, D. and Ogendo, H. (2000) African Perspectives on Governance, Africa World Press, Trenton, NJ.

Hyden, G., Court, J. and Mease, K. (2004) Making Sense of Governance: Empirical evidence from sixteen developing countries, Lynne Rienner Publishers, Boulder, CO.

Ibrahim, J. (2003) *Democratic Transition in Anglophone West Africa*, CODESRIA.

IMF (1998) *External evaluation of ESAF: Report by a group of independent experts*, Washington, DC.

IMF (2001) *Trade Liberalization in IMF Supported Programmes*, Washington, DC.

Independent Evaluation Office, IMF (2004) *Evaluation of the IMF's role in PRSPs and the PRGF*, Washington, DC.

Johnson, C. (1982) *MITI and the Japanese Miracle: The Growth of Industrial Policy 1925–1975*, Stanford University Press.

Johnson, C. (1999) 'The developmental state: odyssey of a concept' in M. Woo-Cummings (ed.) *The Developmental State*, Cornell University Press.

Kanbur, R. (2000) 'Aid, conditionality and debt in Africa' in F. Tarp (ed.) *Foreign Aid and Development: Lessons learned and directions for the future*, Routledge.

Kelsall, T. (2002) 'Shop windows and smoke-filled rooms: governance and the re-politicization of Tanzania', *Journal of Modern African Studies* 40, 4, pp 597–619.

Kelsall, T. and M. Mmuya (2004) 'Accountability in Tanzania; historical, political, economic and sociological dimensions', Paper prepared for Drivers of Change – Tanzania, DfID.

Khan, M. (1996) 'A typology of corrupt transactions in developing countries' *IDS Bulletin* 27, 2, pp 12–21.

Khan, M. (2002) 'Corruption and governance in early capitalism: World Bank strategies and their limitations' in J. Pincus and J. Winters (eds.) *Reinventing the World Bank*, Cornell University Press.

Killick, T. (1995) *IMF Programmes in Developing Countries: Design and Impact*, Routledge.

Killick, T. (1998) *Aid and the Political Economy of Policy Change*, Routledge.

Killick, T. (2004) 'Politics, evidence and the new aid agenda', *Development Policy Review* 22, 1, pp 5–29.

Killick, T. and H. White with S. Kayizzi-Mugerwa and M-A. Savane (2001) *African Poverty at the Millennium: Causes, Complexities and Challenges*, World Bank, Washington, DC.

Kim, K. S. (1995) 'The Korean miracle (1962–1980) revisited: myths and realities in strategies and development' in H. Stein (ed.) *Asian Industrialisation and Africa*, Macmillan.

Kjaer, A-M. (2004) ' "Old brooms can sweep too!" An overview of rulers and public sector reforms in Uganda, Tanzania and Kenya' *Journal of Modern African Studies* 42, 3, pp 389–413.

Koestle, S. (2002) *Rural livelihoods and illness: case studies in Tanzania and Malawi*, LADDER Working paper 19, School of Development Studies, University of East Anglia.

Krueger, A. (1974) 'The political economy of the rent-seeking society', *American Economic Review* 64, pp 291–303.

Krueger, A. (1990) 'Government failures in development', *Journal of Economic Perspectives* 4, 3, pp 9–23.

Krugman, P. (1986) *Strategic Trade Policy and the New International Economics*, MIT Press.

Kwon, J. (1994) 'The East Asian challenge to neo-classical orthodoxy', *World Development* 22, 4, pp 635–44.

Lal, D. (1983) *The Poverty of Development Economics*, Hobart.

Lall, S. (1996) *Learning from the Asia Tigers: Studies in Technology Policy*, Macmillan.

Lall, S. (2000) *Selective industrial and trade policies in developing countries: theoretical and empirical lessons*, Working Paper Series 48, Queen Elizabeth House, University of Oxford.

Lall, S. (2003) *Industrial success and failure in a globalizing world*, Working Paper Series 102, Queen Elizabeth House, University of Oxford.

Lall, S. and C. Pietrobelli (2002) *Failing to Compete: technology development and technology systems in Africa*, Edward Elgar.

Lall, S. and S. Wangwe (1998) 'Industrial policy and industrialisation in Sub-Saharan Africa', *Journal of African Economies* 7, 1, pp 70–107.

Lienert, I. And J. Modi (1997) *A decade of civil service reform in Sub-Saharan Africa*, IMF Working Paper WP/97/179, Washington, DC.

Lieven, A. (2004) *America Right or Wrong: An anatomy of American Nationalism*, HarperCollins.

Lindauer, D. and M. Roemer (1994) eds. *Asia and Africa: Legacies and Opportunities for Development*, Harvard Institute for International Development, 1994.

Lucas, H., D. Evans and K. Pasteur (2004) 'Research on the current state of PRS monitoring systems' [online] http://www.dfid.gov.uk/pubs/files/researchpovertyredstrategymonitoring.pdf [accessed 15 April 2005].

Lucas, S. and S. Radelet (2004) *An MCA Scorecard: Who Qualified, Who Did Not, and the MCC Board's Use of Discretion*, Center for Global Development [online] http://www.cgdev.org/docs/MCAScorecard_0528.pdf [accessed 15 April 2005].

Mamdani, M. (1996) *Citizen and Subject: Contemporary Africa and the Legacy of Late Colonialism*, Princeton University Press.

Mattoo, A., D. Roy, and A. Subramanian (2002) *The Africa Growth and Opportunity Act and its rules of origin: generosity undermined?* Working Paper 02/158, IMF, Washington, DC.

McArthur, J. and F. Teal (2002) 'Corruption and firm performance in Africa', mimeo, Centre for the Study of African Economies, University of Oxford.

McGee, R., with J. Levene and A. Hughes (2002) *Assessing participation on poverty reduction strategy papers – a desk-based synthesis of experience in Sub-Saharan Africa*, Research Report 52, Institute of Development Studies, Sussex.

Melamed, C. (2002) *What works? Trade, policy and development*, Christian Aid [online] http://www.christian-aid.org/indepth/0207trad/whatwork.pdf [accessed 15 April 2005].

Melamed, C. (2003) *What is on the table? An analysis of proposals for changes to Special and Differential Treatment at the WTO*, Christian Aid [online] http://www.christian-aid.org/indepth/308wtotable/wtotable.pdf [accessed 15 April 2005].

Mkandawire, T. (1998) 'Thinking about developmental states in Africa' Paper presented at a UNU-AERC workshop on Institutions and Development in Africa, 14–15 October, Japan [online] http://www.unu.edu/hq/academic/Pg_area4/Mkandawire.html [accessed 15 April 2005].

Mkandawire, T. and Soludo, C. (2004) 'Towards the broadening of development policy dialogue for Africa', IDRC [online] http://web.idrc.ca/en/ev-56330-201-1-DO_TOPIC.html [accessed 15 April 2005].

Mlambo, K. and T. Oshikoya (2001) 'Macroeconomic factors and investment in Africa', *Journal of African Economies* 10, Supp. 2, pp 12–47.

Mmuya, M. (1999) 'Constraints to democratization in Tanzania', *African Review* (Dar es Salaam) 26, pp 171–190.

Moore, M., J. Leavy, P. Houtzager and H. White (2000) *Polity qualities: how governance affects poverty*, Working paper 99, Institute of development Studies, Brighton.

Moncrieffe, J. (2004) 'Uganda's political economy: a synthesis of major thought', Report prepared for DfID Uganda [online] http://www.grc-exchange.org/docs/DOC44.pdf [accessed 15 April 2005].

Mosley, P. (1995) 'The failure of aid and adjustment policies in SSA: counter-examples and policy proposals', Paper presented to a workshop on Sub-Saharan Africa: Looking Ahead, Copenhagen.

Mosley, P., J. Harrigan and J. Toye (1995) *Aid and Power: the World Bank and Policy-Based Lending*, Routledge.

Mosley, P., F. Noorbaksh and A. Paloni (2003) *Compliance with World Bank conditionality; implications for the selectivity approach to policy-based lending and the design of conditionality*, CREDIT Working Paper 03/20, University of Nottingham.
[online] http://www.nottingham.ac.uk/economics/credit/research/papers/CP.03.20.pdf [accessed 15 April 2005].

Murphy, R., A Schleifer and R. Vishny (1989) 'Industrialization and the Big Push', *Journal of Political Economy* 97, pp 1003–1026.

Ndulu, B. and S. O'Connell (1999) 'Governance and growth in Sub-Saharan Africa', *Journal of Economic Perspectives* 13, 3, pp 41–66.

North-South Institute (2004) 'Evaluation of DfID support to trade related capacity building', Consultation Report.

Nyamu-Musembi, C. and S. Musyoki, with M. Mwasaru and P. Mtsami (2004) *Kenyan civil society perspectives on rights, rights-based approaches to development, and participation*, IDS Working Paper 236, Institute of Development Studies, Brighton.

OECD (2004) *African Economic Outlook 2003/2004* Paris.

OED (1997) *Adjustment Lending in Sub-Saharan Africa: An Update*, World Bank, Washington, DC.

OED (1998) *The Special Programme of Assistance for Africa (SPA): An Independent Evaluation* World Bank, Washington, DC.

OED (2004) *Mainstreaming Anti-Corruption Activities in World Bank Assistance: A Review of Progress since 1997*, Washington, DC.

Olivier, G. (2003) 'Is Thabo Mbeki Africa's saviour?', *International Affairs* 79, 4, pp 815–828.

Ostheimer, A. (2001) *Mozambique: the entrenchment of democratic minimalism?*, *Africa Security Review* 10, 1, pp 103–117.

Over, M. (1992) 'The macroeconomic impact of AIDS in Sub-Saharan Africa', mimeo, World Bank.

Oxfam (2002a) *Rigged rules and double standards* [online] http://www.maketradefair.com/en/index.php?file=26032002105549.htm [accessed 15 April 2005].

Oxfam (2002b) *Stop the dumping! How EU agricultural subsidies are damaging livelihoods in the developing world* [online] http://www.oxfam.org.uk/what_we_do/issues/trade/downloads/bp31_dumping.pdf [accessed 15 April 2005].

Oxfam (2002c) *Cultivating poverty – the impact of US cotton subsidies on Africa* [online] http://www.oxfam.org.uk/what_we_do/issues/trade/downloads/bp30_cotton.pdf [accessed 15 April 2005].

Oxfam (2002d) *Mugged – poverty in your coffee cup* [online] http://www.maketradefair.com/assets/english/mugged.pdf [accessed 15 April 2005].

Oxfam (2003) *Evian G8: Time to declare a war on poverty in Africa*, Oxfam Briefing Paper 47 [online] http://www.oxfam.org.uk/what_we_do/issues/debt_aid/downloads/bp47_eviang8.pdf [accessed 15 April 2005].

Page, S. and A. Hewitt (2001) *World commodity prices: still a problem for developing countries?*, Overseas Development Institute.

Page, S. and P. Kleen (2004) 'Special and differential treatment of developing countries in the World Trade Organization', Paper prepared for the Ministry of Foreign Affairs, Sweden.

Poldiano, C. (2001) *Why civil service reforms fail*, IDPM Public Policy and Management Working Paper 16.

Powell, J. (2002) *Cornering the Market: The World Bank and Trade Capacity Building*, Bretton Woods Project, London.

Rakner, L., L. Mukubvu, N. Ngwira and K. Smiddy (2004) 'The budget as theatre – the formal and informal institutional makings of the budget process in Malawi', Draft Final Report to DfID Malawi.

Ranger, T. (1996) 'The invention of tradition in colonial Africa' in E. Hobsbawm and T. Ranger (eds.) *The Invention of Tradition* Cambridge University Press.

Rodrik, D. (1991) 'Policy uncertainty and private investment in developing countries', *Journal of Development Economics* 36, pp 229–242.

Rodrik, D. (1998) 'Why is trade reform so difficult in Africa?', *Journal of African Economies* 7, Supp. 1, pp 10–36.

Rodrik, D. (2000) *The Governance of World Trade as if Development Mattered*, UNDP.

Rodrik, D. (2002) 'After neo-liberalism, what?', Paper presented at a conference on Alternatives to Neo-Liberalism, Washington, DC, May 23–24, 2002.

Rodrik D. and F. Rodriguez (2001) *Trade policy and economic growth: a skeptic's guide to the cross-national evidence*, NBER Working Paper 7081.

Roemer, M. (1996) 'Could Asian policies propel African growth?', Development Discussion Paper 543, Harvard Institute for International Development.

Roemer, P. (1986) 'Increasing returns and long-run growth', *Journal of Political Economy* 94, pp 1002–1037.

Roemer, P. (1990) 'Endogenous technological change', *Journal of Political Economy* 98, pp S71–S102.

Sachs, J., and A. Warner (1995) *Natural resource abundance and economic growth*, Working Paper 5398, NBER.

Sachs, J., J. MacArthur, G. Schmidt-Traub, M. Kruk, C. Bahadur, M. Faye and G. McCord (2004), 'Ending Africa's poverty trap', mimeo.

Sala-i-Martin, X., and A. Subramanian (2003) *Addressing the natural resource curse: an illustration from Nigeria*, IMF Working Paper WP/03/139.

Sandbrook, R. (1985) *The Politics of Africa's Economic Stagnation* Cambridge University Press.

Sen, K. (2002) *Economic reforms and rural livelihood diversification in Tanzania*, LADDER Working Paper 12, School of Development Studies, University of East Anglia [online] http://www.odg.uea.ac.uk/ladder/ [accessed 15 April 2005].

Siggel, E., and G. Ssemogerere (2001) 'Uganda's policy reforms, industry competitiveness and regional integration: a comparison with Kenya' [online] http://www.csae.ox.ac.uk/conferences/2001-NIRaFBiA/pdfs/siggel.pdf [accessed 15 April 2005].

Sindzingre, A. (2004) 'Bringing the developmental state back in: contrasting developmental trajectories in Sub-Saharan Africa and East Asia', Paper presented at the 16th Annual Meeting of the Society for the Advancement of Socio-Economies http://www.sase.org/conf2004/papers/sindzingre_alice.pdf.

Soderbom, M., with F. Teal (2001) *Can African manufacturing firms become successful exporters?*, CSAE-UNIDO Working Paper 4 [online] http://www.unido.org/userfiles/PuffK/CSAE-UNIDO_WP04.pdf [accessed 15 April 2005].

Stein, H. (1995) 'Policy alternatives to structural adjustment in Africa' in H. Stein (ed.) *Asian Industrialisation and Africa*, Macmillan.

Stevens C. and J. Kennan (2003) *Making trade preferences more effective*, IDS Briefing Paper.

Stiglitz, J. (1989) 'Markets, market failures and development', *American Economic Review Papers and Proceedings* 79, 2, pp 197–202.

Stiglitz, J. (1996) 'Some lessons from the East Asian miracle', *World Bank Research Observer* 11, 2, pp 151–177.

Stiglitz, J. (1998) 'Aid effectiveness and development partnership', Symposium on donor coordination and effectiveness of development assistance, United Nations University, Tokyo, June 1998.

Stiglitz, J. (2001) 'Information and the change in the paradigm in economics' Nobel Prize Lecture [online] http://www–1.gsb.columbia.edu/faculty/jstiglitz/download/NobelLecture.pdf [accessed on 30 November 2004].

Subramanian, A. and N. Tamirisa (2001) *Africa's trade revisited*, IMF Working Paper WP/01/33, Washington, DC.

Szeftel, M. (1982) 'Political graft and spoil system in Zambia: the state as a resource in itself', *Review of African Political Economy* 24, pp 5–21.

Tangri, R. and A. Mwenda (2003) 'Military corruption and Ugandan politics since the late 1990s', *Review of African Political Economy* 30, 98, pp 539–552.

Tarp, F. (ed.) (2000) *Foreign Aid and Development: Lessons learned and directions for the future*, Routledge.

Taylor, I. (2002) 'Botswana's "developmental state" and the politics of legitimacy', Paper prepared for a conference on 'Towards a new political economy of development: globalisation and governance', University of Sheffield, 4–6 July 2002 [online] http://www.valt.helsinki.fi/staff/mhossain/state/Botswana.pdf [accessed 15 April 2005].

Temu, A. and J. Due (2000) 'The business environment in Tanzania after socialism: challenges of reforming banks, parastatals, taxation and the civil service', *Journal of Modern African Studies* 38, 4, pp 683–712.

Timæus, I. M. (1998) 'Impact of the HIV epidemic on mortality in

Sub-Saharan Africa: evidence from national surveys and censuses', *AIDS* 12 (supp. 1), pp S15–S27.

Transparency International (2004) *Corruptions Perceptions Index 2004.*

UNAIDS (2003a) *AIDS Epidemic Update*, December, Geneva.

UNAIDS (2003b) *Accelerating Action Against Aids in Africa*, Geneva.

UNAIDS (2004) *2004 Report on the Global AIDS epidemic*, Geneva.

UNCTAD (2002a) *The Least Developed Countries Report 2002: Escaping the Poverty Trap*, New York and Geneva.

UNCTAD (2002b) *World Investment Report 2002*, New York and Geneva.

UNCTAD (2003a) *Development in Africa*, New York and Geneva.

UNCTAD (2003b) *Trade Performance and Commodity Dependence*, New York and Geneva.

UNCTAD (2003c) 'Market access, market entry and competitiveness's Background note by the UNCTAD secretariat, TD/B/COM.1/65 New York and Geneva.

UNCTAD (2003d) *Trade and Development Report 2003*, New York and Geneva.

UNCTAD (2004) *The Least Developed Countries Report 2004: Linking International Trade with Poverty Reduction*, New York and Geneva.

UNDP (1999) *Human Development Report 1999*, New York.

UNDP (2003) *Human Development Report 2003*, New York.

UNDP (2004) *Human Development Report 2004*, New York.

UNECA (2004) *Economic Report on Africa 2004*, Addis Ababa.

UNICEF and UNDP (2002) *The Millennium Development Goals in Africa: Promises and Progress*, New York.

UNIDO (2004) *Industrialisation, Environment and the MDGs in Sub-Saharan Africa*, Geneva and New York.

van de Walle, N. (2001) *African Economies and the Politics of Permanent Crisis, 1979–1999*, Cambridge University Press.

van Donge, J. and A. Liviga (1986) 'Tanzanian political culture and the cabinet', *Journal of Modern African Studies* 24, 4 pp 619–639.

von Freyhold, M. (1979) *Ujamaa Villages in Tanzania: Analysis of a Social Experiment*, Heinemann.

Wade, R. (1990) *Governing the Market: Economic theory and the Role of Government in East Asian Industrialization*, Princeton University Press.

Wade, R. (1996) 'Japan, the World Bank and the art of paradigm maintenance: the *East Asian Miracle* in political perspective', *New Left Review* 217, pp 3–36.

War on Want (2004) *Profiting from poverty: privatisation consultants, DfID and public services*, [online] http://www.waronwant.org/?lid=8740 [accessed 15 April 2005].

Watkins, K. (1999) 'ESAF reform and the poor', Speech at the IMF Global Forum, 24 September 1999 [online] http://www.oxfam.org.uk/what_we_do/issues/debt_aid/imf_esaf.htm.

Weston, A. and M. Tsoka (2004) 'Evaluation of DfID Support to Trade

Related Capacity Building: Case study of Kenya', North-South Institute, Ottawa.

White, G. (1995) 'Towards a democratic developmental state', *IDS Bulletin* 26, 2, pp 27–36.

White, G., and R. Wade (eds.) (1984) 'Developmental states in East Asia: capitalist and socialist', Special issue of *IDS Bulletin* 15, 2.

White, H. (1996) 'Review article: Adjustment in Africa', *Development and Change*, 27, pp 785–815.

Woo-Cummings, M. (ed.) *The Developmental State*, Cornell University Press.

Wood, A. (2002) 'Could Africa be like America?' Proceedings of the Annual Bank Conference on Development Economics, April–May 2002, World Bank, Washington, DC.

Wood, A. (2004) *One step forward, two steps back: ownership, PRSPs and IFI conditionality*, World Vision.

Wood, A. and M. Lockwood (1999) *The "perestroika" of aid? new perspectives on conditionality*, Bretton Woods project and Christian Aid.

World Bank (1981) *Accelerated Development in Sub-Saharan Africa*, Washington, DC.

World Bank (1989) *Sub-Saharan Africa: From Crisis to Sustainable Growth*, Washington, DC.

World Bank (1993) *The East Asian Miracle*, Washington, DC.

World Bank (1998a) *Assessing Aid: What Works, What Doesn't and Why?*, Washington, DC.

World Bank (1998b) *World Development Report: States and Markets*, Washington, DC.

World Bank (2000) *Can Africa Claim the 21st Century?*, Washington, DC.

World Bank (2001) *World Development Report 2000/2001: Attacking Poverty*, Washington, DC.

World Bank (2002) *African Development Indicators*, Washington, DC.

World Bank (2003) *Country Assistance Strategy for Mozambique*, Washington, DC [online] http://www-wds.worldbank.org/servlet/WDSContentServer/ WDSP/IB/2004/07/09/000012009_20040709092054/Rendered/PDF/ 267470corr.pdf [accessed 15 April 2005].

World Bank and IMF (2005) *Heavily Indebted Poor Countries Initiative – Statistical Update April 4, 2005*, Washington, DC.

World Development Movement (2003a) *GATS: From Doha to Cancun*, [online] http://www.wdm.org.uk/cambriefs/gats/gatsupdatecancun.pdf [accessed 18 October 2004].

World Development Movement (2003b) *States of unrest III* [online] http:// www.wdm.org.uk/cambriefs/debt/States per cent20of per cent20Unrest per cent20III_04.03.pdf [accessed 23 October 2004].

World Development Movement (2004a) 'Media briefing: UK Government's Commission for Africa'.

World Development Movement (2004b) *Zambia: condemned to debt – how the IMF and the World Bank have undermined development* [online] http://www.wdm.org.uk/campaigns/cambriefs/debt/zambia/zambia.pdf [accessed 15 April 2005].

World Development Movement (2004c) 'Colludo campaign' [online] http://www.wdm.org.uk/campaign/colludo/colludo.htm [accessed 21 October 2004].

Index

Also in the *Viewpoints* series from

PUBLISHING

Social Progress and Sustainable Development
Neil Thin

'This wide-ranging study...brings the ethics back into development thinking.' *David Marsden, Research Director, INTRAC.*

Paperback • ISBN:1-85339-556-0 • 192pp
£9.95 • €14.95 • Not available from ITDG Publishing in North America

Doing the Rights Thing
Rights-based Development and Latin American NGOs
Maxine Molyneux and Sian Lazar

'This excellent book provides a concise, clearly written overview of the key issues...Wide-ranging and up to date it should be essential reading for staff in development agencies of all kinds, as well as an indispensable text for students and researchers in the field.'
Dr David Lewis, London School of Economics.

Paperback • ISBN:1-85339-568-4 • 176pp
£12.95 • US$23.95 • €18.95
